DEATH
OF AN AMERICAN

David Fleisher
David M. Freedman

DEATH
OF AN
AMERICAN

THE KILLING
OF JOHN SINGER

CONTINUUM • NEW YORK

1983

The Continuum Publishing Company
575 Lexington Avenue
New York, New York 10022

Printed in the United States of America

Library of Congress Cataloging in Publication Data

Fleisher, David.
Death of an American.

1. Singer, John, D. 1979.   2. Church and state—Utah—
History—20th century.   3. Educational law and
legislation—Utah.   4. Education, Compulsory—Utah.
5. Mormons—Utah—Biography.   6. Utah—Biography.
I. Freedman, David M.   II. Title.
BX8695.S4F55   1983   289.3'3   [B]   83-10109
ISBN 0-8264-0231-3

Contents

Acknowledgments

For their generous help, thanks to Michael Leach, Harriët Kohn, Bonnie Norder, Jim Smedley, Kirk Johnson, Kathryn Collard, Gerry Spence, Patsy Ong, and Fred Fogo.

We dedicate this book to our parents.

Chapter 1

ABIDE IN MY COVENANT

R esolute, John Singer walked into the principal's office, clutching a U.S. history textbook that his eight-year-old daughter had brought home from school the previous afternoon.

"I cannot go along with this," Singer told Rex Walker, principal of South Summit Elementary School, Kamas, Utah, in his thick German accent. He opened the history book to a page marked by a scrap of paper and showed it to the principal. "I don't like my kids being indoctrinated with this kind of crap."

It was a drawing of George Washington, Betsy Ross, and Martin Luther King, Jr., with a caption describing the three as great American patriots.

"I don't see anything objectionable here, John," the principal said.

Singer explained, "Martin Luther King was nothing but a Communist-inspired rabble-rouser, and he paid the price of a traitor and got shot. I can't swallow him being called a great patriot."

Rex Walker looked up at Singer. He was not surprised. Singer had a reputation for expressing his beliefs, usually unpopular ones, and standing by his convictions. "There's not much we can do about this, John," Walker said. "The state gives us a list of textbooks to choose from, and we have to choose from it. If you don't like this book, maybe you should write to the state superintendent of schools."

Singer challenged him. "Don't you have the guts to decide for yourself what textbooks are good for the children in this community, Mr. Walker?"

"To tell you the truth, I personally don't object to this one. I think the books we use are just fine for the kids."

"You don't object to a textbook that shows whites and Negroes intermingled? You should know what the scriptures say about it, nay, you're a high priest in the Mormon Church!"

In fact, Rex Walker was one of the high priests of the Kamas Stake—a stake is a unit of the church made up of a number of wards, or parishes—who had a year earlier voted to excommunicate John Singer and his wife Vickie from the church. He well knew that the Mormon scriptures discourage intermingling between whites and the "black race of Cain." The original Mormon doctrine holds that after Cain killed Abel, he and his descendants were thenceforth "shut out from the presence of God" and denied membership in the priesthood. In order to distinguish Cain's descendants from others, God turned their skin black.

John Singer, a wiry, five-foot-ten television repairman and farmer, was a fundamentalist Mormon who lived by the scriptures, and objected to what he considered immoral secular influences his children were subject to in the public school.

Walker invited Singer to sit down and explained to him that public schools must follow a curriculum set up by the state board of education, that he personally could not change the curriculum or choose different textbooks to satisfy anyone's private standard of morality.

Singer stared out the window behind the principal's desk for about ten seconds, then stood up and declared, "Then I'll have to take my kids out of school and teach them myself."

"John!" The principal stopped Singer before he could leave. "Utah has a compulsory school attendance law," he warned. "Parents in this state are required to send their children to public school or to a qualified private school. You better read that law."

Singer looked deeply into the principal's eyes. "You better read the Constitution of the United States, Mr. Walker. It says that the state cannot interfere with my religious beliefs." He walked out of the office, leaving the offending textbook on the principal's desk as if it were a dead fish.

Walker drew in a deep breath and let it rush out audibly past his lips. Although he would be glad to have John Singer out of his hair, he felt concern for the fate of the Singer children. He considered the report he would have to write on this matter for Val Edrington, the school superintendent.

Heidi Singer was doing arithmetic exercises in her third-grade class when the teacher called her name. She looked up and saw the teacher nodding toward the door. Her father was standing there, beckoning to her. Heidi smiled and carefully put her books and papers inside her desk.

This was not the first time her father had called her out of class. About once a week John Singer drove to Salt Lake City to buy television parts and supplies. When he did, he would first gather up Vickie and their three youngest children at home in Marion, then would pull the three older children out of school in Kamas, making the trip to Salt Lake a family affair. After John's business was concluded in Salt Lake, they would visit John's mother or friends, go to a museum or a historical site, and eat dinner at a restaurant.

Heidi assumed this was an unscheduled trip to Salt Lake. She felt disappointed about missing the cowboys-and-Indians game the class had planned for recess that day. Why couldn't they go tomorrow instead?

Heidi waved to her teacher on her way out. John Singer put his arm around his oldest daughter and they walked to Suzanne's second-grade classroom. After collecting Suzanne, they went on to pick up Timothy from his kindergarten class. Timothy was glad to leave school that day because the girl next to him had been trying to kiss him.

Once they were outside the school building, Heidi asked, "Why are we going to Salt Lake, Dad?"

"We're not going to Salt Lake, we're going home. You don't have to come back to this school any more," Singer told his three children. "We're going to have school at home from now on."

The two older girls were relieved. They were aware that their parents had been planning for several months to withdraw them from public school but were waiting for a suitable opportunity. The textbook Suzanne had brought home the day before was concrete evidence that the school was teaching things contrary to their family's religious beliefs. The girls were old enough to understand their parents' objections to the school's "permissive attitude" toward such immoral behavior as sexual promiscuity, drugs, crude language and gestures, rock music, and lack of respect for adults. The Singer children were brought up under a very strong religious faith.

The girls did not have an easy time in school. They were derided for their old-fashioned, pioneer-style clothing, their parents were looked upon as religious fanatics, and their father was considered a social misfit, held in contempt by much of the community.

Timothy, aged six, was happy to be going home. School kept him from doing things he really liked, such as helping his father around the farm and tinkering with machines, motors, and tools.

The Singers climbed into their yellow 1966 Ford Econoline van and headed home. It was March 29, 1973.

South Summit Elementary School is set in the middle of downtown Kamas, three blocks from the junction of U.S. Highway 189 and Utah Highway 150. Across the street from the school is Kamas Lumber and Hardware, and around the corner Cap's Body Shop.

Kamas nestles between the Wasatch and Uinta mountain ranges, about thirty-five miles as the crow flies east from Salt Lake City. The eight hundred residents of Kamas are predominantly conservative farmers and ranchers who belong to the Mormon Church. In fact, most of the people in the neighboring towns connected by U.S. Highway 189 in the Kamas Valley—Francis, Marion, Oakley, Peoa, and Wanship—are Mormons. The Summit County seat, Coalville, is eight miles north of Wanship near Interstate 80.

As Singer drove north past the rich farmland along Highway 189, he told his three children about his plan for their home schooling. He had already spent about two hundred dollars for textbooks in English, math, history, science, health, and geography. He would teach them German; they would have lessons on the Bible and the Book of Mormon. Moreover, they would all have time to pursue their individual interests. Heidi was already making leather moccasins and necklaces; Suzanne liked to paint and draw; Tim wanted to learn carpentry. They would each be given a small garden plot to work on their own. In the future, they might even get the whole family together and build a little schoolhouse with a big blackboard, maybe get a piano, and have square dances.

From Kamas to Marion is about three miles. Marion is a small community with fewer than sixty families and but one retail store, the Kamas Valley Co-op, which sells gasoline, tires, cattle feed, and limited grocery items. Less than five miles due east of Marion is Hoyt Peak, at 10,284 feet. Water running down the west side of the peak enters Hoyt's Canyon and flows by the nearby Singer farm. About forty-five miles farther east is the highest point in Utah, King's Peak, at 13,528 feet.

As Singer entered Marion along Highway 189 from the south, he turned right onto a road that horseshoes around a cemetery, a few small farms, several houses, and the co-op, and meets Highway 189 again about three-fourths of a mile farther north. This is the Upper Loop Road. At the farthest point from the highway on Upper Loop Road, on the curve of the horseshoe, is a 160-acre farm once owned by John Singer's uncle, Gustav Weller. Singer drove past the Weller farm along a private unpaved road for about two hundred yards and arrived at his two-and-a-half-acre farm. The Singer farm stretches eastward to the foot of the Uinta Mountains, where the thick forest, dominated by quaking aspen and cottonwood trees, provides wood for fuel and a place for recreation and quiet.

The Singer homestead remains a scene out of the nineteenth century. John looked with fondness upon the log home that he had built almost single-handedly before he married. John had cut and hauled the logs by truck from Mirror Lake Canyon near Kamas, using only an axe, an adz, and rope, and with the aid of draft horses. His brother Harald had helped him raise the thirty-six-foot center beam which runs the full length of the house, and had helped carry boulders for the seven-by-three-foot fireplace. John reused windows, doors, and fixtures discarded by neighbors and relatives. He did all the carpentry, plumbing, and electrical work.

The big fireplace separates the house into two areas. On one side is the entrance hall leading to the spacious kitchen with a pantry and a dining area. The other side has a living room and, off to one side, two bedrooms with a bathroom between them. Above the bedrooms is a loft where the four youngest children slept.

On the south side of the house is a garden grown with about a dozen vegetables. A little to the east is a ten-by-thirty-foot root cellar, eight feet deep, which John had dug by hand. Here the Singers stored their winter's supply of root vegetables and canned fruits.

Northwest of the house John had built a barn for the animals: chickens, two dairy cows, and a vealer. One end of the barn held John's TV repair shop. The rest of the yard has apple trees and raspberry bushes, and in the summer the walk leading to the house is strewn with flowers. In the forest behind the property are deer, porcupines, and skunks.

John's wife Vickie was inside with the three preschool children, Charlotte, Joseph, and Benjamin, when the van pulled up in front of the house. Vickie had not known, when John left a half hour earlier, what would be the result of his meeting with Rex Walker. When she saw the three oldest children she exclaimed, "He did it!" Her voice was triumphant, yet she felt a wave of apprehension when she thought of the indignation John's act would arouse in the community.

At twenty-nine, Vickie Singer was slim and energetic, and looked as if she could be one of the twenty thousand Mormon pioneers who headed west from Illinois with Brigham Young in the late 1840s to look for a place in the wilderness to call their own. She had long blond hair that was braided and wound into a bun on the crown of her head. Like her daughters, she wore old-fangled long dresses and garments that revealed only the flesh of her neck, face, wrists, and hands. Her face was pretty, with pale blue eyes, a narrow, pointed nose, and an endearing smile. She stood five foot six inches in her boots. Only the wrinkles at the corners of her eyes revealed a rugged life-style. All six children were robust and full of vim, and, like their mother, had fair complexions.

The Singers opened their home school in the living room the following morning, with Heidi, Suzanne, and Timothy in attendance. The first lesson was world geography. Vickie and the children skimmed through the entire textbook, concentrating on pictures of people in different cultures, important cities, and natural wonders, and matching the pictures with a country or region on a big map that Vickie had spread out. The students were invited to ask questions and make comments. The plan was to study each continent in depth, chapter by chapter, in future lessons.

They did not keep track of the time, but stopped when the children seemed restless. Vickie felt there was no point in forcing them to continue if they wouldn't learn much more anyway.

After a short break, they reassembled for reading and writing. This was more disciplined, as the children had to write their sentences over and over until they were correct. For each student a different textbook was used. Eight-year-old Heidi was given the most advanced sentences with the hardest words. Vickie utilized sentences from the McGuffy Readers she had saved since her own childhood.

Again, they did not watch the clock but practiced until Vickie felt the children had made some progress. After another break, John came in and taught arithmetic and religion. The first morning's lessons lasted a little more than two hours.

In the afternoon, each pupil was assigned a job that required learning a practical skill. Vickie started teaching the girls to can fruits and vegetables; John taught Timothy to cut firewood and store it for the winter. All three children were given small garden plots to prepare for planting, with the help of their father. Afterwards the children were free to pursue their hobbies and do their regular chores.

John and Vickie's philosophy of education could be succinctly expressed in this way: Human beings are naturally curious and inquisitive. Learning is satisfying when it is motivated by natural curiosity. Or, put in another way, teaching is most effective when it reinforces this curiosity. When people, especially children, are forced to study and learn things they do not care about, learning becomes a chore and curiosity is stifled. Enforced learning can dull the senses and create "learning disabilities." Children must learn the basics—reading, writing, mathematics, history, and science—so that they can build upon such a foundation. Beyond that, they should be allowed to pursue their individual interests and develop their natural talents, at their own pace. If children are educated with these principles in mind, they will think of learning as its own reward, with no need for grades or honors, and will know the joy of learning for the rest of their lives. They will feel confident that when the need arises they will be able to learn whatever they want to know. Therefore they will not feel helpless in times of crisis, and will not be reliant on other people's charity or on the government's.

Just as important, the Singers believed that children should learn to think for themselves, instead of blindly accepting what they are told by teachers, politicians, the media, or Mormon bishops. Only the word of God as recorded in the scriptures is eternal truth.

On April 12, 1973, two weeks after the Singers withdrew their children from school, Val D. Edrington, superintendent of South Summit School District, visited John and Vickie in their home and invited them to attend the school board meeting the following evening at South Summit High School in Kamas, to explain their action and what they intended to do about their children's education. It would be just a friendly discussion, he said.

The next evening, John and Vickie sat at a conference table with Edrington and the six members of the Board of Education. Besides the Martin Luther King, Jr., incident, which Rex Walker had highlighted in his report to the board, John explained there were other elements of the curriculum that he objected to, including sex education and the teaching of "Darwin's theory." But the most important issue was immoral behavior in the schools. "We feel that our children shouldn't be exposed to this type of atmosphere every day, and so we decided it was time to take them out and keep them clean and decent."

A board member then asked, "Don't you think your kids will be exposed to these things sooner or later when they go out into the world? This is part of growing up, learning how to cope and deal with the different values and life-styles of other people."

John responded, "No, this is modern society's point of view about part of growing up. You see, when you delve into the laws of God, it spells out a different picture altogether. Just because a society has become permissive in its values, that doesn't mean that the laws of God have changed, or the penalties for transgressing those laws. You see," he went on, "when you hear about past civilizations going out of existence, it was because of the permissiveness of the society. You take a society like ours, and if you go and corrupt the youth as they are doing today, you will find out by tomorrow that our nation will be down on its knees and it will be annihilated, because this is usually the consequence of a polluted youth."

With a slight tinge of anger, a board member said, "So you're going to isolate your children from our permissive society; you're going to teach them what *you* want them to know, and not let them go out and see the real world and learn how to deal with it."

Replying calmly, John said, "You know how to take care of a garden, nay? When you want to raise some good plants, the first thing you have to do is make sure that all foreign elements are kept away from these plants, all weeds are kept out, you see, in order that these plants can grow properly. If I was going to follow the rule of this society, I would plant my seed and just let it go and hope for the best, and let the weeds kill it and whatever survives, good and fine, I reap the produce. But no, I am after these weeds, because I want some good plants.

"And this is exactly how I deal with this society and my children. I keep the evil influences away from them, and lay a good foundation within them. And then when they are of accountable age, which I think is about eighteen or twenty years old, and they say, 'Father, now I want to head out into this world,' all right, I will say to them, 'I have given you a good foundation, I have taught you the ways of God and what He wants you to do. Now it's up to you. Up till now, if you've done something wrong, the responsibility rested on my shoulders; from now on as you head out from under my care, the responsibility rests on your own shoulders and you have to pay the consequences for your own misdealings.'

"But you never, *never* send a child out when he does not know anything, to be in this society, and to be trained by these school-teachers that I wouldn't give a nickel's worth of trust to. When it comes to morality and character building, the public school system flunks miserably."

The board members were silent for several seconds. Finally, another said, "John, you know that you are breaking the law of the land by not sending your children to school. Do you think that's a good moral influence on your children, teaching them that they don't have to obey the law?"

John shook his head. "We are teaching them to obey God's law. This is a religious issue. This is an issue of our right, given to us by the constitutional law of the land, to practice our religion without interference from the government. You see, God has entrusted Vickie and me with these children, and it is our responsibility to see after their care and keeping, and see that they are being kept morally clean. Take a look at Doctrine and Covenants, section 68: 'Parents shall teach their children to pray and to walk uprightly before the Lord.' But if they fail to teach their children the ways of the Lord, then the sins of the children will be upon the heads of the parents."

Again the board members were silent for several seconds. Then another asked John, "Don't you think it's possible that one of your kids might some day want to get a particular job that requires a high school diploma?"

"No, definitely not," John answered.

"Suppose one of your children decides he wants—or she wants—to be a doctor?"

"Now, this already is out of the question," John replied. "Because when we get sick in our home we get healed through the power of God. So there is no need for a doctor. Whenever one of my kids gets sick, they call for their daddy to lay his hands upon them, and they do get well. When Vickie got her ankle cracked, she asked for me to administer a blessing, and within two or three days she could walk up the hills again because God healed it, you see. So as far as a doctor is concerned, we don't need one."

"You don't think there's a need for the medical profession at all?" asked the flabbergasted board member.

"Oh, yes, there is a great need for the medical profession. It's for those individuals who haven't got anything better. It's definitely needed there. But for those who have something better, it's not needed, it's obsolete. Do you understand?"

"Have your children told you they don't want to go back to school?"

"You're darn tootin' right they don't."

"But they'll miss out on the junior prom, and basketball games, and many of the important events of a young person's life . . ."

The only woman on the board, one who had taught in the public schools for forty-three years, spoke up for the first time. "There's going to be a time in your children's lives when they're going to go out into the world on their own, and it's not an easy world to live in, and no longer will they have the protection of the parents as when they were smaller. When they get out into this rough world, they will have to associate with other people to make a living. And basically, that's far more important than all the education in the world, to be able to get along with other people. The thing that goes through my mind is, how will your children be able to adjust in the world, on their own, having been isolated from the world itself?"

John responded full of respect, as if this was the first legitimate question of the evening. He reasoned that they had many friends and relatives in Salt Lake City whom they visited almost every week, and these friends often came up to Marion with their children to visit. Also, his brother Harald occasionally came down from Logan with his children. No, his kids were not sequestered from contact with other people.

The Singers were asked about their home schooling and their teaching methods. Vickie described their morning classes and the curriculum material, and the afternoon sessions when the three oldest children were taught practical skills.

What were their qualifications to teach academic subjects, since neither she nor John held teaching certificates? Vickie had gone to college for a year and a half, and John had dropped out of high school when he was sixteen.

How many hours were they teaching academic subjects each day? Two and a half. Was that all?

"Our education is going on every minute of our lives," Vickie responded with spirit, "not just in some little classroom. Our little boys and girls already know what it is like to labor for what they want, and they like it that way. They're already very responsible and are not lazy. They each have interests and talents of their own, and they feel the satisfaction of being able to accomplish things by themselves. Our children may never be star pupils in the academic sense, but, by the heck, I'll tell you something, they're learning a lot of other essential things, and when this economy or this society goes to pot they'll most likely be able to cope with the situation better than those raised in the public schools."

Finally, the board president wrapped up the meeting by telling the Singers that the state compulsory attendance law has set forth conditions under which parents may teach their children at home. The board would contact the state superintendent of public schools and get a copy of the law for them.

On May 26, 1973, two months after the Singers had withdrawn their children from school, they received a letter from Superintendent Edrington, accompanied by a copy of the state compulsory attendance law, which states in section 1 that all parents who have children between ages six and eighteen must send them "to a public or regularly established private school during the regularly established school year" of the district in which they reside. This is followed by two pages of "exceptions, excuses and exemptions," the most pertinent of which are that a child may be excused from attending school provided "that such minor is taught at home in the branches prescribed by law for the same length of time as children are required by law to be taught in the district schools. . . ." The reason for teaching the child at home must be acceptable to the district's Board of Education, "which, if so satisfied, shall issue a certificate stating that the holder is exempt from attendance during the time therein specified."

The law also states, in section 3, that any parent who willfully fails to comply with the law is guilty of a misdemeanor.

Edrington's letter said the following:

> Dear Mr. and Mrs. Singer:
> The position of the Board of Education of South Summit School District is that if you teach the appropriate areas of learning the prescribed amount of time, as shown on the attached schedule, and have your program evaluated periodically by the superintendent and pupil-personnel director, a certificate of exemption will be granted. If you cannot agree with this arrangement, and your children are not in school this fall, the local board will have no alternative but to make a Juvenile Court referral.

The attached memorandum was entitled "Areas of Learning and Time Schedules by Law" and applied to the three oldest children. But it contained the restriction that the teaching of practical skills and working in the garden could not be allowed as legitimate subjects. Edrington's letter requested a written response within thirty days as to whether the Singers intended to comply with the law and apply for an exemption.

John and Vickie thought about the matter for several days. All they wanted was to live their lives in peace and educate their children according to their religious beliefs. In doing so they felt sure they would not be infringing upon anyone else's rights. They felt this was guaranteed by the First Amendment to the Constitution: "Congress shall make no law [with respect to] an establishment of religion, or prohibiting the free exercise thereof." Since Utah's compulsory attendance law infringed on their right to practice their religion, it was thus unconstitutional. They also believed that neither the state nor the local school district should have any right to dictate to them how to raise their children in their own home.

John and Vickie weighed their alternatives. If they complied with the law and allowed the school board to direct and monitor their home education program, they would be compromising their civil liberties. If they defied the law, they would be subject to criminal prosecution and would encounter even more hostility from the community.

For guidance they turned to the Mormon scriptures, and found in Doctrine and Covenants, section 98, a commandment from the Lord:

> And now, verily, I say unto you concerning the laws of the land, it is my will that my people should observe to do all things whatsoever I command them.

This the Singers interpreted to mean that if the laws of the land conflict with the laws of God, the laws of God must be obeyed.

> And that law of the land which is constitutional, supporting that principle of freedom in maintaining rights and privileges, belongs to all mankind, and is justifiable before me.
> And as pertaining to law of man, whatsoever is more or less than this, cometh of evil.
> And I give unto you a commandment, that ye shall forsake all evil and cleave unto all good, that ye shall live by every word which proceedeth forth out of the mouth of God.

John and Vickie took this to mean that laws which are not constitutional are evil and must not be obeyed. This amounts to divine authorization of civil disobedience. But what of the consequences of breaking the law?

> Therefore, be not afraid of your enemies, for I have decreed in my heart, saith the Lord, that I will prove you in all things,

whether you will abide in my covenant, even unto death, that
you may be found worthy.

So regardless of the legal consequences, if a person carries out an
act of civil disobedience against an evil law, God will stand by that
person and prove him right.

John and Vickie now knew unequivocally what course they must
take. On June 16, John wrote a reply to the school board and
delivered it personally to Val Edrington. Edrington waited until
Singer left his office to open and read the letter.

> Dear Board Members:
> According to agreement, I hereby let you know my decision. My
> God has let me know by His scriptures and by His Holy Spirit
> that I am not required to bow under laws which trample upon
> my liberties of exercising rights and privileges, in which liberties
> my God has made me a free man. And also knowing that my
> God is more powerful than you and your illegal laws, and that
> only slaves will bow under these conditions, therefore all I can
> say is "Go to hell, you and your kind, for such unrighteous
> demands."
>
> *Sincerely,*
> *John Singer*

There was not a trace of doubt in John Singer's mind that by
forsaking an evil law he had made a covenant with God; and though
he might transgress the laws of the State of Utah, God would
support him and find him worthy. John fully realized the gravity
of this covenant. Regardless of what the school district or the
juvenile court or the State of Utah might see fit to do with him, he
must from this day forth abide in the Lord's covenant, even unto
death.

In the summer of 1973, no one dreamed it would come to that.

Chapter 2

A PASSION FOR FREEDOM

In John Singer's character there was a paradox, one attributable to his childhood in Germany. On the one hand, he was so repelled by the practices of the Nazis that once he came back to live in a country where freedom was exalted, any infringement on what he considered his constitutional rights was intolerable. On the other hand, he retained one of the traits that the Nazis—including his own father—had literally beaten into him: strict obedience to an infallible central authority. This John transferred to his God.

John's father, Hans Singer, had joined the Nazi party in 1923 in Dresden. Then, party memberships were numbered consecutively. Hans Singer's was 4,278. Adolf Hitler's was 7.

Hans was a merchant seaman during Germany's economic depression, and in 1925, seeking opportunity, he jumped ship in New York City. Subsequently, he lived in Brooklyn for seven years, and there met his future wife, Charlotte Weller.

Charlotte was also a German immigrant, who came with her brother Gustav and two of her sisters to the United States in 1925. Eleven years earlier, in Germany, she and Gustav had converted to Mormonism. Upon their arrival in America, Charlotte and Gustav moved directly to Utah to gather with the faithful, while their two sisters remained in New York. Eventually Gustav Weller bought

160 acres of farmland in the Kamas Valley, although he had never
worked on a farm.

During their first year in Utah, Charlotte had taken a job in Salt
Lake City as a housemaid—something she had done since she was
six years old—to support herself and her brother. Within two years,
Charlotte moved back to New York to find work and live with her
sisters. There she married Hans Singer in 1927. He was then a sailor
in the merchant marine. Their first son, John, was born a U.S.
citizen in Brooklyn on January 6, 1931, although neither of John's
parents were citizens.

In 1932, Hitler was coming to power. Hans, feeling that economic
paradise was about to be restored to Germany, took his family back
across the Atlantic to live in Dresden. John's brother Harald was
born there in 1932, two months before Hitler became dictator.
Constitutional liberties were immediately suspended, including
freedom of speech and the press. Hitler's storm troopers arrested,
terrorized, and murdered people who expressed any opposition to
the Nazi regime.

Charlotte Singer was unhappy to be back in Germany. She was
highly critical of the Nazis; at the same time, her husband denounced
her religious faith and forbade her to practice it or teach it to their
children. After their heated arguments, Hans would often point a
finger at his children and decree, "You are Nazis! You will never
become Mormons!"

Charlotte and Hans Singer also had two daughters, Edeltraud
and Heidi, born in 1934 and 1940.

In Germany the schools were quickly Nazified. New history books
were written exalting Aryans as the master race and denouncing
Jews as breeders of evil in the world. Physical education was given
high priority because of its purported value in building character
and discipline, as well as preparing the German youth for future
military service. A civil service act in 1937 required teachers to be
"executors of the will of the party-supported state," which they
were to defend "without reservation." A local youth office could
obtain a guardianship court order to take children away from
families whose political or religious convictions were questionable,
who befriended Jews, or who refused to enroll their children in the
Hitler Youth. The youth office then placed the children in "politically

reliable" homes. In addition, parents could be fined or imprisoned for withholding their children from participation in party youth activities, even those parents who merely objected that such activities were responsible for the high pregnancy rate among teenage girls.

John and Harald Singer joined the Hitler Youth when each was ten years old, in the early 1940s. At the time it was the largest youth organization in the world, with a membership of eight million. Upon entering, they took this oath: "I swear to devote all my energies and my strength to the savior of our country, Adolf Hitler. I am willing and ready to give up my life for him, so help me God."

Boys in the Hitler Youth learned to read semaphores, lay telephone wire, perform small-arms drills with air guns and dummy hand grenades, and repair bicycles. They were trained in group athletics, farm work, military tactics, and Nazi ideology. Mere children were taught to use lethal weapons, sometimes with lethal consequences.

Hans Singer had moved his family to Berlin and was working for the Nazi party in 1940 when he was drafted into the army on the western front. Before he went to war he enrolled John and Harald in an elite preparatory school in central Germany run by the Schutz Staffeln (SS). His intention was to make good Nazis out of his sons and remove them from their mother's influence.

It was in the regimented, militaristic environment of the SS prep school that John and Harald first developed their hatred of authoritarianism. After a year and half they were both expelled for "rebellious behavior." When they returned home to their mother in Berlin, they spoke out against their father whom they had not seen for almost two years.

Early in 1945 when the Germans were losing the war, Charlotte received word that her husband was in a French prison camp. She also learned that he had been unfaithful to her. By then Charlotte was working to support the family, and she filed for divorce.

It was about this time that the Singers started seeing victims of the concentration camps, much to their horror. Except for a few whispered rumors, the children had heard little about the death camps, and they were aghast at the sight of masses of living skeletons being transported by truck and by rail like sick cattle.

When the Russian army approached Berlin from the east, raping and pillaging along the way, Charlotte and her four children, now ranging in age from four to thirteen, fled westward with the few belongings they could carry. Germany was in chaos. In some parts of the country there was little food to be had, even for those with money, and transportation was disrupted by the bombing. The Russians terrorized the German people. The Singers were kept on the run fleeing from city to city, first west and then south toward Munich, riding what trains were left operating, and walking for miles where there were no trains.

In central Germany the Singers met up with some of Charlotte's relatives, who suggested that to ease her burden Charlotte let John stay with them until she could settle down in Munich. At thirteen John was nurturing a spirit of independence; he consented to remain with his relatives to make traveling easier for his mother.

Three months later in spring of 1945, John got word that his family was safe in the city of Landshut near Munich. He decided to join them against the advice of his relatives, for travel in the war-torn country was perilous, and he had three hundred miles to go.

During his three-day journey, John was on a train which brought him to within five miles of the city of Leipzig. The city had been heavily bombed, the train tracks were twisted and scattered, and passengers had to leave the train to search for where railroad service resumed, or find other means.

It was ten at night and John was lost. Out of a group of German soldiers a sergeant walked over to him and asked, "Well, young fellow, where do you want to go?"

"I want to go to Munich," John answered.

"Wait here for five minutes, and I'll be right back." The sergeant came back five minutes later, motioned to John, and said, "Follow me."

John later told his family that he marched behind the officer through the center of the ruined city to a railroad spur at the other side of town, where a southbound train was just ready to pull out. This walk through Leipzig took seven hours. When John walked onto the platform of the train at five in the morning and turned to look back at the sergeant, the latter had disappeared.

John and Harald were baptized as Mormons in Landshut. Later, when John became acquainted with the scriptures, he bore testimony that he had been guided through Leipzig by one of the Three

Nephites, the three disciples of Christ from the American continent who, according to the Book of Mormon, were granted immortality by the Lord so they could continue their evangelical missions forever.

Germany's economy collapsed at the end of the war, and in Landshut the Singers were forced to scrounge for a living, sometimes eating table scraps. Often they had to run into the forest to escape Allied bombs, and were forced to spend several nights with cows in a barn outside of Landshut.

When the bombing subsided and American soldiers occupied Landshut, John took a job as a baker's apprentice and Charlotte again worked as a housemaid. Being refugees from the north, and Mormons besides, the Singers found that they were socially ostracized in the south. Hearing rumors that Russia would try to take over the rest of Europe and bring on another world war, Charlotte decided to escape with her four children to the United States, where they hoped to find a more secure future. To Charlotte Singer, the condition of Germany in 1945 must have lent credence to Mormonism's claim, which they share with other Adventist sects, that the return of Christ and the end of the world are near at hand.

John was able to immigrate immediately because he was a U.S. citizen, while the rest of his family were placed on a waiting list. At that time the American government had a quota of 2,500 German immigrants each year.

John arrived alone in New York City in 1946 at the age of fifteen, and moved in with his mother's sister and her husband. He attended high school, where he studied English and learned television repair in shop class. After one year he dropped out, but had learned enough to get a job at a television repair shop on Long Island. John's uncle was a carpenter, and taught John much of what he knew about building houses.

While waiting for his family, John became active in the Mormon Church. He attended the weekly sacrament meetings and Sunday worship services, and very soon was ordained as a member of the priesthood, which is open to worthy males over the age of twelve.

Charlotte Singer had obtained a final divorce decree from Hans in Landshut, and in 1949 she immigrated to America with Harald, Edeltraud, and Heidi, over whom she had won custody. They all got jobs in New York City, and by the following year had saved enough money to buy a 1939 Chevy and drive to Utah, the promised land of their faith.

In Salt Lake City, John worked as a television repairman, Harald was a bookbinder, and Charlotte again worked as a maid. By then Harald and Charlotte had become U.S. citizens. In 1951 John was drafted into the marines and was sent to Japan during the Korean War. John found himself still repelled by the authoritarian atmosphere of military service. At one point on leave with his family in Utah, he spoke of deserting; but his uncle, Gustav Weller, talked him out of it.

His brother Harald was drafted into the army in 1953 and was stationed in Munich, where he saw his father again for the last time. It was not a warm reunion. Hans Singer was bitter that his family had left him and his fatherland.

Harald later described the army as "a throwback to Satan's plan. Everywhere you go, you are led. You only have to obey the rules and you don't have to think about anything."

When John was discharged from the marines in 1953 and returned to Utah, Gustav Weller invited John to live with him in Marion, to help him manage his 160-acre farm. Charlotte disapproved of this because she thought Gustav was a religious fanatic and would be a bad influence on her son. She also needed John's substantial income as a TV repairman to help support the family.

Gustav Weller had served in the German air force before the first world war. He sustained major injuries in an airplane accident, including a fractured skull. As a result he was discharged from military service and for several months was confined to his bed at home. It was during his convalescence that he and Charlotte were converted to Mormonism by an American missionary. Gus pursued his new religion zealously. He claimed that in a moment of stress he was visited by Jesus Christ, who personally conferred upon him the power of the priesthood. He developed the ability to heal people through prayer, many instances of which Charlotte claimed to have witnessed. Gustav personally converted more than one thousand people to Mormonism while he was in Germany.

At five foot eleven, Gustav was very fair and had blue eyes. His hair was once red, but after ten children had turned stark white.

Gus settled in the Kamas Valley and achieved some success as a farmer, something he could not have done without the financial support of his sisters in New York. In Marion he acquired several disciples who believed in him as a healer and a prophet of God. His own sons and daughters, unheeding of his spiritual exhortations, all left home. The only member of his kin who would listen seriously to him was John Singer, who had not had a father in ten years.

John decided to move into Gus's house in Marion. He worked on the farm and continued his television repair work in Marion and Kamas. During this time John became a devout student of the Mormon scriptures, and dedicated his life to God.

Some believe that Gus Weller treated John better than he did his own sons because John was eager to learn from him. Every night they studied the scriptures. To John, Gus was a substitute father.

In 1957, four years after John moved into the Wellers' house, Gus gave him two and a half acres of land on which to build his own home. The manner in which the ownership of the property was transferred is a matter of bitter dispute. Several of their mutual friends and relatives, including Charlotte Singer, understood that Gus gave John the land as part of a sacred covenant with the Lord; that the land was to be John's "for time and for all eternity," in payment for the work John had done on the Weller farm.

In his spare time, John put up a wire fence around his property, and with timber from the nearby forest built himself a log house. In 1961, approaching his thirtieth year, John Singer was a strong, independent, industrious man with an unwavering faith in his God.

Chapter 3

A HEAVENLY FEELING

Young Vickie Lemon was a dancer, lithe and svelte, with silky blond hair down to her waist. She performed solo dances in her high school and on church programs. Vickie was elected homecoming queen at South Summit High School; she organized the Twirlerettes drill team, which performed with batons during local athletic events. Folks in Kamas remember her as charming and friendly.

In summer 1961, after graduating from high school, Vickie was teaching tap dance. She wanted to save money so she could study ballet at the University of Utah in the fall. Her parents encouraged her in this. Her father, Grant Lemon, a welder with a fine reputation in several counties and two nearby states, saved his money to help pay her college tuition.

That summer, Vickie decided it was time to get her hair cut short. On that day she met John Singer. He was eating a hamburger at the lunch counter of the Hi Mountain Drug Store, the only one in Kamas. As Vickie walked by to pay her bill she noticed he was staring at her. He suddenly said, "You've ruined yourself!"

Startled, Vickie stopped to look at this confident man who spoke with an accent. His face, bright red from working in the sun, beamed at her, and he gave out a coarse, hearty laugh. "Well, you cut off your beautiful long hair!"

Realizing that this stranger meant no harm, Vickie smiled, embarrassed. John introduced himself to her. "I've seen you dance a couple of times at the ward house [combination Mormon church and recreation center]. You're very graceful."

Vickie thanked him, but wondered why a man who looked so much older than she would flirt with her. Though he was brash, his eyes sparkled with good humor, like a fun-loving child seeking comradery. After a short, pleasant conversation with him, she left the store.

The next day he called her on the phone and asked her out to a movie. Without hesitating she said, "Well, yes." After she hung up she thought, "What the heck did I say yes for, I don't even know him!"

On their first date Vickie had a hard time understanding John's accent, and kept asking him to repeat. However, before the evening was over Vickie was impressed with John's lively sense of humor, his intelligence and self-confidence, his big, strong hands and his immaculate grooming. Although he was twelve years older than she, she readily accepted another date with him.

When Vickie's parents found out, they wanted her to stop seeing him because of rumors about him: He came from Germany and had been a member of the Hitler Youth. He was a religious fanatic, a disciple of Gus Weller who spread false doctrine. He was probably a polygamist.

Even among those who didn't believe the rumors, John was thought of as a rather abrasive person. In the words of one Kamas resident:

> John came into people's homes because he was a television repairman. Most repairmen come in and take care of the problem you have and then leave. But John was conversational. He would crack jokes, and they seemed so silly. He was also very loud. He was talented as far as taking care of my television was concerned, and he did it very well, but all of this conversation and laughing bored me.

Vickie knew her parents felt ashamed that their daughter was dating John Singer. She knew he was a decent man, and deeply religious. He was not coquettish like the boys she had dated before.

That summer John asked Vickie to marry him. But Vickie thought of John as no more than a friend. Besides, reinforced by her parents' wishes, she was set on going to college.

Vickie enrolled at the University of Utah in Salt Lake City. She first majored in ballet, became discouraged, and changed her major to elementary education.

Vickie's heart was not in school. John Singer had planted a desire in her to learn about her religion, and she spent more time reading the Mormon scriptures than studying for her classes. When she went home in the spring of 1963 she decided not to return to school. Her parents were disappointed; they decried her lack of ambition and partially blamed Singer for distracting her with his religious idealism.

Once again Vickie taught tap dance in Kamas. She saw a boy named Bill occasionally, and by the summer of 1963 he started talking seriously about their future together.

Then Vickie ran into John Singer in Kamas on his way to a television repair call. He asked her out, and they had a wonderful time together. They talked intimately about their personal feelings and experiences. They listened with empathy to each other's troubles. John was a social outcast with few friends. Vickie was trying to decide what to do with her life.

Vickie was fascinated by John's independent and self-sufficient life-style in his log cabin. He had dug a root cellar and built a coal shed; had planted raspberry bushes and apple trees, and maintained small vegetable and flower gardens. He never went to doctors but could heal himself through prayer.

One night in August they were sitting together in John's house sharing a book about herbal medicine. A wonderful feeling came over Vickie, a feeling of peace and contentment such as she had never felt before. It was a heavenly feeling that enveloped her whole being. She seemed to be lifted above every care or worry in the world. She told John how marvelous she felt. This feeling stayed with her until John took her home later. From then on she thought more and more about John.

A few days after this, Vickie's friend Bill called from Salt Lake City to say he was arriving in a couple of days to ask her to become engaged to him. He was bringing her a ring. Vickie felt panicked. She was falling in love with John Singer, the social outcast who, at thirty-two, was twelve years older, and whom her parents despised. Her parents adored Bill but he was still a boy in Vickie's eyes. That night before she went to sleep she prayed harder than she had ever prayed before, saying, "Dear God, let me wake up in the morning knowing without a doubt what I should do with my life."

In the morning when she woke, she knew. She sat up in bed and said, with a smile, "I'm going to marry John Singer."

She decided to call John and tell him, but first she would take a bath and wash her hair, for she imagined he would want to come over right away. While she was sitting under the hair dryer, there was a knock at the door. John Singer came in, walked over to Vickie, took out a ring, and proposed to her.

Vickie said yes immediately and beamed at the ring John was putting on her finger. He kissed her on the cheek.

John had also made it a matter of serious prayer the previous night whether or not God wanted him to marry Vickie Lemon. He had pleaded, "Father, I'm going to go over there tomorrow and offer her this ring and ask her to marry me. If she is to be my wife, let her say yes without hesitating. But if she is not to be my wife, let her hem and haw and not give me an answer."

John and Vickie were engaged on September 5, 1963. Vickie's parents were vacationing in Blackfoot, Idaho, when Vickie called them the next day to tell of her engagement. At first they thought she meant to Bill; they were elated and started talking about the wedding celebration. But when Vickie said, "No, I'm engaged to John Singer," they were shocked into dead silence. They became furious—they would never allow it! Grant Lemon spoke to Vickie's brother Carlo and told him to put Vickie on the next bus to Blackfoot. Carlo told Vickie that he would do so the next morning.

In the night Vickie crept out of her house and walked in the dark to stay at her friend Enid's house. Early the next morning Carlo and Vickie's Aunt Eileen came to Enid's house to take Vickie to the bus station. Vickie refused to go with them.

Vickie was in a state of anguish and distress. She asked Enid to drive her to Gustav Weller's place in Marion, to ask him for a blessing. John had told her that Gus had the gift of healing. Enid agreed. Aunt Eileen made a few phone calls before she left.

As Enid and Vickie pulled up to the Weller house, three other cars screeched to a stop too. There were Vickie's cousins, her grandmother and step-grandfather, Aunt Eileen and her husband, and Carlo. Vickie's grandmother grabbed Vickie by the arm and told her that she was mentally ill. Eileen was calmly persuading Vickie to come home with her. At one point Gus's son Jared burst out of the house and Vickie's step-grandfather drew a knife on him. Jared told the old man to put the knife back in his pocket unless he planned to use it. This ended without incident.

Vickie finally agreed to go stay with her aunt Eileen for a while and was getting into her car, when John suddenly appeared and told Vickie to quickly get out of the car. Gus had called John after overhearing that Vickie's aunt was planning to take her to a mental institution in Provo. Gus helped Vickie to struggle free of her captors in the car and she escaped into the Weller house under John's protection. Gus then ordered everyone off his property.

Almost immediately the phone rang. It was Vickie's mother calling from Idaho, threatening that if Vickie married John Singer she would go out and get herself run over by a train. Vickie became very upset and started sobbing but would not agree to leave for Idaho. When she told John and Gus what her mother had said they laughed aloud. Vickie was wringing her hands when they suddenly tightened into fists and became paralyzed. Enid told Gus that Vickie had come up there for a blessing. Gus and John took Vickie upstairs and blessed her, whereupon her hands relaxed.

Then and there John and Vickie decided to elope immediately. John drove Vickie to Salt Lake City, to the home of Gus Weller's daughter, Miriam Jepsen, where she would be safe for a few hours. He drove back to Marion at dusk and bought new car tires at the co-op. There, John heard that the sheriff was looking for him because someone had accused him of kidnapping Vickie. He tried but could not reach the sheriff. Then he called his friend Slim and asked him to take care of his place for about a week. Slim agreed. John hurriedly gathered some clothes and ran out to his car. As he looked north along Upper Loop Road he noticed a string of headlights coming up the road from the co-op toward the Weller place. John turned off his headlights and drove south on Upper Loop Road, passed the cemetery and headed for Salt Lake City.

At the head of the string of cars was the sheriff, followed by Vickie's parents who had rushed back from Idaho, and behind them, several of their relatives and friends. They were going to Gus Weller's to pick up Vickie. Meanwhile Vickie's father and Uncle Bert drove up to John's house a few minutes after John had escaped. Bert was carrying a gun, and the two of them stationed themselves outside John's place for over an hour. Later that night fifty other people from Kamas drove up to John's house, some armed with weapons. Then Slim arrived. He pulled out a pistol and told the mob that John was not there and would not be back. The crowd dispersed.

John reached Salt Lake at midnight. He switched cars with his cousin Miriam, and he and Vickie headed for Elko, Nevada, a town of about 17,000 residents, approximately 275 miles west of Salt Lake. They traveled all night on an unfinished back road that was terribly rugged and desolate, and saw no other cars.

They arrived in Elko early Saturday morning and waited on the lawn of the courthouse until it opened. Vickie had on blue jeans, a sweatshirt, and gym shoes—all the clothes she had with her.

When they checked in at the courthouse and were asked for their identification, Vickie discovered she had left her purse at Miriam Jepsen's in her haste. So they drove all the way back to Salt Lake, spent Sunday night at Miriam's, and started back for Nevada the next morning to get married.

On Monday morning, September 9, 1963, Vickie and John were married by a justice of the peace in the most humble fashion: Vickie wore Miriam's pedal pushers and blouse, both too large for her; John wore a new pair of Levi's, also too large, and a plaid shirt.

After the ceremony Vickie bought some clothes that fit her, and they headed to Oregon to spend a few days with Rachel Summers, another daughter of Gus Weller. While in Oregon, John was offered the opportunity of taking over a co-op feed store. Although this was quite a flattering and tempting offer, John turned it down, saying to Vickie it was a sign that Satan was trying to tempt them to stay in Oregon.

Before returning home to Utah, John persuaded a lawyer, a friend of Gus Weller's, to contact the Summit County sheriff to have the kidnapping charges against him dropped and the arrest warrant voided. Vickie's relatives, who notified the authorities, believed John had kidnapped Vickie and hypnotized her, and they were ready to commit Vickie to the mental hospital in Provo.

As John and Vickie turned off Interstate 80 and approached the Kamas Valley in the evening, a storm entered the valley and ushered them home with thunder, lightning, and torrential rain. There was electrical failure throughout most of the valley. There were no mobs out that night to disturb their homecoming; they believed the Lord was watching over them. John carried Vickie not only over the threshhold but across the wide driveway as well, to protect her from huge puddles of rain.

Chapter 4

APOSTASY

For the first few years after their marriage, an atmosphere of peace and happiness prevailed at their little homestead in Marion. Most mornings John and Vickie woke up in an embrace, and they always treated each other with affection and tenderness.

John would leave early in the morning to milk cows up at Gus Weller's place, and usually would have television repair calls to make during the day in Marion, Kamas, Park City, Coalville, Heber, and Oakley. He'd also spend some afternoons and evenings doing chores around Weller's and his own land.

At first, Vickie felt all alone while John was gone; she locked the doors because she didn't know what to expect out there in the wilderness. But after three or four weeks she grew to appreciate the few hours of solitude she was afforded each day for the first time in her life. Being twenty years old, she had a tremendous amount of energy and liked to run and sometimes skip, like a little girl, along the trails in Hoyt's Canyon. Nobody was around to watch her.

John and Vickie bought some chickens and built a coop for them, soon having their own eggs and meat. They enlarged the vegetable garden and began storing onions, beets, potatoes, cabbage and carrots in the root cellar for the winter. John taught Vickie how to bake bread; she picked raspberries and made jam. They taught each other what they knew about plumbing and heating, seasoning firewood, sewing and cooking; what skills they didn't have they learned from books or from dealers and suppliers. They loved working together and learning together.

Being somewhat isolated and self-sufficient, they were less dependent on towns and free of social pressures, and so Vickie had an opportunity to examine the world with a new perspective. Up at the foot of the Uinta Mountains she tuned in to nature's rhythms and felt the glory of just being alive. Her mother complained that Vickie was cutting herself off from society and becoming a recluse. Vickie explained to her, "This way of life and all this fresh food makes us healthier. Society has become too complex, fast moving and intense; where are people going at such a fast pace?"

Self-sufficiency became an important goal to them, for both practical and religious reasons. John told Vickie about the economic conditions in Germany at the end of World War II when his family could not get food for days at a time, even when they had money. Self-sufficiency is one of Mormonism's basic principles: true believers must always be prepared for times of crisis, such as economic crashes, wars, famines, and natural disasters, that will precede the second coming of their savior.

When John and Vickie drove to Kamas to shop, and when they occasionally attended dances at the church, people in the community would gawk at them as if they were something strange and unusual. Vickie learned that there were rumors circulating to the effect that John had put her under some sort of hypnotic spell. She overhead one of her cousins remark, "When she comes out of that trance, is she gonna be shocked!" One of Vickie's former friends saw her in a store and exclaimed, "You still *look* the same, Vickie!"

At first the stares and derision upset Vickie. John would comfort her, finally saying, "Listen, you've got to learn not to let that stuff bother you. I guess I've become hard-boiled because I had to cope with it for so many years."

John and Vickie studied the scriptures together every night. These included the Book of Mormon, Doctrine and Covenants, The Pearl of Great Price, and the King James Bible. They pondered these documents, prayed for guidance and enlightenment in order to understand their meaning, and rejoiced in the belief that the gospel of Jesus Christ as revealed to the prophet Joseph Smith (1805–1844), the founder of the Mormon Church, was the true gospel.

Some nights they would walk up to the Weller house to read and discuss scriptures with Uncle Gus, whom they now affectionately called Unk. Gus taught them to love the scriptures for their truth and wisdom. He taught that in order to demonstrate one's faith in God, to attain salvation and eternal life in the Celestial Kingdom, it is not enough to merely believe in the gospel, but it is necessary to fully live the gospel.

Vickie began wearing the traditional garments that were required of women in the early years of the church—dresses down to the wrist and ankles and up to the neck, in subdued patterns and colors—even though most Mormons had abandoned the pioneer-type garments long before the church officially allowed modern clothing in 1923.

John and Vickie had read in Doctrine and Covenants about "gifts of the Spirit," including faith healing, revelation, and prophecy. They believed that all those who followed God's commandments faithfully would be endowed with these powers. They learned from Gus the practice of "the laying on of hands," whereby those with the gift of healing place their hands on the afflicted while praying for a cure.

They took literally the passage in the Bible, "If any of you lack wisdom, let him ask of God, that giveth to all men liberally, and upbraideth not; and it shall be given to him" (James 1:5). Doctrine and Covenants further allows that every devoted, faithful, and righteous person may receive personal revelation and guidance from God, in the form of dreams, inspiration, visions, angels, or even the Lord himself. Collectively, the Mormon Church is guided by revelation as well, but it is only the president who can receive revelation on behalf of the whole church. Personal revelation and faith-healing were practices that had fallen by the wayside at the end of the nineteenth century when, after railroad lines through the territory were completed in 1869 and Utah achieved statehood in 1896, Mormons were no longer isolated from mainstream American culture. The church president is to this day considered a prophet of God, who is responsible for making and revising church policy and doctrine through revelation.

There is another doctrine in which John and Vickie placed credence, one that appears in Doctrine and Covenants as a commandment from God, though its practice was banned by the church in 1890: the doctrine of plural marriage.

Such divergence between the Singers' fundamentalist beliefs and the revised doctrine of the modern Mormon church would cause them strife in the years ahead, but in 1964 John and Vickie were occupied with what they believed to be their most important mission on earth—raising their children.

In the life of a Mormon there is no calling more venerable than parenthood. Mormons believe that under the authority of the priesthood a man and a woman can be "sealed" together for eternity and enjoy a never-ending union. Having children is their opportunity to share in God's divine, creative work, and is a step toward the highest form of personal salvation.

According to Mormon theology, previous to this life all humans existed as spirits, waiting for birth into the physical world. If a person closely follows God's commandments during mortal life on earth, he or she can dwell after death in the Celestial Kingdom, progress through three "degrees of glory," and eventually achieve godhood, the ultimate purpose of existence. Conceiving a child, then, is to give a body to a spiritual "god in embryo." The everlasting covenant of marriage is a prerequisite for attaining the highest degree of celestial glory; it also enables families to remain together in their future spiritual lives.

Shortly after they were married, John and Vickie drove to Salt Lake City to have their marriage "solemnized" in the Mormon Temple. In 1964 their first child, Heidi, was born. In that year, the president of the church, David O. McKay, had said: "No other success can compensate for failure in the home. The poorest shack in which love prevails over a united family is of greater value to God and future humanity than any other riches." Few parents believed in that maxim more strongly, and practiced it more diligently, than John and Vickie Singer.

Their second daughter, Suzanne, was born in 1965, and a year later their first son, Timothy, was born. They loved being together as a family. Even when the children were very young John took them along when he drove to Salt Lake City for TV parts, and they'd also visit John's mother and sister. Countermen at the television supply store rollicked with laughter at John's jokes. It was quite a different reception from what he got in Kamas.

As soon as the kids were old enough to enjoy it, John took them along on his daily farm chores and patiently explained to them what he was doing, allowing the kids to be as rambunctious as they pleased, blessing the Lord for sending him such healthy spirits for his children.

John's patience seemed unbounded, Vickie thought. When something went wrong he was always there to aid and comfort, especially when Vickie was sick—John waited on her assiduously, took care of the children, cooked meals, and saw that clothes were washed, in addition to attending to his TV business and farm chores.

After their first three children were delivered by doctors at the Coalville hospital, John and Vickie decided to deliver their future children at home. They studied books about natural childbirth, and Vickie exercised and walked a mile every day. Many of Vickie's friends and relatives and even Gus Weller warned her of the dangers of home childbirth and urged her to go to the hospital, some offering to pay the doctor's bills. Vickie told a close friend in Kamas that she was relying on the Lord to see her through safely, to which this friend had said, "But the Lord doesn't always answer your prayers." In 1968 Charlotte was born in the log home, the only adults present being her two parents. When Vickie called her friend to announce jubilantly that Charlotte was born without a problem, her friend offered no congratulations and almost seemed disappointed.

The first home childbearing experience was physically painful for Vickie, though she would not have traded it for a bed in the hospital. Their three youngest boys, Joseph, Benjamin and Israel, were also born at home; each time they went through that sacred and trying ordeal the bonds of love between Vickie and John grew stronger.

After Charlotte was born, John bought a Holstein and later a Jersey cow. The Singers started producing their own milk, butter, cheese, cottage cheese, buttermilk, and ice cream. Any extra milk and cheese they sold to neighbors. In 1969 and each year thereafter, they bought a calf to raise for beef. By now the Singers were raising almost all their food on the two-and-a-half-acre farm. They cut wood from the forest behind their property to use for fuel. Their only expenses were food staples, electricity, gasoline, and the telephone. The two hundred dollars or so that John made each month from his TV repair business was more than enough to pay the bills and feed and clothe his family.

As his own family grew, John found less and less time to help Uncle Gus manage the Weller farm, and also spent fewer evenings at Unk's house studying scriptures. The Singers' relationship with Gus Weller at this point might be considered tragic, and perhaps bizarre. Gus began calling at all hours of the day and night to ask for John's help on his place. Vickie would tell Gus that John was busy working in the garden or fixing the house or away on a TV call, to which Gus would reply that John had become irresponsible. The Weller farm, Gus said, was dedicated to the Lord as a place for Mormons to gather in the millennium, when the earth will be renewed, the wicked burned like stubble, and only the pure-in-heart of Zion will remain. It was John's religious obligation, Gus demanded, to help maintain the farm as a holy place.

John understood Gus's lofty purpose, and he had his eye on that goal whenever he helped out on his uncle's land. But John had been working for the Wellers for seventeen years; his only recompense was the two-and-a-half-acre plot of land that was now his home. He had never been paid otherwise. In those seventeen years John had milked cows morning and night, dug irrigation ditches by hand, mended fences, plowed fields, mowed, raked and baled hay, fixed farm machinery, helped to build a garage and a barn, pioneered a spring for drinking water, hauled rocks from fields, and even invested his own money in an irrigation pipe and a sprinkling system for the benefit of the Wellers. When John lived in Gus's house, he paid all the utility bills and more than his share of the food. Now he had a growing family of his own to support and could no longer spare the time.

But there were other reasons for the disharmony between Gus and John. A few years after John and Vickie were married, Gus's son Jared and wife Carol moved back to the farm and built their own house. John and Jared were at first like brothers; they had served in Japan together during the Korean War. Then Gus's daughter Esther and her husband Dick Watson also moved back, followed by another daughter Miriam and her husband Don Jepsen. There were frequent quarrels between Gus's sons and daughters, and at one point Gus told his neighbor, Shirley Black, "I hope my family don't all devour each other." Dick Watson did not like John Singer, and there was always trouble between the two. There was perhaps some jealousy over the fact that Jared, Watson, and Jepsen each received half an acre on which to build their homes, whereas John had been given two and a half acres. All this tension made Gus irritable. Vickie thought Uncle Gus was getting senile. "You either blew into Unk's horn in those days or you were in his doghouse. If you couldn't agree with him you were an apostate."

But perhaps the real reason for the split between John and Gus was their fondness for Shirley Black. Shirley was an attractive blond-haired woman one year older than John, who was born and raised in Kamas. She had dropped out of high school to marry Dean Black, a construction worker from Coalville. Years later in a custody trial Shirley would testify that Dean was a heavy drinker, that he physically and mentally abused her and their children, had a "vulgar, foul mouth and dangerous temper," and "persecuted" his family for practicing religion in the home. Dean would deny those allegations, and the judge would rule in his favor.

Shirley met John Singer in 1958 when she and Dean lived in Coalville and John came over to fix their television set. Shirley was one of the few people who enjoyed John's jokes, his laughter, and his scripture quoting. A year later the Black family moved to Marion when Shirley's father offered them his ranch on Upper Loop Road. Their closest neighbors then were Gus and Margaret Weller, and John Singer.

Through their association as neighbors and during his occasional repair visits, John taught Shirley a bit of the gospel, sparking her interest in religion. Dean and Shirley were both Mormons, but neither had been active in the church. Shirley began studying the scriptures and going to John and Gus, and later Jared Weller, for religious instruction.

Around 1961 Shirley developed a bad back. She went to several chiropractors to try to find out what the problem was, but none of them could determine the source of her pain. It bothered her most when she woke up in the morning; occasionally it got so painful that she would pass out as soon as she got out of bed. Finally she went to Gus Weller to see if he would heal her by the power of the Spirit. Gus laid his hands on her head and blessed her. By the following morning her back was completely healed, never to bother her again.

She ascribed this as being a testimony to the truth of the scriptures, and turned devout. Her inspiration came also from John Singer's gift of wisdom and teaching. She wrote in her diary:

> John was a powerful example. I saw him dig a great big trench by hand, and I don't see how any man could have done it. He said the Lord helped him do it. And the Lord helped him build that house. He did many things that I think would have been impossible without the Lord's help.

Dean and Shirley moved to Kamas in 1963, the year John and Vickie were married. Two years later their oldest daughter was married in a temple service, and she had asked her parents to have their own marriage solemnized at the same time. Shirley knew she could not agree to an eternal marriage with Dean Black. Her interest in religion had caused even a deeper rift between her and her husband. But the pressures from her relatives to have their marriage sealed were great. Worried about her eternal welfare, Shirley fasted for twenty-four hours and prayed to God for guidance. She recorded the answer she received in her diary:

> The Lord actually spoke to me through my mind and spirit and said that He loved both Dean and me, but that we don't belong together in the Celestial Kingdom. He said that I belong with John and Vickie, that some day I would be a member of their family. But I should be patient, for this event would not take place for several years.

Shirley did not disclose this revelation to anyone but John and Vickie until 1968, when the split between John and Gus Weller was first brewing. Nobody knows how he got the notion, but John suspected that Gus wanted to take Shirley as his second wife. No doubt Gus had strong fatherly affections toward her and was jealous because she was going more and more to John, and less to Gus, for spiritual guidance. But if Gus ever had any intention of marrying her, Shirley was never aware of it. In any case, when she told Gus late in 1968 that God had revealed to her three years earlier that she would some day be John Singer's plural wife, Gus flew into a rage. "If you don't deny that, our friendship is over!" he screamed at her. But Shirley could no more deny her revelation from God than renounce Mormonism.

That ended Shirley's association with the Wellers, and it was also the end of the father-son bond betweeen Gus and John.

The Singers' righteous path was becoming increasingly singular. In the years following their split with Gus Weller their faith would be severely tested. The first major test came in 1972 when they were forced to choose between recanting their fundamentalist beliefs and surrendering their membership in the Mormon Church.

Parts of the Mormon doctrine have been substantially revised and some of it abandoned since 1890 in response to intense persecution against the church during its formative years. Modern church leaders considered it essential to the unity, survival, and respectability of the church to insist that their members support the modern doctrine. They went so far as to excommunicate those who strive to maintain all the beliefs and practices set forth in the original scriptures of the mid-1800s.

The Mormon religion was founded in 1830 by the prophet Joseph Smith, Jr., as a restoration of the Church of Jesus Christ "in the latter days." The members of the church called themselves Latter-day Saints, but later sanctioned the nickname Mormons, which was originally used by their detractors because the religion spread through the dissemination of the Book of Mormon.

In 1843 Smith announced the revelation that became section 132 of the Doctrine and Covenants. It began:

> I, the Lord, justified my servants Abraham, Isaac, and Jacob, as also Moses, David and Solomon, my servants, as touching the principle and doctrine of their having many wives and concubines.

Plural marriage was thus introduced as a restoration of biblical mores. Between 1850 and 1890, approximately five percent of married Mormon men had more than one wife. Almost all the church leaders during that period practiced polygamy and considered it the ideal form of marriage.

But polygamy became the rallying point for widespread and

hostile anti-Mormon sentiment. Governor Lulburn Boggs of Missouri, where the Saints had gathered in the 1830s, had proclaimed, "The Mormons must be treated as enemies, and must be exterminated or driven from the state." Joseph Smith's assassination in Carthage, Illinois, in 1844, was accomplished with the collusion of Illinois Governor Thomas Ford. Indeed, after Brigham Young led the Saints to the Salt Lake Valley, Abraham Lincoln campaigned for president on a promise to eliminate "the twin relics of barbarism, slavery and polygamy."

In 1879 the U.S. Supreme Court upheld a law that made polygamy a felony. "Laws are made for the government of actions," the court held, "and while they cannot interfere with mere religious beliefs and opinions, they may with practices."

The United States perceived the Mormon Church—which eastern journalists called "a theocratic dictatorship holding sway by terror and ignorance"—as a threat because of its extraordinary political solidarity and its control over the territorial economy. In 1887, after Brigham Young's death, Congress disincorporated the church and confiscated its property, worth about a million dollars. In 1890, church president Wilford Woodruff, "acting for the temporal salvation of the church," issued the Manifesto which banned plural marriage. The church's escheated property was returned, and in 1896 Utah became the 45th state in the union.

Most church leaders and members, realizing the practical limits of religious freedom in America, regarded the Manifesto of 1890 as a "creative adjustment," necessary for the church's survival. But fundamentalists called it an "accommodation," and believed the church fell into apostasy by bartering the sacred covenant of plural marriage for statehood.

Since 1896 church leaders have abandoned more of the original doctrine, including the importance of personal revelation and the gathering principle ("The righteous shall be gathered out from among all nations, and shall come to Zion.") Today as much as two percent of the five million church members worldwide still believe in all the doctrine of the early church.

The conflict that led to the excommunication of John and Vickie Singer began in the Marion Ward. During the weekly sacrament meetings there was normally a teaching session for adults, presided over by volunteers from the community. Mormons who attended the weekly meetings and worship services were considered active members in the church.

John Singer began attending sacrament meetings when he moved to Marion in 1953. He considered it wrong and humiliating that some of the teachers were women, presiding over men in the priesthood. Moreover, he was irritated because many of the teachers were not studying the scriptures, but merely reading lessons from class manuals prepared by church leaders. On some points the manuals were not consistent with the scriptures, in which case John would raise his hand and point out the discrepancy or contradiction. "Why don't we look and see what the Doctrine and Covenants has to say about that," he would say, or, "Let's take the words of God, instead of the opinions of men." He would quote the Book of Mormon, quote Joseph Smith and Brigham Young, and urge members of the Marion Ward to accept the literal interpretation of the scriptures.

The teachers would retort, "We must accept the teachings and advice of the current church president, who is God's living prophet." They would refer to a message from the General Authorities (the president, his counselors, and the Council of Twelve Apostles) of the church to all the ward teachers in 1945:

> When our leaders speak, the thinking has been done. When they propose a plan, it is God's plan. When they point the way, there is no other which is safe. When they give direction, it should mark the end of controversy. Any Latter-day Saint who denounces or opposes, whether actively or otherwise, any plan or doctrine advocated by the General Authorities of the church is cultivating the spirit of apostasy.

John once had the audacity to compare the mentality of those church members who blindly follow their leaders to the obedience of the German people to Hitler during World War II. That obedience was not condoned by the judges at Nuremberg, he pointed out.

Members of the ward became fed up with John after several years of his intrusive comments. Vickie too became an active church member and supported John during the ward meetings. She knew the scriptures as well as most members of the ward, and understood the conflict between fundamentalists and the modern church.

John and Vickie became increasingly unpopular in Marion. Finally they withdrew from active membership in the ward and stopped paying tithes, the ten percent of their incomes that Mormons give to the church. John built a baptismal font in the woods behind his property and as a member of the priesthood performed his family's religious sacraments himself, including the baptism of his children when they reached the age of eight.

In 1970 the Singers' fourth child, Joseph, was born. In the same year the president of the Mormon Church, David O. McKay, died and was succeeded by Joseph Fielding Smith, whose grandfather's brother was the founder.

John had had personal dealings with Joseph Fielding Smith. When John was nineteen years old he went to hear Smith speak as one of the Twelve Apostles. After the speech, John stayed to meet the man personally. Thirsting after knowledge, John inquired earnestly, "Brother Joseph Fielding Smith, you are an apostle of the Lord, tell me: was Jesus married?"

Smith replied that it was better not to delve into such mysteries.

Surprised, John entreated, "Well, Jesus is my prototype. I'm supposed to follow his example. The prophet Joseph Smith said that we should drink deeply into the mysteries of godliness."

Joseph Fielding Smith shook his head vigorously and walked away from the seeker after truth.

John met Smith again in 1964 when he went to President David O. McKay's office in Salt Lake to appeal his uncle's excommunication for teaching false doctrine. John was told that McKay was ailing and could not receive visitors, and was referred to the Chief Apostle, Joseph Fielding Smith. John asked Smith to reconsider Gus's case, pointing out that Gus was very knowledgeable about the scriptures, and therefore should be welcomed into the church, not kicked out. Smith promised to review the case. Despite repeated visits and importuning by John, Smith never fulfilled his promise.

When Smith succeeded McKay in 1970, John made no secret of his opinion that the new president was a coward, and certainly not a prophet of God.

In 1971 Gus Weller died.

In May 1972, John and Vickie were called in to a meeting with the president of the Kamas Stake, to which the Marion Ward belonged. They were asked why they had left the ward, to which John calmly replied, describing their conflicts with ward members over the years. A week later, two high priests from the stake personally delivered a notice to the Singer home requesting that John and Vickie appear before the stake high council and be tried for their church membership.

On the last day of May, John and Vickie entered the Kamas Stake house accompanied by Harald Singer, who had come to testify in his brother's behalf. Harald had spent two years in Australia as a Mormon missionary after the army (Mormon men are expected to give two years at their own expense to missionary work). He then attended Brigham Young University on the GI bill, where he earned a bachelor's degree, then later on a master's degree in accounting at Indiana University. In 1968 he and his wife settled near Logan, Utah, where Harald became a CPA. Harald had accepted his brother's fundamentalist beliefs, though he was nowhere near as outspoken as John in his criticism of modern church leaders.

John, Vickie, and Harald entered the room in which the stake president, his two counselors, and the twelve high priests were seated in a semicircle. The Singers sat facing the assembly.

The president started to question them. "John Singer and Vickie Singer, do you accept fully and endorse and endeavor to make part of your life the present-day teachings of the General Authorities of the Church of Jesus Christ of Latter-day Saints?"

John responded, "No, we cannot—"

"Please confine your answers to yes or no," the president cut in and continued. "Do you sustain Joseph Fielding Smith as the prophet, seer, and revelator of God, and in doing so accept his teachings as coming from the Lord, and do so without any reservation?"

John and Vickie both responded no. As they did so, they noticed several high priests shaking their heads in dismay. One of them was Rex Walker, the school principal.

"With respect to the subject of plural marriage, do you accept and endorse the present policies and teachings of the General Authorities of the Church of Jesus Christ of Latter-day Saints, and accept the Manifesto of 1890 as the word of the Lord?"

"No."

The president asked Harald if he was prepared to testify as a witness in behalf of John and Vickie. Harald replied he was, and proceeded to defend John and Vickie on the basis that they strived only to follow the Mormon scriptures, to which they had dedicated their lives. On the subject of accepting the teaching of the current church leaders without reservation, Harald quoted Joseph Smith: "I will not seek to compel any man to believe as I do, only by force of reasoning, for truth will cut its own way." With respect to plural marriage, Harald repeated the words of Brigham Young: "If any of you will deny the plurality of wives, and continue to do so, I promise that you will be damned."

The Singers left the room while the council deliberated. When they returned, John and Vickie were informed that they were excommunicated.

To the members of the Kamas Stake High Council, it must have been the ultimate affront when John Singer, upon learning that he was excommunicated, said to them, "When Christ comes the second time, I will be on his right-hand side and the rest of you will be cut asunder as wheat in the field."

In most rural communities of northern Utah, excommunication can mean economic hardship for families that are not self-sufficient. Even in Utah's major cities of Salt Lake, Ogden, and Provo, employees have been fired from their jobs expressly because they were labeled apostates by the church. There is at least one case of a man being fired when his employer learned that the man's stake president was considering excommunicating him.

Many fundamentalists carefully keep their religious beliefs and loyalties secret for fear of losing their jobs or the esteem of their colleagues. On the other hand, some fundamentalists, including the Singers, accept excommunication as a blessing. They feel the Mormon Church has abandoned the gospel in pursuit of wealth and power, and is no longer the true church of Jesus Christ; it is therefore their mission to preserve the true gospel by maintaining the practices and beliefs brought forth by Joseph Smith and Brigham Young.

Some fundamentalists have established self-sufficient, polygamous colonies in southern Utah or in the outlying areas of Salt Lake County, in anticipation of the day when "one mighty and strong" will arise from their ranks to restore the true gospel to the church as predicted in the Doctrine and Covenants:

And it shall come to pass that I, the Lord God, will send one mighty and strong, holding the scepter of power in his hand, clothed with light for a covering, whose mouth shall utter words, eternal words; while his bowels shall be a fountain of truth, to set in order the house of God.

They believe this setting in order of the church will immediately precede the millennium, for, as the Bible states, "Judgment must begin at the house of God." Doctrine and Covenants further speaks of the vengeance, destruction, and mourning that will afflict the unrighteous on that day of judgment. When that day comes, the fundamentalists, the bastions of righteousness amid a majority that has turned away from the Holy Commandments, will become the pillars of the true church of Jesus Christ, and will walk alongside the Savior when he returns to preside over the Kingdom of God.

This fundamentalist vision of an upheaval within the Mormon Church must threaten the status quo of the church, whose annual revenues are said to exceed a billion dollars. That is perhaps one of the reasons that the church discourages its members from attending fundamentalist meetings and demands absolute loyalty to the modern doctrine.

Much of John Singer's TV repair business dried up in the Kamas Valley after word spread that he had been cut off by the church. He was forced to advertise and seek customers in Park City, a twenty-minute drive west from Marion and one of the few non-Mormon towns in Utah. Park City was an old mining town that since the early 1970s has developed into a popular ski resort.

Within a year John's TV business was thriving. After the birth of his sixth child, Benjamin, in August 1972, he found it necessary to spend between thirty to thirty-five hours a week working to pay the mounting bills.

Chapter 5

IN ACCORDANCE WITH THE LAW

The Singers were already treated coolly when they were excommunicated in 1972. Withdrawing their children from public school the following year aroused shock and anger throughout the Kamas Valley. Most people believed that only outlaws and subversives, or else elitists, would do such a thing. On their shopping trips to Kamas, John and Vickie would encounter burning stares of rage and hate from the people.

The members of the local school board must have felt pressure from the electorate when they met to decide on how to proceed with the Singer case. As Walter D. Talbot, State School Superintendent, testified later, Utah's compulsory attendance law is not enforced uniformly throughout the state; it is largely left to the discretion of each local school board whether to bring charges in juvenile court against parents.

In 1973, all six members of the South Summit Board of Education were Mormons. One of them had been on the high council that excommunicated John and Vickie, and had been warned by John that when Christ returned he would be cut asunder as wheat in the field. Another member of the school board was the brother of a high councilman who was told the same thing by John. Val Edrington, the local superintendent, was active in the church and would later be appointed executive secretary of the Kamas Stake.

One event that summer influenced the board not to act immediately when they reconvened in September. On a Saturday near the end of July, two boys were playing on a raft in the middle of a fifteen-foot-deep reservoir just south of the Singer farm. The raft overturned, throwing the boys into the water. Neither of them could swim. Heidi Singer was working in the garden and heard their shouts for help. She ran over to see what had happened, then ran back into the house yelling that two boys were drowning in the reservoir. John dashed out of the house. As he came over the hill and jumped the fence he saw a head between two flailing arms go under. He dived in and pulled the boy safely to the bank and then, still wearing his boots, dived back in to look for the second boy.

Meanwhile, Vickie and Heidi arrived to aid the very pale, coughing boy who was lying face down, soaking wet on the bank. When his coughing subsided, Vickie asked the boy his name.

"Jeff Edrington," he replied. And then, recovering his senses, he asked, "Where's Spencer?"

"You mean Spencer Smith?" Vickie was alarmed.

"Uh huh," the boy nodded.

"John's looking for him," Vickie said.

They both peered out into the reservoir and saw John dive, come up and search, and dive again. Jeff started to cry.

Vickie asked him, "Are you Val Edrington's boy?"

"Yeah," the boy answered, starting to shiver under the hot sun.

Vickie told Heidi to stay with Jeff while she ran back to the house and called Val Edrington and Ron Smith, Spencer's father, who lived on Upper Loop Road.

John searched about twenty minutes for the second boy, to no avail. Finally, exhausted, he gave up. When he walked up to the bank and saw Val Edrington kneeling beside his son, John was startled. With a humble and grateful countenance, Val took John's right hand in both of his and said, "It might as well have been two boys drowned if it hadn't been for you, John." There was a peculiar feeling between these two men who were destined to be adversaries.

Ron Smith and another neighbor arrived, and after a short search they found Spencer's body.

School opened in September but the Singer children were not in attendance. Three months went by and John and Vickie had not heard from the South Summit School Board.

Val Edrington had told the board in September that John Singer had saved his son's life, and for that reason he would feel loath to file a complaint against the Singers in juvenile court. Respecting the superintendent's position, but also feeling reluctant to let the Singers off, the board asked Edrington to inform State Superintendent Talbot of the Singer case and ask for his advice on how to proceed. On October 4, 1973, Dr. Talbot wrote in his reply: "I have discussed this matter with personnel in the Office of the Attorney General and we are in accord that action should be initiated by your board of education in accordance with the law." Dr. Talbot's two-page letter excerpted pertinent sections of the compulsory attendance law, including section 4 which gives each local school board the duty to report violators to the juvenile court in its district.

At their October meeting the school board decided they had no choice but to refer the Singer case to the Summit County Juvenile Court in Coalville. Edrington then obtained a copy of the juvenile court code, which he read to the board at its November meeting. According to the code, a neglected child is one whose parents "fail or refuse to provide proper or necessary subsistence, education, or medical care." The parents of neglected children are guilty of a misdemeanor and are punishable by imprisonment of not more than six months or by a fine not exceeding $299, or both.

On December 6, 1973, the school board filed a complaint in juvenile court and the case of *State of Utah* v. *John Singer and Vickie Singer* was commenced before Judge Merrill L. Hermansen.

> The undersigned, being duly sworn, complains and alleges that the above defendants ... did on the 29th day of March, 1973, commit the crime of contributing to the delinquency and neglect of Heidi Singer, Suzanne Singer and Timothy Singer, children under the age of 18 years, by withdrawing said minor children from school, and failing to comply with policies and standards set out for the education of said children as provided by the Utah Code ... and against the peace and dignity of the State of Utah.

It was signed Val D. Edrington.

The first time the Singers heard of this action against them was when a Summit County deputy sheriff knocked on their door on the afternoon of December 7 and handed Vickie a summons ordering her and John to appear before Judge Hermansen in three days to answer the charges against them. When Vickie read the words "the crime of contributing to the delinquency and neglect," she exclaimed to the deputy, "What is this? Delinquency and neglect!" She pointed to Suzanne and Charlotte who were playing with their year-old brother Benjamin in the living room. "Do those children look neglected to you?" She pointed out the window to where John, Timothy, and Joseph were carrying bales of straw from the van to the barn, to where Heidi was washing vegetables in the kitchen.

The officer smiled and said, "No, they sure don't. But I'm not the judge."

He departed. Vickie sat down by the fireplace. The crackling and hissing of the damp cottonwood seemed to express her sentiments toward the people who had brought these charges against her.

John came in shortly wanting to know the purpose of the deputy's visit. Vickie read him the summons. John's initial reaction was to feel deeply insulted. He could not understand how parents who spent so much of their time teaching and caring for their children could be accused of neglecting them. They both agreed that they would never, under any circumstances, let the state force them to send their children back to public school.

But they were also frightened. The court date was three days away. They did not know of any other parents who had gone through the same thing. Nor did they know what the penalties were if they were convicted of delinquency and neglect of their children. They thought and prayed about what to do.

Court convened on December 10 with Judge Hermansen presiding. Attending the hearing were Val Edrington, Principal Rex Walker, and the assistant county attorney as the prosecutor. They waited for John and Vickie to arrive. When they failed to appear, Edrington presented the facts of the case. Rex Walker then confirmed that John Singer had withdrawn his three oldest children from school nine months earlier and that the children had not been in attendance since that time.

The prosecutor requested that the judge issue a warrant for John Singer's arrest, and a bench warrant was issued. The task of serving the arrest warrant fell to Deputy Sheriff Leon Wilde of Kamas, who had known John Singer for several years.

Leon Wilde knocked on the Singers' door the following day. John had seen Leon coming, and had a pretty good idea of what the deputy's mission was. He opened the door, neither stepping outside nor inviting Leon in.

"I have a warrant for your arrest, John. You'd better come in with me," Leon said.

John asked where the warrant came from.

"Judge Hermansen issued it, because you didn't show up in court yesterday."

"Why don't you tell Judge Hermansen that we don't think it's the state's business to have their noses down our necks telling us how to educate our children."

"John, you're charged with a misdemeanor, and you have to go to court to defend yourself. That's the way this system works."

"I'm not guilty of neglecting my children. The judge can come over here and see for himself."

Leon looked down for a moment. In some respects he admired the way the Singers lived. They were a clean, rugged, hard-working, freedom-loving frontier family, the kind that made this country great. "You coming with me, John?" He knew what the answer would be.

"No."

Deputy Wilde was not interested in precipitating a violent confrontation in the Singers' home. He left with a warning: "We're going to have to bring you in sooner or later if you don't come in voluntarily. The judge could send ten guys out here to break your door down to get you."

"If that's the case," John responded, "then there will be bloodshed."

When Leon Wilde returned empty-handed to the sheriff's office in Coalville, Summit County Sheriff Ron Robinson decided to assume full responsibility for the arrest of John Singer.

A month later, on January 11, 1974, Sheriff Robinson and Deputy Fred Eley were riding in their squad car, passing through Kamas on routine patrol. It was bitter cold and snowing. Robinson saw a yellow Ford van in front of him make a right turn off Highway 189.

Suspecting the van was Singer's, he asked Eley to run a "10-28," which is the code for a license plate check, through the radio dispatch, while they slowly followed the van. The dispatcher quickly confirmed the van was Singer's.

John Singer parked in front of a house three blocks from the highway. He was collecting his tools in the back of his van when Sheriff Robinson pulled up. The two officers got out of their car and walked around to the side of the van where they expected John to emerge.

When John opened the side door to climb out, the officers put him under arrest. Surprised, John dropped his tool box on the fresh snow. He held in his left hand a long thin screwdriver. As Robinson grabbed John's left elbow John ripped a hole in the sheriff's sleeve with his screwdriver, causing a minor scratch on the sheriff's arm. Fred Eley grabbed John's right arm and was preparing to put handcuffs on him when John abruptly forced his arms down and escaped the grip of both officers. He dropped his screwdriver and said quickly, "I'll go peacefully, but don't put the handcuffs on me."

John spent the night in a Coalville jail cell. This was only the second time in his marriage without Vickie by his side; the first time had been on a hunting trip in the High Uintas Primitive Area.

The next day John was able to see Judge Hermansen. The judge was friendly. He gave John a copy of the complaint charging him with child neglect, and asked if he had an attorney or could afford to hire one. John said he couldn't afford a lawyer.

The judge then said, "I'll tell you what we'll do. This court will appoint a lawyer to represent you. It won't cost you anything. Now, if you'll agree to meet with this lawyer, and work out a program for educating your kids at home that will satisfy the school board, and if they'll issue you an exemption from sending your kids to public school, then I'll let you go home and we'll dismiss these charges against you. How does that sound?"

'What other choices do I have?" John asked.

The alternatives, the judge said, were to send his children back to public school, or stand trial on a misdemeanor charge. If he chose the latter and was convicted, he'd probably have to go to jail or send his kids to public school anyway, or both.

John explained that it was his religious duty to educate his children in the ways of the Lord and protect them from an immoral society, that he could not compromise this stand because he had made a covenant with God. He asked the judge whether he didn't think the compulsory attendance law was unconstitutional since it interfered with his religious liberty.

Judge Hermansen said that he did not have the jurisdiction to rule on the constitutionality of a state law. "The only way to have a law declared unconstitutional is to get convicted of breaking it and then appeal the conviction to the state supreme court," he said. "Or you can try to get a declaratory judgment, but you'll need a real good lawyer for that. Or you can petition the legislature to change the law."

One night without freedom had been too much for John. He did not understand the court system, and felt powerless to change the laws. He feared that if he were convicted of a crime he would be locked in a cell and left there to rot. He did not want to spend another day away from his family—his profound love for them, and theirs for him, as well as the religious ordinances that bound them, took precedence over all other matters. Under the circumstances, he felt he must accept a court-appointed attorney and work with the school board. It would be humiliating and it would mean compromising his liberties. But it was the best of the alternatives.

The judge expressed great pleasure and relief at John's decision. He said that the attorney would call John within a few days. John picked up his keys from the clerk and drove home feeling subdued, but was glad to feel the cold wind coming through the half-opened window, stinging his face as he drove west along Interstate 80.

On January 14, the court appointed attorney James D. Smedley of Heber City to represent the Singers. After talking with John by telephone, Smedley met with Superintendent Edrington to make sure he understood the requirements for obtaining a certificate of exemption from the school board. The Singers were to write up and submit a schedule for each day of the week, including five and a half hours of instruction each day in the required subjects, taught at the appropriate level for each school-age child, and using textbooks and materials approved by the school board. Edrington agreed to allow the use of the educational television channel as an aid in teaching health education, art, music, and science.

Smedley met with John and Vickie at their home and helped

them draw up a daily schedule. As an example, Monday's plan was as follows:

8:45–9:00	Exercises
9:00–9:15	Health (Channel 7)
9:15–9:45	Language arts
9:45–10:00	Social studies
10:00–11:00	Math
	Lunch, one hour
12:00–1:00	Phonics, reading, writing, spelling
1:00–1:30	English grammar workbooks
1:30–2:00	Science workbooks
	Recess, ten minutes
2:10–2:45	Art (Channel 7 and review)

Smedley submitted the weekly schedule and a list of textbooks and materials the Singers were planning to use, some of which they would buy or borrow from the school district, to the board for its approval.

In a meeting of March 8, 1974, the school board decided to issue a certificate of exemption to the Singers on the condition that the school district administer a Basic Skills Achievement Test to the four oldest Singer children twice a year, starting that fall. Tony Powell, school psychologist for the South Summit District, was appointed to conduct the tests and monitor the Singers' home education program.

On June 10, 1974, Smedley returned to juvenile court and presented Judge Hermansen with evidence that the Singers had complied with the provisions of the compulsory attendance laws. The judge dismissed the complaint against John and Vickie, who expressed their gratitude to Smedley for his efforts on their behalf.

Many people wish that could have been the final chapter of the Singer story.

John and Vickie tried diligently to comply with the conditions of their exemption, but after a few months they began to feel that their lives were being run by the school district.

With students ranging from kindergarten to the fourth grade,

John and Vickie found that for some subjects, especially math and reading and writing, it was necessary to split the children into two groups—John teaching the older girls, Heidi and Suzanne, and Vickie the younger ones, Timothy, and Charlotte, who was six. They also had to watch the youngest children, Joseph and Benjamin, who were now three and a half and one and a half. Their days were long and demanding. They followed the schedule throughout spring 1974, took a break in the summer, and resumed in the fall.

Tony Powell came to the Singer home in October to test the four oldest kids to compare their academic progress to that of their peers in public school. The kids liked him. He was easygoing, casually dressed, and seemed to have a genuine interest in the welfare of the children. He explained the purpose of the test to them, but they were not aware of the consequences if they should fail to do well.

The tests took a little more than an hour each day for four days. It was tiring for the younger ones, who had never taken a test before and were nervous. Heidi accepted the test as a challenge as she did most tasks in life, and thought it was fun.

The tests showed that the Singer children were slightly behind their public school peers. Suzanne was significantly behind in science and Timothy in English. Powell took into consideration that the children were not accustomed to taking tests, for he observed that they were otherwise healthy, bright, industrious, and harmonious. He advised the school board that he found the Singers' educational program to be satisfactory. The board voted to extend the family's exemption for another year.

But John and Vickie were becoming increasingly dissatisfied. They still felt they were slaves in their own home, still believed the education of their children to be their exclusive domain. They began to modify their schedule, reducing the daily hours first to five, then to four and a half hours. They started using their own choice of textbooks in social studies and science. They added formal religious instruction to the curriculum, and allowed the kids to proceed at their own pace instead of enforcing a fixed schedule of lessons.

John told stories from the Book of Mormon in his religion class. Soon John and Vickie used the book for handwriting and spelling lessons and abandoned the board-prescribed workbooks. All these changes were made without the knowledge or consent of Powell or the school board. They had "bowed down to that bunch long enough."

When Powell returned to test the children in April 1975, he found them to be further behind their peers than they were six months ago. He discussed the scores with John and Vickie, and pointed out to them that the children would continue to fall behind unless they were returned to public school.

"It's an impossibility," John said. "We will not send them back to public school."

Vickie explained to the psychologist that their children were not interested in competing with their peers or with anyone else. Their children did not want to be molded and guided by a society whose vision had become cluttered. "My children will seek first the Kingdom of God," she told Powell, "and the Lord will let each of them know, individually, what his or her life's mission will be. They will progress at their own pace and learn the things they need to know to fulfill that mission."

Powell was torn between his duty to uphold certain educational standards and his feeling that the Singers did not deserve to be labeled as criminals. Like many others, he did not agree with the Singers' religious beliefs but knew they were sincerely held, and he respected their devotion to them. He decided to wait and check on their progress in the coming fall before making any recommendations to the board.

Meanwhile John Singer developed grandiose plans for his children's education. In May, when the weather turned warm and dry, be began building a one-room schoolhouse across the lane from their log home. It was to be a wood-frame structure, twenty-one by seventeen feet. He planned to furnish it as a classroom: tables, chairs, bookshelves, blackboards, maps, globes, and all kinds of teaching accessories. There would be a lectern for experts to come and lecture; there were going to be seminars and debates. Eventually there would be a piano, and a movie projector to show educational films. Also, in a few years the older children would be able to teach the younger ones—Vickie was now pregnant with their seventh child, and Heidi, the eldest, was eleven. Sometimes friends of theirs from Salt Lake would bring their kids to Marion and assist in teaching.

Among the friends from Salt Lake who came to visit and help with building the schoolhouse was Bonnie Norder, who at that time had only met the Singers once before. Bonnie was an energetic woman with a warm personality, and an articulate, ingenuous manner. She had grown up in New Jersey and taken degrees in secondary education and home economics from the University of Massachusetts. Later she taught grammar school briefly in New York City where she converted to Mormonism in 1972. She moved to Utah that year, but left for St. Louis the following year to help out a sick relative.

While in St. Louis Bonnie met distant relatives of Vickie Singer's, and in April 1973 traveled with them to Utah for the Mormon Church's semi-annual general conference. On this occasion Bonnie visited the Singer farm for the first time. During her visit John was intermittently watching the general conference on television. Bonnie remembered she was shocked by the bluntness with which John openly criticized the general authorities of the church, especially the new president Harold B. Lee, whom John called a "crap shooter." However, Bonnie liked the Singers and admired their life-style.

Bonnie returned to St. Louis and made a living as a home economist. She became involved with a quasi-fundamentalist off-shoot of the Mormon Church that dated back to the Latter-day Saints' Jackson County days in the mid 1800s. Early in 1975 several members of this group moved to Utah. Bonnie traveled to Utah in June that year, this time to scout out job prospects for herself so that she too could move there later in the year.

This time she brought three friends from St. Louis to meet John and Vickie. After they had raised the walls of the schoolhouse, everyone sat around the log home and talked religion. Bonnie noticed that John was a good listener but did not allow anyone to change what be believed. Over the years Bonnie would find that John was the most stubborn and intractable person when it came to doctrine. John hearkened unto the Lord, and nothing else. But she grew to love him like a brother.

In fall 1975 Bonnie moved permanently to Salt Lake City and found herself living very close to John's mother, whom everyone called Grandma—because she had more than twenty-five grand-children. Bonnie frequently drove Grandma to the Marion farm, and was gradually accepted as a family member. Besides, as a certified schoolteacher she was keenly interested in the developing conflict between the Singers and the county over the education of their children.

The one-room schoolhouse was completed that June. John and the three oldest kids painted it red. They sanded and refinished furniture for the classroom. John installed a blackboard and a wood-burning stove. They made repairs on an old phonograph and an ancient sewing machine. Grandma donated a brand-new globe.

Classes were held in the red schoolhouse as soon as it was finished. They enjoyed it so much that they all decided to skip the summer break. The schoolhouse gave them a sense of independence, and they soon forgot about the restraints the school district had imposed on them.

John and Vickie no longer followed a schedule. They took care to teach the basic subjects every day, but in whatever order and for whatever duration they felt like. The school day usually lasted two or three hours. It would begin with ten or fifteen minutes of group exercises, followed by a prayer seeking the Lord's guidance in their education, and a song from the church hymnal. John would always write the song on the chalkboard to explain its meaning before leading the singing. Then classes would begin. If necessary, after formal classes Vickie took one or two of the children aside for remedial lessons.

John and Vickie found that the most difficult task was how to make the lessons interesting. Vickie confided to Bonnie Norder that she had been bored to tears when she was in school, and for that reason had no enthusiasm for it. "The kids will learn more in two hours," she said, "if you make the classes interesting and they're alert and enthusiastic, than if you teach all day and they're tired and restless."

Bonnie asked Vickie how the children would learn algebra when neither John nor Vickie knew it, and whether the kids would get an opportunity to dissect a frog or work in a chemistry lab.

"Listen, I took algebra in high school and it went in one ear and out the other, and I've never needed to use it," Vickie replied. "And we couldn't care less about dissecting a frog or learning chemistry. I took that too, and I can't remember one darn thing about it, it was the driest junk you ever heard of."

Vickie explained, "My job is to give them the basics and the incentive to search and learn things on their own, to stand on their own feet; and when the time comes that they need to know algebra or some of those things, they'll have the motivation and the confidence to study it and learn it."

One day Heidi asked about the "big bang" explanation for the beginning of the universe that she had heard on television. John explained to the class: "No matter which way you twist or turn, if you look at the whole universe or the smallest particles, if you go into the animal life, tree life, or plant life, no matter which way you delve into it, the only way that any creation ever comes about is through male and female. There is no other way that you can organize or create anything unless it's on that principle. If you delve into the animal elements, no matter which way you look, an offspring will only come about in that fashion. Not just by chance or all of a sudden being there, no."

This was typical of the way John gave his children a simple and unsophisticated view of the world. He taught concepts that the children could grasp from their own experience—not abstract theories in a book that may be replaced by new ones in the future.

That summer the Singers hired Mitzi Black, daughter of Dean and Shirley Black, who had just graduated from high school, to come in once a week for three hours to teach the children. This freed John to spend more time repairing televisions, and gave Vickie, who was pregnant, a little respite from the daily routine.

There was a well-established routine at the farm. They would rise before seven and do chores for fifteen minutes. Vickie would fix breakfast while John took care of farm affairs. Heidi and Timmy milked the cows. Suzanne and Charlotte milked the goats, which the family had acquired in 1974, and Joseph fed the baby goats. Then the children would all come back into the house; each picked a room, and together they would straighten up the entire house. After breakfast at eight-thirty, school would start and run without recess for two or three hours, after which the children would go out and play.

In the afternoons the kids learned practical skills—gardening, pruning, animal husbandry, house painting, varnishing furniture, cooking, repairing equipment, canning, and cutting firewood.

Timothy loved to work in the shop. He liked building small vehicles such as wagons, carts, and trains out of wood and metal pipe. From John he learned at age nine to make furniture and fix lawn-mower engines. Five-year-old Joseph also liked working in the shop and made toy wooden boats to play with in the irrigation ditch.

Heidi, eleven, made Indian necklaces and leather moccasins for herself and as gifts. She studied Indian lore and had discovered a sacred Ute burial ground in Hoyt's Canyon. She collected flint arrowheads that she had dug up around the property, and used them in making her necklaces.

Suzanne, who was a year younger than Heidi, was artistic. She drew pictures of the surroundings and made gifts out of portraits of her brothers and sisters using watercolors and colored pencils. She also made dolls out of discarded clothing and materials.

Charlotte, seven, could sew. She mended clothes and, with Vickie's help, had made a skirt for herself. She also loved to hike in the mountains to look for deer and smell the wild flowers.

A few times the kids got together after school and built a small clubhouse, which would usually last a few months before they tore it down to reuse the materials for other projects. Over the years they managed to build a log cabin, tepees, huts, and tree houses. They also played baseball and soccer, especially when Harald's children or friends from Salt Lake were visiting.

John's TV repair business brought in just enough money to support his family. John never had a bank account, and never attempted to save money or build up a business. He had decided to spend as much time as he could working on the farm with his family to maintain self-sufficiency.

Every Sunday John conducted religious services in the home. He would read from the Bible and the Book of Mormon, teach the gospel, and bless the sacrament. The service would last thirty minutes to an hour, and no one but the immediate family participated. He still took the whole family to Salt Lake once a week to pick up TV parts, and they made a day of it.

The Singers did not see doctors even in the event of a grave illness. They relied entirely on the power of God for healing. Vickie explained how this worked: "God's spirit is in and through all things. It is the very light that makes us alive. When you understand this, you can learn to draw this light, this power within you, and send it out to others for the healing, for the well-being, for the blessing of individuals. You can send forth this Holy Spirit, through your administration, into an individual and cast out all darkness. Whatever is in disorder can be set in perfect and restored order."

Later Vickie gave testimony about their reliance on the power of the Spirit:

Q: Did any of the children ever become seriously ill during the period of time when you didn't go to doctors or dentists?

A: Yes.

Q: In July of 1974 the three youngest had what you diagnosed as whooping cough. Is that right?

A: Yes.

Q: And they were deathly ill for three weeks or thereabouts?

A: They were very ill.

Q: Is it true that Charlotte almost choked to death?

A: At one time she had blood coming out of her nose, I think, and had a hard time breathing just for a minute.

Q: Did you ever consider that the children probably ought to receive some medical help?

A: No.

Q: That is because of your belief and John's belief?

A: Because we had been healed so miraculously all the other times and we knew the Lord would see us through.

Q: What did the children think about this when they were deathly ill? Did they ever say, "I want to go to the doctor"?

A: No. They asked Daddy to bless them.

Q: You mentioned something earlier which I thought was interesting and it was something to do with the Lord fixed your washing machine. Tell me about that, will you?

A: I think there were two incidents when it wouldn't work and it was a fairly new machine, I believe, and I needed it to work so I prayed to Heavenly Father, "Please fix it, whatever is wrong, please fix it," and He did.

Q: That happened twice?

A: Yes.

If healing did not take place within a short time after the administration of a blessing, it was considered a test of the afflicted person's faith. It meant that person needed to study the scriptures and pray to replenish his faith. When that was accomplished, healing would take place. Healing, then, was more than just relief from illness. It was a reaffirmation that the Lord considered a person faithful and worthy of being blessed by the Holy Spirit.

Daily the Singers sought the Lord's will concerning their lives through prayer and personal revelation. Many revelations came through dreams. John kept a diary of his most important ones from the time he first arrived in Marion. Vickie started a journal in 1971 in which she recorded her children's dreams as well as her own, and accounts of the important events in their lives.

One of the most significant revelations for John came in a two-part dream that he had around 1970, two years before excommunication and three years before withdrawing his kids from elementary school. In the first part of the dream, John had built a log fortress at the entrance to his property, and was standing in front of it wearing a buckskin outfit and armed with a long rifle, a pistol, and his Bowie knife. Down the lane, Jared Weller and some other men were also armed; they were expecting some sort of invasion. The air was quiet and still. Then John saw his old friend Slim running up the lane toward him. Slim was frightened; he was seeking protection from the mobs that were on their way to Marion to start a battle. John gave Slim a pistol. Everyone, including Jared's group, began preparing to defend themselves and their families.

In the second part of the dream, John was standing in the doorway of a Mormon chapel. The assembly hall was filled with people whose faces were hewn out of grayish-brown rock. He heard a voice tell him, "From here is where you can expect your trouble."

Afterwards John wrote in his journal: "This two-part dream showed me that the Devil has taken over in the Mormon Church. Also that these so-called Latter-day Saints will be the cause of blood spilling."

Another significant dream that John had early in his marriage was one concerning the doctrine of plural marriage. He was at the foot of a mountain, at the top of which were two women. In the dream he understood that these women were to be his wives. He started to climb the mountain, but an angry mob of people pursued him and tried to keep him from reaching the top. The mountain was so rugged and steep that most of the pursuers fell behind, except for a few who kept up. As John neared the top, suddenly a huge iron gate fell from the sky and lodged between him and his enemies, and they had no more power over him.

It was clear to John that the dream meant it was God's wish that he should have plural wives. His wives were at the top of a mountain because he must first become righteous and learn to live by all of God's commandments before he could have them. In many of his and Vickie's dreams, the Kingdom of God was represented as the summit of a mountain, to be attained only by hard work and devotion to the scriptures. The mob in John's dream symbolized the opposition by the church and the state to plural marriage. But once the Kingdom of God was reached, those forces would have no more power.

John and Vickie had discussed the doctrine of plural marriage and both agreed that someday they would practice it. The idea made Vickie anxious, however. One night she lay awake in bed thinking about it. She felt a panic come over her; she felt conflicted between her desire to live according to God's will and the pain of having to share her husband with other women. A lump appeared in her throat, making it painful to swallow. She prayed silently, "Heavenly Father, please help me. Please bless me and show me the light. I want to do what's right. I want to do thy will, but it hurts to think about it."

The next morning Vickie had a revelation while she was making the bed. She wrote in her journal:

> The most marvelous peace came over me and I was shown a higher order of God. I was shown the celestial order of God where one man would have many wives, and it was the most marvelous, the most joyous feeling I can ever describe. It was the most marvelous love, the most beautiful, joyous love; I would love all the other wives as I love myself and there was no reason for jealousy or any bad feelings whatsoever, but the most marvelous joyous happy feeling I have ever felt. I realized that the Kingdom of God is a higher existence that we are not familiar with, and I rested assured that when these events were to come about I would be able to receive comfort and strength. This was revealed from Heaven.

The Singer's seventh child, Israel, was born on October 3, 1975. A few weeks later Vickie began having severe toothaches. She had had problems with her teeth ever since childhood, but had quit seeing the dentist after her marriage, and her toothaches became more frequent.

When Tony Powell called at the end of October to make arrangements for the tests, John told him it was an inconvenient time since

Vickie was ill and the older girls were caring for the new baby. He told Powell they had held school throughout the summer, so the children were probably caught up. Powell agreed to postpone the testing until spring.

Vickie's illness grew worse. Her gums became abscessed and swollen, and the infection spread to her ears. She could not take any solid food for days at a time. She was in great pain and was confined to bed most of the day. John prayed and laid his hands on her several times. Suzanne, almost eleven years old, took care of Israel as if he were her own child. The other children pitched in around the house and helped John with his farm work. Vickie's illness lasted five months, during which they did not hold school.

Near the end of January 1976, Bonnie Norder visited the Singers and, knowing that Vickie was sick, brought her presents. She was alarmed by Vickie's condition. Vickie was pale and had lost fifteen pounds, down to 105. She hadn't been able to eat for several days and was so weak that she had to be carried to and from the bathroom. John had stayed awake the night before kneeling in prayer beside the bed. All the kids looked very worried; they were afraid Vickie was going to die. Still, they refused to call a doctor.

Bonnie's visit lifted Vickie's spirits and marked the turning point in the illness. By the end of February Vickie was teaching school, cooking meals, and taking care of Israel again. Her family considered her long illness a supreme test of their faith. They had passed the test by relying on God's healing powers alone; now they were a step closer to the Kingdom of God.

As their faith renewed, their conviction grew that they must get out from under the thumb of the local school district. John and Vickie decided that when Tony Powell next called, they would refuse to allow him to come in and test their children.

Powell called on April 1, 1976. John was out on a TV call. Vickie steeled herself to break the news to Powell. "We don't want our children tested by the school district anymore," she told him. "We have decided to restore the freedoms that have been lost to us, one of which is the freedom to educate our children according to our religious beliefs without interference from the government. And this being the bicentennial year, it's a good time to make such a stand."

"Vickie, I sympathize with your feelings, but if you don't comply with the education laws the school board will prosecute you. I know they will," Powell reasoned.

"We are responsible for our children, not the school board. They don't support or raise them, we do. We are true Americans, and the Lord has let us know that He will protect our constitutional freedoms. It is a corrupt government that passes a law that takes children away from their parents, and those people who try to enforce that law are tyrants. Do you know what Thomas Jefferson said? 'Rebellion to tyrants is obedience to God.' He was one of our founding fathers. And I want to tell you something else: in the very near future, sooner than you believe, this government is going to be replaced by a theocracy."

As an executive of his ward in Woodland, Utah, Powell understood what Vickie meant by theocracy. But he was concerned with the fate of Vickie's family. "Are you saying that you shouldn't have to worry about obeying the laws now because the millennium is right around the corner?" he asked her.

"I'm saying, or we believe, that the Kingdom of God will be established *before* the millennium, and man's law will be replaced by God's laws. When this is accomplished, Christ will return."

"Do you think this will be accomplished by a revolution?"

"Well, it will be accomplished as a result of social unrest, and crisis, and natural disasters, and great political upheaval. And an ensign will be lifted here in these mountains for people to gather, the people from all nations who are interested in setting up a society based on the laws of God."

"And you think this will happen soon."

"Yes, very soon."

"I certainly don't want to argue with your religious beliefs. But I sincerely hope you'll face this school issue on a secular level, because that's how the juvenile court is going to handle it," Powell concluded.

Chapter 6

PRESSURE

U pon learning of their refusal to permit testing, the South Summit School Board decided to invite John and Vickie to one of its future meetings in order to determine whether there was any reason not to withdraw the exemption it had issued to the Singers. Before the proposed meeting, the board petitioned the juvenile court to appoint an attorney to represent the Singers there.

In summer 1976, Summit County was transferred from the Third Juvenile Court District of Judge Hermansen to the First Juvenile Court District of Judge Charles E. Bradford. In September, Summit County Attorney Robert Adkins appeared in court on a motion in support of the school board's petition. Quite properly, Judge Bradford refused to appoint an attorney for the Singers on the grounds that there were no criminal charges pending against them. During the discussion of the motion, the judge confided to Adkins that he sympathized with the Singers because he believed that "parents should have substantial latitude in the education of their children."

Adkins presumed from Bradford's comment that the judge was averse to enforcing the compulsory education law. Adkins, thirty years old and only four years out of law school, wrote to Val Edrington on October 4 to advise him that the judge had dismissed his motion. He added, "I don't believe that we would receive too much help out of the juvenile court, if another criminal action were filed against the Singers. Judge Bradford apparently takes the position that a parent should have substantial discretion in the type of education, or lack of it, which his child receives."

In November, Edrington wrote to State Superintendent Walter Talbot to bring him up to date on "the intriguing saga of Mr. and Mrs. John Singer." Edrington informed Talbot of Judge Bradford's "alleged flexible attitude" toward the compulsory attendance law, and enclosed a copy of Adkins's October 4 letter. "I have tried to keep this situation low-keyed," Edrington wrote, "but the board is putting pressure on me to carry the issue through to its legal end. I certainly don't want to put you in the position of taking on the juvenile court system and their failure to enforce the state statutes."

For reasons that are still unclear, Edrington believed that Walter Talbot then contacted the Utah attorney general's office in an attempt to have the attorney general persuade Judge Bradford to change his attitude. Edrington made this report to the South Summit School Board in February 1977: "Since the last board meeting, Superintendent Talbot has directed me to go ahead with the complaint against the Singers. He has the assurance of Judge Bradford that he will carry out the compulsory attendance law even though it is contrary to his personal beliefs. It seems that Dr. Talbot contacted the attorney general's office, and the attorney general's office apparently called in Judge Bradford and put the pressure on him. Then the judge called Superintendent Talbot and informed him of his intent to carry out the law."

To gain an understanding of Edrington's claims it is necessary to go back a few months to the fall of 1976. An informant told Judge Bradford that Walter Talbot had written a letter to the governor complaining that the judge had refused to hear cases relating to the compulsory education law.

The judge called Dr. Talbot, who explained he hadn't written to the governor but had learned of the judge's position from Superintendent Edrington's recent letter to him. The judge told Talbot that it was a "gross misperception" of his attitude. He explained his concerns about the compulsory attendance law, even stating that he thought it should be amended so it wouldn't force people like the Singer children to go to school. "But my personal philosophy absolutely does not affect the performance of my duties as a judge to carry out the law," Bradford stressed.

Talbot later testified that in fact as state school superintendent he communicated with the attorney general's office frequently. But apparently Bradford was never contacted by anyone in the attorney general's office.

Another wrinkle in this convoluted issue is the fact that Bradford's six-year term as juvenile court judge was due to expire in August 1977. In order to be reappointed he had to be recommended to the governor by a Juvenile Court Commission which screened candidates for appointment to the juvenile court bench. In 1977, one of the five members of the commission was Walter Talbot, and Judge Bradford knew this.

Walter Talbot, who was fifty-four, had worked in the Utah public school system for thirty-two years and had served as state superintendent since 1972. He was also counselor to the president of his stake. He considered the compulsory attendance law a serious matter, and admitted that his vote as a member of the commission was influenced by whether or not judges intended to enforce that law.

When Val Edrington told the school board in February 1977 that Judge Bradford had been pressured into enforcing the law, the board decided to take the Singers to juvenile court. But first the board invited John and Vickie to its March meeting. There John told the board that he would no longer allow the school district to monitor his home school or test his children. He reiterated that the schools were breeding places of immorality and it was his religious duty to protect his children from corruption, and that he refused to be enslaved by unrighteous laws.

After John left, the board voted to withdraw the Singer's exemption. Edrington notified them of the board's decision by mail, in which he also noted that unless the Singers reinstated their children in the district schools by March 18, 1977, their case would be reported to the juvenile court.

The Singers did not take any action. Edrington filed a complaint charging John and Vickie with contributing to the delinquency and neglect of Heidi, Suzanne, Timothy, Charlotte, and Joseph Singer. Two days later the Singers received a summons to appear in juvenile court for arraignment on June 7. Except for Benjamin and Israel, the children were all of school age.

During this time Vickie had more trouble with her teeth. In late 1976 she was again in great pain from an infection. She told John she might go out of her mind if the pain continued much longer. John fasted for four days and prayed vigorously. On the morning of the fifth day, he laid his hands on Vickie's head and prayed, and as soon as he uttered "Amen" the pain left her.

The infection returned in early 1977. This time Vickie received a revelation that God had tested her and accepted her sacrifice of pain and suffering, that now she should go to a dentist and have the pain cast out for good. A dentist in Heber City pulled four of Vickie's teeth. It was then revealed to her through a dream that someday she would grow a new set of teeth to replace the four missing ones. Expecting that prophecy would be fulfilled, she declined to wear false teeth. "All things are possible to those who believe," she insisted.

John and Vickie appeared in juvenile court before Judge Bradford on June 7, 1977. Assistant County Attorney Terry Christiansen and Val Edrington were present.

The judge read the charges of the complaint. He gave John and Vickie the option of pleading guilty or not guilty, or remaining silent. If they pleaded guilty, they could each receive jail sentences of up to six months, or fines of up to $299, or both. If they decided to plead not guilty or remain silent, they would be granted a hearing with the power to subpoena and examine witnesses. They chose to remain silent.

Judge Bradford then gave them the choice of hiring their own attorney, having a court-appointed attorney, or waiving the right to one. The Singers chose the latter. They did not believe that a lawyer would accept their religious beliefs as basis for their defense, and, besides, they had received personal testimony from God not to employ a lawyer. The judge set the next hearing for August 23.

When Christiansen and Edrington had left the courtroom, Judge Bradford informally gave John and Vickie some advice. He said in a kindly manner that he himself had once tried to take his kids out of public school and teach them at home, but was unsuccessful. He told John and Vickie that he believed they might have a constitutional basis for refusing to cooperate with the school district, but that it would probably be futile to attempt to prove it through the

Utah court system. He advised them to send their kids back to school and compensate for any false teaching they would receive by deprogramming them at home—that was what he did with his own nine children.

"But if you swim in a sewer every day," Vickie said, "no matter how much you wash you still smell bad."

A month later Judge Bradford received a telephone call from the governor's office, informing him that he had not been recommended by the Juvenile Court Commission for reappointment.

Bradford was disappointed. He made a few phone calls and learned that one of the three applicants recommended for his position was a law partner of one of the members of the commission, Clyde Patterson. Bradford learned that Patterson had not abstained from voting, despite the obvious conflict of interest.

Bradford then called Walter Talbot, who confirmed what the judge had heard about the voting. Talbot promised that he would personally request that the commission reconvene and look into Patterson's action.

When the commission reconvened it added Bradford's name to the list that was submitted to the governor. However, Governor Scott M. Matheson had by then decided to appoint his Summit County campaign manager, L. Kent Bachman, to the juvenile court bench.

Charles Bradford, who was fifty-one, did not return to the practice of law but began a new career in real estate and investment banking. His last order in the Singer case, issued a week before his term expired, was to appoint a guardian *ad litem* for the Singer children. A guardian *ad litem* is someone who appears in court to protect the interests and welfare of a "party incapacitated by infancy or otherwise." Utah state law permits the appointment of such a guardian regardless of whether the parents were present in court or whether they consented to such an appointment.

John and Vickie received notice on August 4 that Attorney Robert F. Orton had been appointed guardian *ad litem* of their children. Not knowing the legal definition of the term, they were nevertheless incensed that their role as protectors of their children had been appropriated. They were convinced it was illegal.

"The state has gone over its boundaries too far," John said to Vickie. "They are slowly trying to take over our children. This is exactly what Hitler tried to do, nay? He said, 'Give me the youth and I have the nation.' And they are doing this now here in America.'' Vickie agreed.

They turned to section 98 of Doctrine and Covenants on which they had based their defiance of the compulsory education law in 1973. Section 98 also provides a method of beseeching one's enemies for peace, and, if the entreaty is disregarded, going into battle against them.

> This is the law that I gave unto mine ancients, that they should not go out unto battle against any nation, kindred, tongue, or people, save I, the Lord, commanded them.
>
> And if any nation, tongue, or people should proclaim war against them, they should first lift a standard of peace unto that people, nation, or tongue;
>
> And if that people did not accept the offering of peace, neither the second nor the third time, they should bring these testimonies before the Lord;
>
> Then I, the Lord, would give unto them a commandment, and justify them in going out to battle against that nation, tongue, or people.

John and Vickie felt it was time to raise the first standard of peace in seeking to reclaim their rights and liberties from the state. John addressed a letter to Judge Bradford, unaware that Bradford was about to be replaced on the bench.

> Marion, August 7, 1977
>
> Dear Mr. Bradford!
>
> I have received your orders by which you appointed Robert F. Orton as guardian of my children.
>
> My reply:
>
> You, Mr. Bradford, by making a court order of this nature are, according to the laws of the land, a law breaker and to pursue this matter further against me & my family makes you also the law breaker in the eyes of Allmighty God. I have lost all confidence in you as an officer of Justice & as a man of God. God's remedy of restoring confidence is that the transgressor repents.
>
> I have never yet turned a person away from my home, if they acted half-way decent. This will apply to Mr. Orton also. But if he comes here as the guardian of my children, I personally will throw him out.

You, Mr. Bradford, have placed me in a very peculiar situation, namely, either to transgress the laws of my God & obey men's corrupt laws, or obey my God's laws & defy men's corrupt laws. I, fearing God more than men, have chosen the latter. Now, in order to be justified before my Maker because of pending troubles, I now lift the *first* standard of peace unto you people according to the laws of God (D&C 98:32–38) hoping you will see my side & we can come to an agreement in truth & righteousness, which is my desire, greatly.

Sincerely,
John Singer

On the morning of August 10 John took his three guns, one carbine rifle and two pistols, to the baptismal font in Hoyt's Canyon, and dedicated his weapons to the Lord. He had used these guns for hunting when food and money were scarce. He prayed that he would be inspired to use the weapons only in the name of truth and righteousness, or for procuring food during times of need. He promised his God that he would never use his weapons as an aggressor, or in the name of vengeance, but only in the defense of his family and their God-given rights and liberties.

Chapter 7

GIVE ME THE YOUTH

On August 10, 1977, Assistant County Attorney Terry Christiansen filed a petition in juvenile court in support of the school board's charges of child neglect against John and Vickie Singer, and charging their five oldest children with habitual truancy. Christiansen was twenty-eight years old; between college and law school he had spent two years in Brazil as a Mormon missionary.

On August 15, L. Kent Bachman was elevated to the juvenile court bench. At thirty-eight, Bachman had practiced law in Utah for ten years. At the time of his appointment to the bench he was a Mormon bishop; two years later he was appointed to his stake high council.

When Charles Bradford left the bench he had not seen John Singer's first standard of peace addressed to him. It came to Judge Bachman's attention when he reviewed the Singer file before the next hearing on August 23. Bachman gave a copy of John's letter to Robert Orton because the letter contained the warning that if Orton attempted to visit the Singers he would be thrown out.

John and Vickie and their three oldest children fasted for twenty-four hours prior to the juvenile court hearing on August 23. John prayed for utterance, as he was going to appear without representation by an attorney. Thus spiritually armed, John and Vickie set out for the Coalville courthouse, leaving thirteen-year-old Heidi in charge of the other children. Bonnie Norder accompanied them to court. On their way into the courthouse they learned that Judge Bradford was no longer presiding over the juvenile court, and assumed that this was due to John's standard of peace.

More than half the seats in the small Coalville courtroom were occupied. John had subpoenaed all six members of the South Summit Board of Education, not because he planned to call them as witnesses, but so that they would have to sit through the proceedings "because it was their doings" that brought him into court. John and Vickie took seats at the counsel table with Terry Christiansen. Bonnie sat in the gallery with John's brother Harald, who had come to testify. Vickie held the Book of Mormon in her lap.

Judge Bachman was about five foot nine, had blond hair, and looked very fit. He began the proceedings by asking John if he was absolutely sure he wanted to represent himself and waive the right to an attorney. John was sure. The judge then read the allegation of the complaint and asked John whether the allegation was true or not. Remaining in his seat, John answered it was true they had kept their children out of school. He looked quite respectable in his light-colored, long-sleeved shirt open at the collar, and dark pants; though every other male in the courtroom except for the bailiff wore a suit and tie.

"To that extent are you admitting, then, that the children are neglected?" the judge asked.

"I do not admit that at all," John answered. "The children are not neglected but they have been kept out of school."

The judge made a note, then called on Robert Orton. Orton, the father of six children and an active Mormon, had served as Summit County Attorney for four years before going into private practice. He had appeared in juvenile court more than a dozen times, both as prosecutor and as defense counsel. He was about the same height and weight as John Singer, though at forty-one he was five years younger. The judge asked Orton if he had visited the Singer home. Orton said he had not because of the tenor of John's letter to Judge Bradford. Orton continued to say that he had contacted a psychologist at the University of Utah named Victor Cline, who would be willing to interview and examine the Singer children in order to testify as an expert in this case.

The tall, clean-cut, well-dressed Christiansen, acting as prosecutor, then made a brief opening statement at the lectern, and began to list the significant dates and events of the case, from March 1973 when John made his protest in Rex Walker's office, to the withdrawal of the Singers' certificate of exemption in March 1977 and the subsequent filing of the complaint by the School Board.

John was then given a chance to make a statement to the court. He rose to the lectern and began slowly, looking around from face to face as he spoke. "The issue here is a religious issue and only a religious issue. Every action that we have taken in behalf of our children was because of our religious beliefs. It is for that reason that we have made these decisions, and our religious beliefs are that we live amongst a people that are losers—or as the Lord puts it, they're going to be destroyed one day. I believe that is not in the too far future. We could go into detail on this if you would prefer it, but this is just my opening statement."

The state's first witness was Rex Walker. A big, burly man, Walker had been principle of South Summit Elementary School for twenty-two years. He was also a member of the stake high council that excommunicated John and Vickie.

Walker described the "friendly, low-key argument" he had with John on March 29, 1973, the day John withdrew his children from school. The textbook John had complained about, showing Martin Luther King, Jr., beside Betsy Ross and George Washington, was introduced into evidence.

Christiansen asked the principal whether John had ever complained about immorality in the school before then, and was told he hadn't.

John's cross-examination of Walker consisted of one question: "Are you a Mormon?" Walker replied he was.

Robert Orton then asked Walker how the Singer children were doing in school prior to their withdrawal. Walker replied, "To the best of my recollection, Heidi was coming along quite well. Suzanne was not doing quite as well. Timothy was in kindergarten and we felt that he was fairly well adjusted." Walker testified that the children were well behaved, were not rebellious, and although the girls dressed differently from the other children, they were not mistreated because of it.

Terry Christiansen's second witness was Val Edrington. Edrington discussed the school board's decision to issue the Singers an exemption in 1974, the Singers' failure to comply with its conditions in 1976, his correspondence with State Superintendent Walter Talbot, and the consequent filing of the complaint. Christiansen asked Edrington about John's letter of June 1973, in which he told the school board to "go to hell." The letter was produced and placed in evidence.

John began his cross-examination of Edrington by asking, again, "Are you a Mormon?"

"Yes."

John then asked, "Who is this Mr. Talbot you always get in touch with?"

"Walter D. Talbot, the state superintendent of public instruction."

"Don't you know how to make your own decisions without running to Mr. Talbot every time something happens?"

Christiansen calmly stood up and turned to the judge. "Your honor, I object to this line of questioning."

"Objection sustained," the judge ruled.

John continued questioning Edrington. "Didn't I save your boy from drowning?"

Christiansen was on his feet again. "Objection. The question is irrelevant and beyond the scope of the direct examination, your honor."

"Sustained."

But John forged ahead, ignoring the ruling. "I have never asked for any reward for saving your boy, but what I do ask is the decency and respect for my beliefs—"

The judge interrupted, admonishing John to stick to the issues of the case and to ask questions instead of making statements to the witness.

John had no more questions for Edrington.

It was Robert Orton's turn. He asked Edrington whether it would be in the best interests of the Singer children to readmit them to public school.

Edrington replied that he could not make such an assumption at that point. Orton went on to ask if Edrington felt having the children

examined by a psychologist might help in determining their educational plan. Edrington agreed that it would help. Then Orton
returned to his seat.

The prosecutor then called Tony Powell to testify. Powell described
the testing he had conducted with the Singer children in fall 1974
and spring 1975. When asked to give the results of the California
Achievement Tests administered in spring 1975, Powell reported
that both Heidi and Suzanne were a year and a half behind their
peers in public school, and that Timothy was proficient in math
but two years behind in all the other subjects.

Anticipating the question from Orton, Christiansen then asked
whether Powell had an opinion as to whether the Singer children
should return to the public school system.

"That's difficult to answer," Powell replied. "What grade would
we place then in? If we put them in classes with younger students,
there may be problems with their socialization. And I think that
because of the way they dress, the girls would be taunted by some
of the other kids. One alternative would be to have a tutor go into
the home to teach the children, at least until they are caught up
academically with their own age groups. But this would be a
problem because I don't think there are any qualified tutors available
in Summit County.

"I think also," Powell added, "that you'd have to consider the
fact that the older children probably share the parents' view about
education, and would not want to go to public school again."

When it came time for John to cross-examine Powell he implored
the judge to allow him to make a statement first. Given the okay,
John addressed Christiansen. "You're not even treating the issue
that's important here. What we're doing is like the tree out there.
You're picking up one leaf here, another leaf there, another leaf
there, and you're never coming to the basic stem of the tree."

John then commenced his questioning of Powell. Picking up the
file with test scores that had been introduced in evidence, John
asked him, "In order to have a properly educated individual,
wouldn't you also have to have a category here that would say how
well an individual handled an axe? How well an individual can
handle a saw? How well an individual could handle a hammer?
Wouldn't that be correct?"

Christiansen objected to this as being irrelevant and the judge upheld his objection.

John approached the bench and began to argue about the merits of practical skills, but the judge cut him off, "Mr. Singer, as I explained earlier, you will have an opportunity to make an argument after the testimony is concluded."

John returned to the lectern and asked Powell the same question he had asked all the others. "Are you a Mormon?"

"Yes, I am."

"Do you sustain—"

Christiansen rose indignantly and addressed the judge. "I'm going to object to this line of questioning. The witness's religious beliefs have no relevancy in this case." His objection was sustained.

"Okay, I have no more questions," John said, and took his seat.

At this point, John leaned toward Vickie and said softly, "They keep cutting me off from stating our reasons and beliefs. They don't want the religious issue entering into the case."

Vickie agreed. "They seem to finagle things according to their own whims," she said to John.

Once again it was Orton's turn to examine the witness on behalf of the Singer children. "Mr. Powell, in your opinion, would further testing of the children be advisable to determine what their education should be in the future?"

"Yes, I think it would be."

"What kind of testing would you recommend?"

"I'd prefer a complete psychological battery, including I.Q. as well as social, emotional, and skill level as related to the public schools."

"Conducted by yourself or by someone outside the school district?"

"I'd prefer an expert outside the district."

"Would it be in the best interests of the children that Mr. and Mrs. Singer also be interviewed by a psychologist or sociologist or a psychiatrist?"

"I think so."

Orton then asked Powell, "Do you think the Singer children are capable of interacting with children of their own age in their community?"

"Yes, if they so desire."

"In your opinion, do the educational beliefs of the parents and the children have anything to do with a decision as to what is ultimately going to be in the best interests of the children?"

"Yes, I think it does."

"In what respect?"

"Mr. Singer has stated that religiously he feels that the world can come to an end, that all the wicked—and most of us would be included in that group—would be destroyed, and that would leave them here to carry on." There was a hint of sarcasm in Tony Powell's answer.

"Your honor, may I say something?" John asked, rising to his feet.

"I have no objection," the judge replied.

"It seems like here is only opinions, back and forth opinions," John began. "But the wise man once said, 'The opinion of a man is like a crackling of thorns under a truck.' And that's exactly what I get out of this trial. I believe, your honor, that the only thing that I have to prove to this court is that my children are not being trained for any delinquency actions or any criminal actions, and this is the only thing that I have to prove, nothing else."

At this point Judge Bachman announced a recess for lunch.

As John and Vickie walked out of the courtroom, Bonnie, following behind them, saw one of the school board members in the gallery turn to the man next to him and say in a mocking tone, "Aw, look, she's got her scriptures with her." And both men chuckled. Bonnie could sense the contempt and animosity the two men felt toward the Singers.

When court convened at one-thirty, the state rested its case. Now John was given an opportunity to call his witnesses. He called his brother Harald.

Harald had been excommunicated from the Mormon Church in December 1972, six months after he had testified at John and Vickie's excommunication trial. The official reasons given by his stake president in Logan were that he refused to acknowledge Joseph Fielding Smith as a prophet, he did not believe that the church's 1890 Manifesto outlawing polygamy was a revelation from God, and he believed in the fundamentalist Adam-God doctrine, introduced by Brigham Young, but officially repudiated early in the twentieth century. This doctrine holds that Adam, the first man on earth, ascended to the Celestial Kingdom after his death and became God. Harald's wife was not excommunicated, however, and their seven children all attended public schools in Logan.

At forty-five, Harald was stockier than his brother with a dark complexion, and large bright eyes. He spoke with a slight accent and had retained some Germanic grammatical patterns.

"Could you explain a little bit to the court why the state is trying to take my children away from me?" John asked his brother. Harald was prepared to compare the compulsory education law to Hitler's youth movement, but not before Terry Christiansen rose to his feet to object.

"Your honor," the prosecutor pleaded, "I don't believe the witness is qualified to state that opinion."

"Sustained."

Then John asked Harald to tell the court what he thought of the way he and Vickie were teaching the children.

Harald turned to the judge. "The observations that I've had of my brother's children is that he has always tried according to his best ability to be a good example, religiously as a moral citizen and also as a good provider for his family. He is interested that his children learn how to read and write because this is one of the basic, fundamental aspects of his religion, that they do read and write, otherwise they would not be capable of reading and comprehending scripture."

"Those are all the questions I have," John said. As the prosecutor declined to cross-examine, Harald stepped down.

John decided to take the stand and testify in his own behalf. Judge Bachman carefully advised him that he was not obligated to testify, but if he did he would be subject to cross-examination by the state. John decided to go ahead, and was sworn in. After answering some preliminary questions from the judge, John said:

"As I have stated before, my actions in this matter have not been of a malicious nature, but rather of a responsibility which almighty God gives to every parent here on this earth, and every parent on this earth should take this responsibility upon their shoulders to rear their children in a proper manner. I have studied the things of God, and as I read the promises of Almighty God to us it states this: that children are a heritage of God. That means actually they are an inheritance given to the individual who has them. Now, if the Lord would have meant that the children are the heritage of the state, then I could understand the trouble that I'm in. But since He has just said that He has given me the responsibility in my life to rear our children, I believe that I have the right to do so and educate them according to my beliefs.

"At this time my rights before God have been treaded upon by people who actually say that they believe the scriptures, like the Book of Mormon, Doctrine and Covenants, and Pearl of Great Price . . . but when it comes right down to it I can see by their actions that they want to take these rights away from me as a parent.

"Now, for instance, when our first child was born, Heidi, there was a tremendous price paid by my wife. When Suzanne, my second child, was born, it was so severe that when I took this child to be blessed the evil spirit actually tried to drive me out of my body, so severe was the attack upon me, until I could seal this child up against the powers of the destroyer. But the warfare was tremendous, I can tell you this. When Timmy was born, the warfare that was fought, as we took him to the hospital down in Provo, the fears that had to be fought down and everything like this, in which the Lord showed me that he let me overcome these type of feelings. Then the last four children we have had at home, of which I was the only one there at home to help my wife have these children. Again, people ridiculed me and said that I'd done something that's not right. But through the graces of Almighty God everything went well, because we trusted wholly in Almighty God. . . . One of the children that was born, just before delivery, my wife went paralyzed and after we had administered to her—"

"Your honor," interrupted the prosecutor, "I don't mean to interrupt Mr. Singer, except for the fact that he's stating things that are obviously important to him, but they're just absolutely irrelevant to the proceeding that is before this court. Not only that, your honor, but in taking the witness stand I think he should recite facts; what he's trying to do, I believe, is to make an argument, a closing argument, which he is entitled to after he presents his testimony. And I think that if he wants to use this line of argument then, I would have absolutely no objection."

The judge asked John whether he understood the objection.

"I understand what he's saying, but I am trying to relay that I am a responsible parent and that I do care for my children, that I'm not negligent of which I was charged, and that I do care exactly what happens to my children, more so than I think many people do."

"All right," Judge Bachman said. "Now, I think the court has understood that. If you would get to the issue of contributing to the delinquency of these children by not permitting them to attend formal schooling here in this particular district. If you would give us the facts regarding how you educate the children and why you would not permit testing of the children, their educational progress or lack of progress. You address those issues, and you would be in an area of relevance."

John addressed Terry Christiansen. "The things that I have said up till now were facts. The testimony that I listened to before lunch were opinions, but from me facts are expected. Before, I had to listen to opinions. Now, I'd like to know what makes you so privileged to listen to all these opinions and me—"

The judge again cut in. "But now we're arguing. I don't want to confuse you, Mr. Singer, I want you to have your opportunity to give your testimony, but I don't want you to argue with the county attorney. I want him to have the right, as well as every counsel, to object to certain testimony when it is not responsive to the allegation. You give, once again, that testimony which goes to the facts of whether a crime of contributing to the neglect and delinquency of a minor has been committed. That is the only thing I can really listen to at this particular stage."

John resumed his testimony. "As far as my children go, and I was laying the groundwork for that, I don't have to send them to school because this is my religious belief as far as God and me is concerned. Now there is a statement which God has made that the glory of God is intelligence, and I believe that a hundred percent. But I also believe that this type of intelligence cannot be found in this school system. Now, for instance, the reason I have taken my children out is because I specifically want to keep my children clean. As the Lord has dictated to us, he says, 'Be ye clean that bear the vessels of the Lord, be ye separate,' and this is exactly what I am doing. I'm keeping my children separate in order to keep them clean so they will not be brought up in these things of immorality and sex education which you people have, and thereby place within their reach the idea of trying things out, or things like that. No, I will not send my children to school to see filthy pictures which the superintendent of the school board has no power to control. I will not let my children come in contact with drugs either, which is already a proven fact that it cannot be controlled here in this school system. This is what I'm sheltering my children from, and this is why I want to keep them clean, in order that they have a chance of survival when the judgment of God comes upon them. And this is what I wanted you people to understand."

Terry Christiansen was making notes in his file as John testified. He stated later that he had grave doubts about the sincerity of the Singers' religious beliefs, and thought it possible that they wanted to keep their children at home merely to do household and farm chores.

John's testimony continued. "Why am I not given the right to stay away and live my life the way I want to and educate my children according to the dictates of my conscience which God has guaranteed to me? That's the reason I have said to the court before, the only thing I really have to prove to the court is that my children are not being trained up in criminal activities. Thereby, they would become a burden upon society and thereby they would tresspass on the rights of other people. But I don't think that anybody in this room here could prove that my children have ever trespassed or done any harm to anybody.

"Now, you have a law in your books that says I must do so and so. Now, if I go into scriptures and read what the Lord dictates, he says as pertaining to the laws of the land, he says, 'I want you to live my laws first of all.' And then if the laws of the land comply with the laws of God, by which they guarantee me my free conscience and liberty in doing these things, then I will accept the laws of this kind. But if a law is contrary to the law of God and your honor wants to put me in slavery, so to say, or make me bend under something which is against my conscience completely, then I have to obey the laws of God and not the laws of the land. . . .

"We have taken proper care of our children. We have properly provided shelter for them. I built a schoolhouse for them where we can have recreation in it and we can do everything else in it. Just because my plan does not exactly parallel with the plan that you people have marked out, so I am in such great transgression?

"I can show you my little fellow who's only ten years old now. He has built himself a little outhouse already, of which I have helped him nothing. . . . When I look at my daughter, she has taken art and she can put almost a picture together like you see hanging on that wall back there."

Almost everyone in the courtroom turned around to look at the painting on the back wall.

"When I look at my oldest daughter, she does cooking, she does anything in the house. When my wife was sick there for five months straight, my second girl completely took care of the newborn baby. Do you want to tell me this is all no education? Just because it's not accepted by you, it's no education? As far as I stand before my Maker and myself, this is the most marvelous education that I can see for my children."

Judge Bachman let the sentence end, and interjected. "Mr. Singer, once again I've let you go a little too long, once again you're arguing the point. State the facts. What have you been doing as to the instruction of your children? Have you complied with the policies or standards set out for the education of your children?"

John retorted, "But it seems like the standards which have been set out there are not the same standards that I believe in. Now, for instance, we have put this to the test about teaching our children literally five and a half hours a day. It's an impossibility. If any of you have children, you try it. You put your little children for five and a half hours exactly to the schedule that is supposed to be what they have prescribed, and you will find out that these children will not be able to take more than two and a half hours of this.

"And I can see in your school system, you are not following the rules yourselves. Because they have so much goof-off period of time in between their lessons that it would amount maybe to the education of two and a half hours per child per day."

At this point, Terry Christiansen made a lengthy objection, and Judge Bachman warned John that if he could not restrict his testimony to whether or not his children were being taught reading, writing, arithmetic, science and social studies, the judge would not allow him to testify further.

In a rare display of anger, John replied, "Okay, according to the laws of God, then, I'm very strict with you there, and I say it's none of your business if my kids learn!"

"Is that the conclusion of your testimony?" the judge asked him. "Yes."

John started to step down, but Christiansen stood up and the judge asked him, "Do you have any questions for Mr. Singer?"

"Yes, your honor," the prosecutor said. John took a step back and sat down again in the witness's chair. "Mr. Singer, you've listened to the testimony that was given this morning by Mr. Edrington and Mr. Walker and Mr. Powell. Are the facts that they testified to substantially correct to the best of your knowledge?"

"There are certain facts that I acknowledge as far as those papers are concerned."

"Well, let me start out—"

"You see, I do not care about those idiots!" John blurted out.

"Just answer the questions, please," Christiansen said, trying to remain in control. "Did you in fact go to the office of Mr. Walker in March of 1973 and withdraw your children from school?"

"Yes."

Christiansen took John one by one through all the facts that the state's witnesses had testified to that morning. John confirmed that each fact had been stated correctly, until they came to the question of whether he had followed the schedule for their home school which had been submitted to the school board by attorney James Smedley. Instead of answering the prosecutor's question, John pointed a finger at him and said, "Let's get down to the basics. Have you got even the right to force my children under any form of education? This is the thing!"

The judge ordered John to respond to the question, which he did, and the cross-examination continued. Christiansen asked John which textbooks he used to teach his children, and John could not remember the names of most of them. Nor could John remember how many hours per day he had taught certain subjects to his children. Nor could he say how many days of classes each of his children had missed because of illness.

Vickie turned and whispered to Bonnie that she believed the prosecutor was trying to harass John.

"You've mentioned very frequently, Mr. Singer, that your religious beliefs caused you this conflict with the state as far as the education of your children is concerned." Christiansen was laying a foundation for his argument. "I'd just be interested if you would tell us what religious group you are affiliated with?"

"I don't belong to any group. I believe in the Mormon scriptures, the Bible, Book of Mormon, Doctrine and Covenants, and Pearl of Great Price," John said.

Christiansen changed the subject. "Do you feel that your children have learned the basic fundamentals as far as reading, writing, arithmetic, spelling, science, social studies, on a comparable level with those children who attend public schools?"

"My children are not in competition with anybody. As far as I'm concerned my children are getting a darn good education in reading, writing, and arithmetic, plus."

"Do you feel that it is comparable to the education the other children in the area are receiving in public schools?"

"I don't go out and try to test other children to find out."

"I have no further questions, Your Honor."

Robert Orton had a few questions to ask John. "Do you think it's important that your children learn to read?"

"I think it's important." John calmed down in response to Orton's questions, after being visibly agitated by the prosecutor.

"Is it important that they learn mathematics?"

"Very important."

"Is it important that they know about science?"

"Yes."

"And social studies?"

"Yes."

"Have you taught all of these subjects in your home?"

"More or less."

"Can you explain what you mean by that?"

"Well, we've dealt on many things. You see, I was brought up in very great regimentation, and this is what I do not want my children to have. I do not want them to be regimented in any type of system because I have gone through this and I see the pitfalls therein. You see, I have grown up to be in the Hitler Youth. That's the reason anything that has to do with regimentation I am against. You see, even though in your school system here they paint Hitler as a real bad, bad man, but his philosophy they have accepted one hundred percent as far as the educational plan is concerned. Forced education.

He said, 'Give me the youth and I've got the whole nation.' That was exactly his plan. And the next thing you know, in order to enforce this, he went after the parents, and put jail sentences upon them if they didn't send their children to public schools or into his youth movement. That's the reason I'm very liberal or flexible."

"You don't object to the concept of school, but you object to the regimentation as a part of the school system?" Orton asked.

"The learning process I am full in favor of, but the regimentation I am not in favor of."

"Do you have any recommendation as to what kind of system your children could be educated under other than the public school system and the system you've been following at home? Can you think of an alternative?"

John paused to consider the question for several seconds. "I think we're very pleased, my children and myself, because we are a marvelous unit, and I can see the public school is not really education but just drives a wedge into my family unit."

"Do you see any other alternative?"

"No, and I wouldn't want any other alternative."

"Do you think, Mr. Singer, that when your children reach the age of eighteen and have to go out into the world to make a living, or whatever age that comes, they are going to be prepared to do that? That maybe is the key issue in this case: Will they be prepared?"

"In my opinion, they will, yes, very much so. If you ever would see their actions you would have to say the same thing."

"Do you think other people's opinions are worth considering? Do you think that other people's opinions are worth considering on the question as to whether they will be prepared?"

"The only time that I would consider other people's opinions is if they had the spirit of the Lord within them, otherwise I would reject them downright."

"Would you be willing to have someone examine and test your children to determine what might be in the best interest—"

"No, I'd never let you do that."

"Would you be willing to be interviewed?"

"Me interviewed?"

"Yes, by someone in an attempt for that person to determine what's in your children's best interests?"

"No."

"In other words, you're unwilling to accept anyone's opinion or recommendation other than that of your own?"

John shifted uneasily in his chair on the witness stand, trying to think of the right words. "I know one thing for a fact. I don't know what you know, but I know what I know, and the experiences that I've had, and I think I'm a pretty good judge of this myself. I do not have to lean on anybody for that."

Orton concluded his examination by eliciting from John the fact that he had not graduated from high school and did not have a teaching certificate. The judge then called a short recess.

When court reconvened, Robert Orton requested permission to address the court. The judge told him to proceed, and Orton said: "Your honor, a petition has been filed with the court alleging that Mr. and Mrs. Singer have neglected their children. I think that there are some conflicts which have got to be resolved and I, as guardian *ad litem* for the children, don't think that I'm prepared to make any recommendations to the court at this time as to what course of action would be in the best interests of the Singer children. As a matter of fact, I haven't heard any witness here today who did say that he could make such a recommendation. I suggest that the court withhold its decision in this case until we have an opportunity to allow Dr. Cline at the University of Utah, or another qualified psychologist, to examine the children. I also feel that the physical, mental, or emotional condition of the parents may be a factor in the neglect of the children, and they should be tested as well."

Terry Christiansen told the court that he knew Dr. Cline to be reputable, and that he had no objection to having the Singers tested by him. Orton also suggested that the Division of Family Services pay for the examinations, since the Singers most likely could not afford to pay the fees. The judge made some notes, and asked the prosecutor to give his summation.

After a review of the testimony, Christiansen said, "Mr. Singer's contention in this case is that because of his religious beliefs, he does not feel that he has to subject himself or his children to the laws of the State of Utah. And I may indicate that the religious beliefs that he has, he does not share with any organized sect."

He then cited three previous court decisions which he felt supported his contention that the Singers should be found guilty of child neglect, and which he urged Judge Bachman to use as legal precedents in making his final decision.

The first citation was a 1955 case before the Utah Supreme court, referred to as *In re State* v. *Black*. In the Black case, a polygamist had been convicted of child neglect and lost custody and control of his children because the state charged that he encouraged his children to "violate the law of Utah regarding marriage and sexual offenses" by teaching them to believe in polygamy. The defendant had claimed that polygamy was a religious belief protected by the Free Exercise Clause of the First Amendment. But the conviction was upheld by the Utah Supreme Court.

By citing the Black case, Christiansen meant to show that parents could not rely on religious beliefs to justify breaking a state law where the welfare of their children was concerned. But John and Vickie Singer, sitting at the counsel table, thought the prosecutor was attempting to prejudice the judge by implicating that the Singers were polygamists. Vickie later told a friend, "I'm pretty sure that Mr. Christiansen must have dug this information out of the Kamas sewer system, where all gossip is started."

The second case cited by Christiansen was *Wisconsin* v. *Yoder*, in which a group of Amish parents refused to send their children to public schools after the eighth grade, in violation of Wisconsin's compulsory attendance law. In the Yoder trial, the parents had testified that they did not object to sending their children to school through the eighth grade to acquire "basic educational tools," but felt that the high schools taught principles contrary to their religious beliefs, and therefore the compulsory attendance law infringed on their religious freedom. The state court convicted the parents of breaking the law, despite expert testimony that the Amish parents were capable of teaching their children adequately at home. But in 1972 the U.S. Supreme Court reversed the lower court, based on the Free Exercise Clause, stating in its opinion that indeed the religious freedom of the entire Amish community had been threatened by the state's compulsory attendance law.

Now, when John and Vickie Singer heard the prosecutor cite the Amish case, they looked at each other, thinking that it might be used in their favor.

But Christiansen proceeded to turn the citation to his own advantage. He pointed out to Judge Bachman that *Wisconsin* v.

Yoder must be distinguished from the Singer case because the Amish were competent to teach their own children, whereas, in his opinion, the Singers were not. Also, the Amish belonged to an organized religious sect and shared their beliefs with a whole community, while the Singers' religious beliefs were "a matter of personal preference," ones not shared by an organized group or by the community. Therefore, Christiansen said, the Singers were not entitled to be acquitted on the basis of the Free Exercise Clause as were the Amish.

In the gallery, Harald Singer quickly hunted through a file folder, found a document and started underlining particular sentences on it.

Christiansen's third citation was a case in which an American Indian father in North Carolina refused to enroll his two children in public school because the school did not teach American Indian history. The parents were convicted of child neglect, and a North Carolina appellate court upheld the conviction, noting that refusing to provide a basic education was injurious to the welfare of their children.

At this point, Harald penned a note to the document he had been studying, and passed it to John by way of Bonnie Norder.

Christiansen concluded his summation by directing the court's attention to the allegations against the Singers. "I don't believe, your honor, that any testimony was presented, nor was any intended to be presented, that Mr. and Mrs. Singer are neglecting their children in any manner other than education. But I think it can be seen in this case that refusing to provide them with a sufficient alternative education or training constitutes neglect. So I think that without a doubt the parents are guilty of the misdemeanor that was brought before this court in the complaint. But before I could make any recommendation to this court, and it's been indicated by Mr. Orton, and Mr. Edrington also, I think additional testing and evaluations should be made."

The young prosecutor took his seat, and Judge Bachman motioned to John: "Would you like to take the lectern and argue to the court concerning your position? Now is the time. As I cautioned you during your testimony, you had the right at that particular time to state facts. Now you're given the opportunity to argue against what the county attorney has stated."

John went to the lectern. "I think I have a simpler solution to the whole thing," he said. "Couldn't Your Honor just rule this law unconstitutional which creates this compulsory action? This would place the responsibility on the individual parent and make him responsible before his Maker, and would relieve the burden from His Honor's shoulders in order to make a decision of this type, because of this Yoder case." Referring to Harald's document, he said, "There was also a Chief Justice Burger who said toward the end of this, he says, 'This case involves the fundamental interests of parents, as contrasted with that of the state, to guide the religious future and education of their children. The history and culture of Western civilization reflect the strong position of parental concern for the nurture and upbringing of their children. This primary role of the parent in the upbringing of their children has been established as an enduring American tradition.'

"This is the only thing that I ask for," John concluded, "to be made responsible before my Maker for the upbringing of my children, and not have somebody else carry the burden."

"Is that all?" the judge asked.

"Yes," John replied as he sat down.

"Do you have anything further to say in regard to this, Mr. Christiansen?"

The prosecutor stood but did not go to the lectern. "Only, your honor, that the Supreme Court in the Amish case did not declare the compulsory education statute unconstitutional. It just determined under the conditions of that particular case that after grade eight the Amish could, in fact, teach their own children." He too sat down, and the matter was then in the hands of the man who had been a judge for little more than a week.

"Mr. and Mrs. Singer," Bachman began, looking down from the bench upon the couple, "the responsibility is placed upon the court to make a decision. That decision is one which I look at with a very, very great deal of concern. It's also a decision that is not really that difficult to make, considering the technical aspects of the compulsory attendance law here in the State of Utah. Pursuant to Section 53-24-1 of Utah Code Annotated as amended, the court finds beyond a reasonable doubt that a violation of this law has taken place.

"Now, I'm sure you see nothing but a great deal of respect for your religious beliefs here in this court today, a respect for your attempt to raise your children as God would probably have it, shielding your children from the turmoil that is in the world today, from the types of conduct that the other children are involving themselves in because they are out mingling with the society. And this is very admirable. But likewise, you are subject to the laws of the State of Utah. Likewise, I am subject to those same laws and the upholding of those laws. I think the only way we are really going to see the overruling of those types of laws which you feel are wrong for your children would be some type of legislation or some type of declaration that these same laws are unconstitutional. I won't rule that they are unconstitutional. I will uphold them.

"The finding of this court is that there has been a neglectful situation. Not neglect in terms of raising the children to believe in God, not neglect in terms of feeding the children or giving them clothes or nurturing them, or teaching them the basics of survival. In these areas, I am sure you've been training your children and taught your children far beyond the capacity of other children in the surrounding areas and in the cities. You're to be commended for that.

"But you made a commitment to the school district to educate your children in a certain manner, and you have failed to abide by it. Therefore, it is the disposition of this court that evaluations be made of the children by this Dr. Victor Cline at the University of Utah Department of Psychology. Now, how are you disposed, will you follow the orders of the court?"

John stood. "I have a tough decision to make, your honor. If I obey you I will be breaking a covenant with my God."

"I will make it a little easier for you to make that decision," the judge offered, "because I'm going to temporarily place your children in the care, custody and control of the Utah Division of Family Services. Not to remove the children from your home, but to make sure that the children are taken before the evaluating psychologist, Dr. Victor Cline, and that you likewise be examined so that this court can make further disposition of this case. So this takes the decision away from you, Mr. Singer. Those children are now placed in the temporary custody of the Division of Family Services, and the DFS will pay for the examinations.

"It is further ordered that you are to pay a fine, each of you, in the amount of two hundred and ninety-nine dollars, and to be committed in the county jail for a period of sixty days, the same sentence and the same fine to be suspended upon your compliance with the orders of this court that you and your children be tested and evaluated by Dr. Cline. I still have the right, in the discretion of this court, to amend that particular order as new information is given to me. As soon as this hearing is adjourned you can get together with Mr. Orton and he will arrange an appointment for you to see Dr. Cline."

John and Vickie were stunned.

The judge opened his calendar. "I will set a conclusionary dispositional hearing for September thirteenth. This court is adjourned."

Chapter 8

SHAKE OFF THE DUST

On September 6, 1977, Victor B. Cline, professor of psychology and practicing clinical psychologist, interviewed and tested the four oldest Singer children in his office at the University of Utah for eight hours, and for five more hours in their home on September 27. In between he met with Rex Walker, Terry Christiansen, and Robert Orton to obtain background information.

Dr. Cline was a respected, much published author of books and magazine articles. His specialty was parent-child relationships and marriage counseling.

To each of the children individually Dr. Cline administered the Rorschach Test, Wechsler Intelligence Scale for Children, Sentence Completion Test, Gray's Oral Reading Paragraphs, Projective Drawings and Questions, and Thematic Apperception Test. Heidi, Suzanne, and Timothy, the eldest ones, were also given the Short Form Test of Academic Aptitude. He found that the children did not seem nervous during the tests, that they were pleasant, good-humored, motivated, and cooperative. All four told him that they did not want to attend public school because they enjoyed being taught at home by their parents. Cline also set up an appointment to test John and Vickie at his office a week later.

During this time, Bonnie Norder met a member of the Utah State Board of Education named Keith Steck, who suggested that if the

Singers were to establish their own private school and enroll their children in it, the government would have no power to regulate their educational program since no law existed which gave the state or the school district any control over private schools. Steck also said that although Utah's compulsory attendance law recognizes attendance in a regularly established private school as satisfying its attendance requirements, nowhere in the statute is the term "regularly established" defined. Bonnie eagerly relayed this information to John and Vickie.

On September 29 the first article about the Singers appeared in one of Park City's weekly newspapers, the *Park Record*. Under the headline "Family Faces Legal Battle over Education, Religion," the full-page feature set out a brief history of the Singers' struggle and included information on their elopement, excommunication, conflict with the school board, the juvenile court conviction, and even John's childhood in Nazi Germany. The last paragraph of the article stated, "In one sense, the case involving the Singer family threads down to one question: Who should have the final say concerning a child's education? The state or the parents?"

Richard and Karla Lance of Riverton, Utah, saw the article and called up the Singers to offer help. The Lances had withdrawn their children from elementary school in 1974, had incorporated their own private school, and had been teaching their seven children at home with the help of professional tutors. The Lances said they objected to what they called the "sheep syndrome" in public schools. "The schools are just the state's youth camp," Mrs. Lance said. The Lances were Mormons, and did not like their children mingling with students of different races.

In 1977 the Lances founded Liberty Bell, a nonprofit corporation that provides information, educational materials, and legal assistance to private and home schools. On Liberty Bell's staff were a curriculum director, a social director, a musical director, and an attorney. Its curriculum is designed to prepare students to enter college at the age of sixteen.

Richard Lance advised the Singers that the best way to establish a private school was to incorporate their home school under state law. The Singers immediately set about doing this, in the belief this would get them out from under the jurisdiction of the juvenile court permanently. With the assistance of Bonnie Norder and Harald Singer the application was mailed on October 7 to the secretary of state. They named their school High Uintas Academy.

Shortly after the publicity of the *Park Record* article, a television reporter interviewed the Singers on the evening news. The next morning the *Salt Lake Tribune* had a feature article on them, and a radio station in Salt Lake City aired a live telephone interview with Vickie.

The Singers started getting calls from people all over the state offering them suggestions on how to beat the school district and juvenile court. Confirming what the Lances had said, Joyce Kinmont of Brigham City told Vickie that there were no laws in Utah governing the establishment of private schools, and that there were hundreds of private and home schools in Utah that had never been regulated or monitored by the state. Since 1974 Mrs. Kinmont had taught her own children at home with no state interference, and in fact wrote a book on the subject named *American Home Academy*. She had appeared on the "Phil Donohue Show" because of her book.

Tom and Mary Bergman of Porterville, Utah, drove to Marion to tell the Singers about their home school, Pioneer Trails Academy. After being educated at home their oldest daughter had enrolled at the University of Utah at the age of fifteen. The Bergmans gave John and Vickie a copy of a letter they had received from State Superintendent Walter Talbot in 1974, which stated: "Insofar as I know there are no legal requirements in this state on meeting educational standards in private schools."

Feeling bolstered by this new development, John called Victor Cline to cancel their appointment on September 27. He informed Cline that they were in the process of establishing a private school. John added that he would consent to be tested only if all six members of the South Summit Board of Education were also required to be tested. "Let's see if they are more capable than we to decide what is best for our children," he said to Dr. Cline.

On October 7, 1977, the State of Utah issued a certificate of incorporation for High Uintas Academy, Inc.

Upon learning from Dr. Cline that John and Vickie had failed to submit themselves to testing, Terry Christiansen filed a motion asking that the Singers appear in court to show cause of failure to fully comply with Judge Bachman's orders. The Singers were summoned to appear in juvenile court on November 1.

The little courtroom in Coalville was packed when Judge Bachman brought down his gavel on November 1. Among the spectators were Harald Singer, Bonnie Norder, several of the Singers' friends from the Salt Lake area, Keith Steck, Val Edrington, Tony Powell, an army of reporters, and three sheriff's deputies.

Terry Christiansen opened the proceedings by introducing an affidavit signed by Dr. Cline, which stated that John and Vickie Singer had refused to submit to testing unless the entire school board submitted to the same tests, and that therefore he could not make a complete and adequate recommendation to the court what course of action would be best for the Singer children.

The judge addressed John. "I thought we agreed that since counsel for the state and counsel for the children are not experts in this field, we would rely on the recommendations of Dr. Cline as to the best interests of the children."

Approaching the bench, John said, "But what we figured was for the best interest of our children is to incorporate our private school, and therefore we have enrolled our children into private school now." He handed the certificate of incorporation to the judge, and resumed his place at the counsel table.

The judge did not look at all impressed. "That is very interesting," he said coolly. "This private school you're referring to, then, is set up according to the standards set forth by the state board of education? And it has received approval of the state board of education?"

"It has been approved by David S. Monson, Secretary of State of Utah," John proudly said.

"He's the secretary of state, but he's not the state board of education," Bachman retorted. "Do you have the state board of education's approval and consent? Just answer me yes or no to that extent." In response, John read from his copy of the 1974 letter from Walter Talbot to Thomas Bergman.

"Mr. Singer, I doubt very much that we could say there are no legal requirements for private schools," said the judge, who had been presiding in juvenile court for two and a half months. "There are minimum requirements to receive a diploma of graduation. I find it very difficult, without having that particular law before me to research it myself personally, to understand why any Tom, Dick, or Harry or Jane or Joan could go out and start their own private school and be able to avoid then the requirements of compulsory attendance at a school."

At this point Terry Christiansen joined in. "Your Honor, I think it's a moot question whether or not Mr. Singer has established a private school at this time. As a result of our hearing on August 23 they were found guilty of a misdemeanor, and the court ordered that the fine and sentence be suspended on compliance with the provisions of the order. I would indicate to the court that based upon the affidavit of Dr. Cline, they have not complied with that order. I think, Your Honor, that it's quite clear that Mr. and Mrs. Singer have blatantly disregarded the order of the court. I don't think there is any excuse for it. Now, the fact that they say that they've established a private school, I think, is moot for this reason."

Disturbed, Judge Bachman called the Singers, Christiansen, and Robert Orton into his chambers for a private conference. He took off his black robe and sat across from the others.

Bachman's first concern was the Singers' continued refusal to have a lawyer represent them. He urged them to accept a court-appointed defense counsel.

John once again emphasized that the case was one involving a conflict between scriptural law and the law of man. To obey man's law would place his salvation and the salvation of his children in jeopardy. Lawyers are trained only to uphold man's laws, and therefore he and Vickie were under God's instruction to not have a lawyer.

As a Mormon bishop, Judge Bachman said he realized that man's law may be inferior to God's law, but his job was to enforce the former. "I don't have an ecclesiastical court here; it is a court of the law of the land," he said.

John talked at length about the lessons of the 1945 Nuremberg trials, during which Nazi leaders were condemned for obeying the laws of their country when they should have observed a higher moral law.

"I don't think we're getting anything accomplished here," Bachman said as he stood up and donned his black robe again. The party returned to the courtroom and the proceedings resumed.

In open court Judge Bachman stated to the Singers, "Now, you have not been in compliance with my orders of August 23. I am going to place you in jail for sixty days and fine you each two hundred and ninety-nine dollars. Is there a reason why I shouldn't do that, Mr. Singer?"

"There is a moral reason, Your Honor."

"Is there a legal reason?"

"Let God in Heaven tell you," Vickie said, speaking for the first time in court.

Robert Orton now stood and asked the judge to grant a stay of execution so that the Singers would have an opportunity to reconsider seeing Dr. Cline. "I'm concerned about the fact that the children perhaps will be in a worse situation if the parents are in jail," he told the judge. "I'm extremely anxious to get a final recommendation from Dr. Cline."

Judge Bachman granted a stay of one month. "At the end of the month, if you have not fully complied with my order of August 23, there will be incarceration for both of you," he said sternly to the Singers. "The children are still placed in the custody of the Division of Family Services. We will give the latitude to the DFS if it sees fit at any time to remove those children from the home if Mr. and Mrs. Singer are not evaluated and examined by Dr. Cline by the first day of December."

Two days after the court hearing, John and Vickie drove down to Dr. Cline's office. They were interviewed by Dr. Cline and given the Wechsler Adult Intelligence Scale, Rorschach Test, Minnesota Multiphasic Personality Inventory, California Psychological Inventory, and Sentence Completion Test. The testing took six hours.

Two days later Victor Cline completed his written evaluation of the Singer family.

> The Singers have put together a remarkably cohesive and happy family of nine people. The husband and wife have a strong marriage with much love and affection and mutual support between the two. They are greatly committed to the task of

raising obedient, loving, responsible and resourceful children and are doing a truly remarkable job of this. This is a rare "Old Testament" type family with the father as a strong, vigorous patriarch who has the full support of his wife and the genuine support, love and respect of his children. They are to some degree isolated socially and economically with total self-sufficiency being an extremely important goal for them.

According to Dr. Cline's report, Vickie had an I.Q. of 108, which put her in the top thirty percent compared with other women her age. He described her as "mentally competent, of sound mind, knows clearly what she is doing, and is overall a remarkably resourceful and adequate woman."

John's I.Q. was measured at 121, placing him in the top eight percent compared with other men his age. Dr. Cline described him as a "tough, competent, resourceful, sometimes stubborn, shrewd self-made man. There is absolutely nothing suggestive of pathology or mental illness."

The emotional soundness of the children was described in glowing terms:

> I found them to be happy, kind, affectionate to each other, dutiful to their parents, and I found a remarkably powerful chemistry that bound them together with the parents totally committed to the unity of the family regardless of what sacrifices had to be made.

However, the difference between the children's I.Q. scores and those of their parents were "shocking."

> They scored on an average 34 I.Q. points below their parents. Since intelligence is to a great extent inherited, the only logical reason for these children scoring so low would be (a) not having adequate educational experiences and (b) their isolation from other children who might stimulate them intellectually.

The result of the academic achievement test showed that Heidi and Suzanne had "profoundly low" scores, but Timothy compared favorably with other children his age. The reason Timothy had scored poorly in 1975, Cline presumed, was that he had not been trained to take tests. This time Dr. Cline spent a considerable amount of time training the children to take tests.

Cline's report concluded with his recommendations:

> Mr. and Mrs. Singer have, probably unwittingly, in their concern
> to protect their children from unsavory experiences and influ-
> ences, denied them important types of intellectual growth
> stimuli by taking them out of school four years ago. This has
> profoundly interfered with the children's mental growth in the
> area of academic type of subject matter. Also, as their children
> move into adolescence and adult life there is no way they can
> overprotect them from every adverse experience. It might be
> wiser to teach the children how to cope with these while they
> grow up rather than let them experience only a protected unreal
> life at present.
>
>   I would suggest that the parents be apprised of these facts
> and be given a brief period of time to recommend a program
> whereby their concerns for their children's moral and character
> growth might be taken into account, but that also the children
> be given appropriate remedial education experiences, and that
> the concerns of the school board and state statutes be taken
> into account. I would feel that to take the children away from
> their parents would have devastating psychological and emo-
> tional consequences for the children. Peaceful negotiations with
> the parents toward the end of getting these children back into
> some kind of high-quality educational experience would be seen
> as most important.

He sent copies of the report to Judge Bachman, the Utah Division
of Family Services, and John Singer.

As the Singers had finally complied with his order, Judge Bachman
scheduled a trial for December 16, 1977, in order to reach a final
disposition on the neglect and truancy charges. On November 5 he
called John and Vickie to Coalville for a pretrial conference, where
they met with Christiansen and Orton to attempt, as Victor Cline
had suggested, to work out some sort of compromise by peaceful
negotiation, and possibly avert a trial.

Urged to consider remedial educational experiences, John once
again stressed that it was their God-given right and duty to educate
their children as they saw fit. They were supported legally by the
Constitution, and they would not compromise their liberties.

After more than two hours of discussion, Judge Bachman decided
to give the Singers one last chance. "It is my job to uphold the laws
of this state. If I dismiss the charges against you I'll lose my job. If

you won't compromise and give your children a more adequate education, as they're entitled to under state law, the court may be forced to remove them from your home and place them in a foster home, and you may never see them again. I don't want that to happen. Help me." He looked back and forth between John and Vickie, hoping for a conciliatory sign. None was forthcoming.

The judge then moved the conference into open court. In the gallery, Sheriff Ron Robinson and Deputy Sheriff Leon Wilde took seats directly behind John and Vickie, in readiness to take them into custody should the judge order their arrest.

Terry Christiansen entered a motion to vacate the fine and jail sentence: "I think they have substantially complied with the prior order; I see that it would do no good to have them pay a fine or spend some time in jail."

"I concur, Your Honor," Robert Orton added.

Bachman granted the motion, to the relief of both attorneys and John and Vickie, but ordered the latter to come up with an alternative educational program that would provide their children greater intellectual stimulation and more association with their peers. If they would submit an acceptable plan to the court before December 16, there would be no need for a trial. But if they still refused to compromise by that date, they would be tried on the neglect charges. The judge added, "I will admonish you again. You do have the right to have an attorney represent you at any future hearing or trial. Do you understand?"

"Yes."

"Now, you are to bring your children to court with you on December sixteenth, that is, the four oldest children, if we do have a trial. Do you understand that?"

"Yes." And the hearing was adjourned.

As they left, John and Vickie noticed the two sheriffs sitting behind them, and two other officers standing by the doors in the back.

There were already two feet of snow in the Uintas, while forty miles to the west in the Salt Lake Valley the grass was green and some of the trees still had their leaves. John and Vickie could see their breath inside the van as they drove home from Coalville. Before they reached Upper Loop Road they had decided they would not attend the December 16 trial. As they saw it, the judge had improperly disregarded their efforts to form a private school; he had threatened to take their children away from them, and the sheriffs would do just that in the courtroom in December. Compromise was out of the question. There could be no recourse from the juvenile court.

As soon as they got home they went into the bathroom and washed their feet, as was commanded in Doctrine and Covenants, section 60: "And shake off the dust of thy feet against those who receive thee not . . . and wash thy feet, as a testimony against them in the day of judgment." They would have no more business with any of the court personnel. They were entrusting their fate solely to the Lord.

In the aftermath of the November 15 conference, both of Salt Lake City's daily newspapers, the *Tribune* and the Mormon Church–owned *Deseret News*, as well as the *Park Record* and *Summit County Bee* and two local television stations, all ran stories on the Singers. By now the story had spread throughout Utah and had aroused the concern of Alex Joseph, perhaps the best-known and most politically influential polygamist in the whole country. Joseph was the leader of a loosely confederated group of polygamists based in the Glen Canyon area near the Utah-Arizona border, a group dedicated to "restoring the culture of ancient Israel." Joseph estimated the number of adult males in his confederation at fifty.

Joseph's group had established a private school in Glen Canyon which the members' children attended. In 1975 the juvenile court brought charges against members of the group because they had not obtained exemptions from the local school board. But because of the group's size, the high quality of its educational program, and their ability to finance a long, hard legal battle, the juvenile court dismissed the charges and never bothered the group again.

Alex Joseph visited the Singers in Marion with one of his ten wives, Elizabeth, who was in her third year of law school at the University of Utah. Elizabeth gave John a list of U.S. Supreme Court decisions relating to compulsory education. These included a 1925 opinion in *Archdiocese of Portland* v. *State of Oregon:* "There has never been compulsory education in the United States, and it is the legal, moral, and constitutional duty of the parents to educate their children in any manner they see fit."

In the 1963 case of *Abington School District* v. *Schempp*, Justice William J. Brennan, Jr., wrote,

> Attendance at the public schools has never been compulsory; parents remain morally and constitutionally free to choose the academic environment in which they wish their children to be educated. The relationship of the Establishment Clause of the First Amendment to the public school system is preeminently that of reserving such a choice to the individual parent, rather than vesting it in the majority of voters of each state or school district.

And in 1971 the court in *Booher* v. *Oregon State Board of Education* wrote: "Parents may teach their children, and the state does not control that which it does not fund."

Alex Joseph told John about his own juvenile-court fight and offered him free legal help. "You have to resolve this through the system," Alex said. "You can't fight these people while you're living in the middle of them without respecting the rules of their game."

John turned down Joseph's offer of legal assistance. He was convinced he would not get justice through the courts, and was determined to demonstrate his faith by leaving the matter solely in the hands of God.

Joseph concluded from their brief meeting that John was a religious fanatic who only listened to himself. His sympathy for the Singers waned. "You're going to get yourself killed, John," he said before departing.

John decided it was time to issue the second standard of peace to the officers of the juvenile court. Since they had proclaimed war against his family and refused to accept his first offering of peace, according to scripture he must make a second and a third offering of peace before he would be justified in going into battle against them if they still would not make peace.

On December 3 John wrote a long letter nonstop from ten in the morning to five in the afternoon. The next day Vickie spent nine hours typing the letter, which was addressed to Kent Bachman, Terry Christiansen, and Robert Orton. This second standard of peace was ten pages long, single-spaced. A copy of it was mailed to each addressee accompanied by a copy of the first standard of peace that had been sent to Judge Bradford four months earlier.

In his letter, after a four-page history of the *State* v. *Singer* case, John quoted the U.S. Supreme Court decisions on compulsory education that Elizabeth Joseph had given him. This was followed by four pages of quotes from scriptures and a sermon on education given by Joseph Smith:

> Their teachings should be such as are calculated to turn the hearts of the fathers to the children, and the hearts of children to the father; and no influence should be used with children contrary to the consent of their parents or guardians.

The letter closed with a warning:

> We have not reviled against you people, nor did we seek revenge, but we were always in hopes that you people's hearts would be softened and show fairness to our beliefs and freedoms. But now, since this has not been the case, and the threat that my children would be taken out of our home still exists, I now warn you in the name of Jesus Christ, my Lord, to cease your mischief against my family and myself.
>
> This letter is also my second Standard of Peace that I raise to this court, and all others concerned. Hoping you people repent is my deepest desire.

When Vickie was typing the letter, several times her bosom burned and swelled with such joy that she had to stop and clap her hands, and once she got up and prayed to the Lord in gratitude. When she was done praying, she felt a powerful assurance that the decisions they had made were the right ones. She was filled with a feeling of peace and renewed faith.

Not long after, one of John's friends printed up several extra copies of the letter and mailed them on behalf of the Singers to Val Edrington and all six members of the school board, Sheriff Robinson, Walter Talbot, Dr. Cline, and members of the press.

On December 9, at the request of Walter Talbot, the Utah attorney general's office released an opinion regarding the definition of "regularly established private school." The opinion stated:

> Since the legislature has not defined precisely what a regularly established private school is, the local boards of education . . .

have the responsibility of determining whether or not any school
is a "regularly established private school."

When John and Vickie did not appear in court on December 16,
Judge Bachman issued a bench warrant for their arrest and set bail
at three hundred dollars. The trial was continued to January 3,
1978. "On that date the trial will proceed with or without the Singer
family," the judge declared. This time there were six uniformed
sheriff's deputies in the courtroom.

Half an hour after court was adjourned, the Singers' log house
was filled with friends, relatives, and reporters who had come
directly from the courthouse to inform John and Vickie about the
arrest warrant, and to record their comments for the evening news.
John told reporters that he would resist any attempt by law officers
to take him away from his family, "even if it means using force."

Most of the friends and relatives present tried to persuade John
and Vickie to hire a lawyer and fight within the system for their
rights, and warned that if they resisted arrest someone was bound
to get hurt. Among the gathered were Bonnie, Harald, John's sister
Edeltraud, and one of John's close friends, Fred Collier.

Fred Collier was born a Mormon in 1949 and was ordained into
the priesthood. He was employed by the church in Salt Lake City
as a typesetter. While working in the church's archives, Fred had
gained access to some unpublished historical documents that supported fundamentalist doctrine which he believed had been suppressed by the modern church. He quit his job in 1976 and published
a book entitled *Unpublished Revelations of the Prophets and Presidents
of the Church of Jesus Christ of Latter-day Saints.* One of the
revelations in the book, said to have been given to third church
president John Taylor a year before his death and four years before
the 1890 Manifesto banned plural marriage, was the following:

> I the Lord do not change in my word, in my covenants, in my
> law, and as I have heretofore said by my servant Joseph: all
> those who would enter into my glory must and shall obey my
> law. I have not revoked this law, nor will I, for it is everlasting,
> and those who will enter into my glory must obey the conditions
> thereof, even so, amen.

In 1974 Fred met a man named Curtis Plexico who had been a

disciple of Gus Weller, and who at one time believed that Gus was the "one mighty and strong" sent by the Lord to set the church in order. After Gus died, Plexico aligned himself with John Singer's doctrinal beliefs, although John discouraged Plexico from following him as he had followed Gus. Plexico introduced Fred Collier to John, and, finding that they shared many views concerning religion and education, John and Fred became friends.

In 1975 Fred was excommunicated. The official reason given by the church was his belief in the Adam-God doctrine. Already married with eight children, Fred became a polygamist by sealing a second and later a third wife to himself by the authority of the priesthood. Eventually Fred devoted himself to researching and writing about Mormon history. Like Bonnie Norder, he became emotionally involved with the Singers' fight over the education of their children. Fred felt that the government was intruding into the private affairs of families, and assuming responsibility for establishing moral standards that should be left to parents. He expressed this philosophy in his writing:

> When you distribute the responsibility for correct living to the people of a nation, then each one individually can carry his own weight or sink under it. But he won't take the whole nation down to hell with him. If you give the responsibility to the government, woe unto this people. All you have to do is get one corrupt man, and you've got them all. And our country was not made great by one Abraham Lincoln or one George Washington, it was made great with a whole country filled with such people.

A few years later, Collier would withdraw his own school-age children from public school and teach them at home.

On December 30, Sheriff Robinson called John and asked whether he would consent to being arrested. The sheriff knew that John had threatened to resist arrest with force, and did not want to risk harming the Singer children. John told Robinson that he intended to resist arrest.

John felt no animosity toward the sheriff. In fact, he knew Ron Robinson to be a decent, hard-working, compassionate man who treated everybody, including the Singers, with respect.

That night, John and Harald drafted the third standard of peace.

Dear Judge Bachman,

I was informed through various sources that you have issued a bench warrant for my arrest setting bail at $300. It pains me to realize that you had to go to such a measure rather than dismiss the action against me. Dismissing this law suit would have been a blow for freedom and liberty and would have been the means of clearing your conscience between God and man. You chose not to follow this course of action. On the other hand, I must remain true and steadfast to the spirit of freedom and liberty as guaranteed under the Constitution of the United States and which the Doctrine and Covenants teaches I must insist upon in order to be accepted of God.

I have tried to raise the standard of peace twice before. Your decision to have me arrested is an indication that you ignored my attempts to live at peace in this community. Therefore, in accordance with the law of God I am raising the third standard of peace and implore you in the name of the living God, the God of Abraham, of Isaac and of Jacob to dismiss all charges against me and my family. I am doing this not only for my benefit, but also for the benefit of you and your family's eternal destiny.

Sincerely yours,
John Singer

After the letter was mailed, John pinned up a sign on the bulletin board in the living room and called his family in to read it. It was a quotation from a Captain Parker during the American Revolution: "Hold your ground, don't fire unless fired upon. But if they mean to have a war, let it begin here."

Chapter 9

THE OLIVE BRANCH

"**T**he children have been deprived of intellectual stimulation, and it's had a profound effect upon their intellectual development. . . .

"Despite the parents' good intentions, they have mistakenly isolated their children from associating with other children. . . . I see these children as not being able to cope, both intellectually and later socially.

". . . Massively deprived intellectually."

On the basis of that testimony by Dr. Cline, John and Vickie Singer were found guilty of child neglect on January 3, 1978. The truancy charges against the children were dismissed, on the basis of Robert Orton's motion that they had been prohibited by their parents from attending public school.

Judge Bachman ordered Heidi, Suzanne, Timothy, Charlotte, and Joseph to submit to daily tutoring under the supervision and at the expense of the South Summit School District. The tutoring would be in "the subjects prescribed by law through the State Board of Education, with the understanding that the interests, feelings and beliefs of John and Vickie Singer will be taken into consideration." The children's academic progress would be monitored by Tony Powell and Dr. Cline by means of testing every two months, and the tutoring program would continue until the children could be reassimilated into public school or an accredited private school.

The school district was ordered to submit a tutoring program to the Singers by February 1, 1978. The Singers would then have five days to approve the program or voice their objections to it. If they refused to comply with the order, they would be held in contempt of court. The children would remain in the custody of the Division of Family Services, but allowed to live at home with their parents until a further court order. The DFS would also continue to pay Dr. Cline's fees.

"I will not let a tutor come into my home," John told the *Park Record*. "I will not let them monitor my children either. I will not sell my liberties to these people. This is a fight for freedom which they are trying to take away from me inch by inch."

Soon after the January 3 trial Val Edrington and Terry Christiansen each issued press releases regarding the Singer case, after being besieged by calls from the press. Both releases emphasized the fact that John Singer had objected to school textbooks that taught racial equality. This was the first time the issue of race had been brought to the public's attention; those who already saw Singer as a religious fanatic and an outlaw now held racism against him as well.

Edrington denied in his press release that there was any drug abuse or immorality in the district schools, which prompted Vickie to call him "either a damned liar or a stupid fool."

John was quoted in one newspaper as saying, "We're not really as strange as people think. We're just common ol' folk. We're not trying to tell other people what to believe or how to live, we just want to be left alone and mind our own business."

But life at the Singer farm had become disrupted by a steady stream of calls and visits from reporters who had become enamored of their nineteenth-century life-style. There were frequent visits from friends and relatives, and from strangers—including college professors, state congressmen, and political activists—who wanted to meet the celebrated Singer family. Vickie, Heidi, and Suzanne spent hours cooking and serving food to guests. John found himself repeatedly explaining why he did not intend to comply with Judge Bachman's orders: Their three standards of peace had invoked God's law, and they were not to be bound by anything less.

Most of the callers urged the Singers to hire a lawyer and fight their battle in court to set a precedent for other parents. John and Vickie dutifully explained that their fight was over a religious, not an educational issue.

Only their closest friends truly understood the devotion the Singers felt for their cause. John and Vickie had come to believe that they were on a mission to restore God's law to the earth. The more they perceived themselves as persecuted, the more convinced they became of the importance of their mission.

Under the threat of arrest, not one of the Singers set foot outside their farm. The isolation of the place, with the Uintas guarding its eastern boundary, provided an illusion of safety; besides, they felt the Lord would protect them there because they had dedicated the property to Him as a place of refuge for the Saints during the millennium. Still, John wore a pistol much of the time when he worked outdoors.

Unable to make television repair calls, John sold his electronic equipment and retired after thirty years in the business. He and Vickie worried about how they would pay their bills, but Harald offered to help out. The Singers at this time were growing most of their food and relied entirely on wood from the forest for heat. Despite their poverty, their visitors always found hospitality in the Singer home.

After his retirement, John was able to spend more time teaching in the red schoolhouse. He added a class in the German language to the curriculum. But his grandiose plan for his children's education—debates, seminars, and guest lecturers—foundered amid the swarm of guests and the legal pressures.

One activity that John and the older boys devoted more time to was house building. Over the years, John had begun work on houses for Grandma and Harald's family, expecting that when the millennium arrived they would all be gathering at the farm in Marion. At the end of 1977 Grandma's two-story house was completed on the northwest corner of the farm, at the edge of Don and Miriam Jepsen's property. Harald's house, built over the root cellar with two thousand dollars' worth of scrap lumber, was nine months from completion.

As the pressures upon the family mounted, so grew their conviction that the millennium was imminent, and, in fact, was to be the solution to their problems with the law. This belief increased their fervid home-building activities. Moreover, John and Vickie had revelations that during the millennial period John would have several more wives, and they began laying the foundation for yet another house on the southeastern corner of the farm.

In mid-January 1978, the whole family came down with an illness that lasted about a month. Entries in Vickie's journal attest to the debilitating effects of the recent pressures.

Jan. 21, 1978: For the last three or four days we've had deathly sickness come upon the whole family. It saps all strength out of you. I've been able to wait on others some today, but yesterday I could hardly move. We all lay like corpses in bed. High fever, chills, aches, vomiting, terrible headaches, terrible sore throats, violent coughing. The children cry out for help and look pitiful. John had been down terribly sick. He suffers terrible pain in his head along with everything else. He's lost weight and is starting to resemble a corpse.

It's almost as if Satan is trying to kill us. . . . If we don't have deliverance from this tribulation soon, we feel that the only thing left will be to go to the spirit world. We are so horribly weary from our sojourn—here we are old and worn out and suffer almost constantly in one way or another under our decrepit bodies. We pray that the Lord will deliver us from this awful darkness *soon*.

Jan. 23, 1978: Since last entry—no let up of this horrible plague. The children cough violently and are terribly weak. Heidi and Suzy just crawled out of the bathtub from soaking—they have coughed so hard Heidi's tongue started going numb—every time she coughs Suzy's stomach hurts terribly. Charlotte is getting so skinny in her face—she's almost coughed her poor self to death it seems. Benjamin is having a very hard time of it, too, as with everyone else. I've been able to wait on everyone the last couple of days, thank Heaven. What would we do if I were still down so sick. Our only friend in the valley, Shirley, has this same thing with her little daughter. She brought us some soup today.

Our lives have been nowhere near what you might call normal—we are truly in the hard, long tribulations before our redemption cometh, these tribulations having gone on now for many years.

John's teeth are so horribly rotten—some broken off to the roots, others hanging in pieces. His breath is really bad and he can't chew too well. My top front tooth that is left in the front

is partially broken off and has a sharp jagged edge, besides
sticking somewhat out, and cuts into my bottom lip which is
not comfortable. We're truly sad cases, I'll tell you.

We need the Lord to do some great rebuilding on us when He
comes—that's our *only* hope.

Feb. 2, 1978: Some of the childrten are finally getting better,
but they still cough so loudly and hard—John too. I'm worn
thin of patience hearing these loud barking coughs continu-
ously—it's getting to me badly.

Feb. 19, 1978: Situation has much improved.

Near the end of January, the juvenile court judges voted to
transfer Summit County from the First to the Second Judicial
District, because the District 2 Detention Center in Salt Lake County
was closer to Coalville. The Singer case was reassigned to Judge
John Farr Larson, who had served on the juvenile court bench for
fourteen years. Before his appointment to the bench he was director
of children's services for nineteen years. He had also been a stake
high councilman, and was the father of five children.

Larson disregarded John's three standards of peace, as he explained in his testimony almost three years later:

> Larson: We have a way of dealing with constitutional questions
> and it isn't by letters through the mail. That isn't the way
> you raise constitutional questions in the laws of this state.
> Question: The second standard of peace not only talked about
> constitutional issues but cited you a whole series of United
> States Supreme Court cases, didn't it?
> Larson: I think it possibly did.
> Question: Did you pay any attention to the cases?
> Larson: No, I didn't.
> Question: Did you read them?
> Larson: No, I didn't.
> Question: Were you ever aware of the Amish case?
> Larsen: I'm not aware of that.

Personnel from the South Summit School District, some of whom
were irritated at having to shoulder the burden and expense of
providing a remedial education for the Singer children, drafted a
"Daily Home Tutoring Educational Plan" and mailed copies of it
to the Singers and to the juvenile court on January 30. The six-page
plan provided individual tutoring schedules for Heidi and Suzanne

and a group schedule for Timothy, Charlotte, and Joseph. A certified tutor was to be in the Singer home 180 days each year from eight-thirty to four. Attached to the plan was a schedule of public school assemblies, dances, athletic events, and other activities which John and Vickie were encouraged to take their kids to to "foster socialization."

When John and Vickie received the plan, they again told the press that they would not allow a tutor into their home. "This is dictatorship, this is no longer freedom," John said. "I will not bow to these people who try to inroad themselves and drive a wedge between me and my children."

The Singers had been given five days to respond. Having heard nothing after the five days, Terry Christiansen filed a motion for an order to show cause. Judge Larson promptly issued an order for the Singers and their children to appear in court on March 14, 1978, to show cause as to why they should not be held in contempt and the children not be taken from their home and placed in the custody of the state.

Sheriff Robinson called John to say he would be driving out to deliver a notice of the March 14 hearing. "I'll park my squad car outside your gate and I'll leave my gun in the car," he promised.

When Ron Robinson arrived at the farm to serve the court papers, John told the sheriff he had no ill feelings toward him personally, but he would fight anyone who came into his property to enforce the court's orders. "I'd rather die than go against my religious beliefs," John said.

On February 21, Val Edrington met with the Citizen's Group, a committee of Summit County residents formed to provide community input to the school districts. One member of the group said he thought the school board was "pursuing the Singer issue" too zealously. Edrington replied that he intended to "press the matter to the very ultimate." Several members of the group urged that the "issue should not be pushed or pressed to the point that John Singer would be killed." One of the group, Nadalee Noble, who was present, later signed an affadavit stating that Edrington said, "John Singer has broken the law, and if pressing the issue means that John Singer will be killed, then that's the way it will be."

John and Vickie did not attend the March 14 hearing in Coalville. Bonnie Norder, Fred Collier, Shirley Black, and John's sister Edel-

traud Lawrence were there, along with the press and other spectators.

The only witness called by the state during the hearing was
Sheriff Robinson, who testified that John was prepared to use force
to defend his family against arrest.

When Robinson stepped down, Fred Collier rose to his feet in the
gallery and called to the judge, "Your Honor, can I say a few words
on behalf of the Singer family?"

"Sir, will you identify yourself?"

"Yes, my name is Fred Collier, and I've been a friend of the family
for some time and attended most of these court proceedings. I fail
to understand why the court has refused to acknowledge the fact
that Mr. Singer legally incorporated a private school and has
enrolled his children in that school, and according to Utah law
there are no laws regulating private schools or how they are tutored."

"Thank you," the judge said. "I think the question of whether the
private school met legal requirements was litigated in previous
hearings. Is that right, Mr. Christiansen?"

Christiansen rose. "Your Honor, it's the state's position that a
private school is required to meet the approval of the local board
of education, and Mr. Singer has not applied to the board to get its
approval. If he's unwilling to do that, I think that this private school
is simply a sham that's designed to circumvent the educational
requirements of Utah.

"I would also like to indicate to the court," the well-dressed
prosecutor continued, "that the issue of neglect has already been
adjudicated and the only matter before the court today is the order
to show cause. This is the third time the Singers have failed to
appear in court, and I think Your Honor should take that into
consideration in proposing any fine or jail sentence."

After a short recess, Judge Larson announced his decision. "This
is a very perplexing case," he said slowly. "Here we have parents
who believe that the law requiring them to send their children to
public schools is in violation of their religious beliefs. But the basic
question as I see it at this stage in this proceeding is whether the
rule of law shall prevail in resolving disputes between opposing
parties. . . . I think that the experience in this country in the last
few years, especially the Watergate affair, has brought us to the
conclusion that no man is above the law, whether he be president
of the United States or one of us ordinary citizens. Now, the Singers

were given ample opportunity for due process of law. To say that this matter is above the law and in the hands of God it seems to me invites only chaos and the destruction of a system which we developed in this country over a number of years.

"I'm going to make my orders based upon Judge Bachman's previous findings and orders, and direct that the children be taken into custody and placed in the custody of the Division of Family Services. The court finds John and Vickie Singer in contempt and directs that bench warrants be issued for their arrest. This court does not take lightly the problem of severing the relationship of parent and child. My whole professional life has been spent trying to preserve families. But Mr. and Mrs. Singer should understand that they're not above the law. I will stay these orders for a period of seven days to give Mr. and Mrs. Singer an opportunity to file an appeal. If there is no appeal filed by the close of business on March 21st, a week from today, I will issue an order to the sheriff to commit John and Vickie Singer to the Summit County Jail for thirty days and order each of them to pay a fine of two hundred dollars.

"I want to say this, believing that my words may be carried to Mr. and Mrs. Singer: The olive branch is still out. But this court cannot tolerate just a complete ignorance of the system. This is the system. This is the way it's going to be settled."

After the hearing was adjourned, Shirley Black spoke with Ron Robinson outside the courthouse. Ron had been best man at Dean and Shirley's wedding thirty years before. The sheriff told Shirley that he was quite distressed over the possibility that he might have to go up to arrest John and Vickie and take their kids away from them. "I don't know if this job is worth it," he told her.

That afternoon more than a dozen friends, relatives, and reporters rushed up to the Singer farm and literally begged John and Vickie to appeal Judge Larson's decision to the state supreme court. "The olive branch is still out," they chimed.

"The olive branch is just another subtleness of Satan," Vickie countered. "The judge's statement is sentimental and touches the emotions just enough to blind the eye of reason for those who don't understand the importance of our stand. If we appeal to the supreme court it would make null and void our three standards of peace," she reiterated, "and allow Satan to thwart the purpose of the Lord."

The day after the court hearing, Robert Orton drove out to the

Singer farm to try to persuade them to appeal their conviction. He spent two hours at the homestead in Marion, during which he met for the first time the children whose interests he was charged with protecting. Orton was unsuccessful, of course, in his attempt to get John and Vickie to take their case to the supreme court. But he did form a favorable impression of the children. "If they were turned out into the world to fend for themselves," he later told a journalist, "they probably would be better prepared to take care of themselves, from a physical standpoint, than most kids their age who had been educated in public schools."

Ron Robinson and a Summit County commissioner also visited the Singers and urged them to file an appeal, to no avail.

"It seems there is no way to make people understand," Vickie wrote in her journal. "They agree that there is a God, but their words and actions deny it. . . . It seems the words of God lie dormant on a cold page and are only there for looks, as far as most people are concerned, because when it really comes down to it, most people we've talked with don't take the word of God in the scriptures seriously."

On April 6, when no appeal had been filed, Judge John Farr Larson dissolved the stay of execution and ordered the sheriff to arrest John and Vickie and commit them to the county jail, and to deliver their children to the Division of Family Services Detention Center. Judge Larson's statement from the bench was quoted in almost every newspaper in Utah, and was carried by United Press International to news bureaus all over the world: "By law, children in this state have a right to an education and a duty to attend school. Children are no longer regarded as chattels of their parents. They are persons with legal rights and obligations. The rights of parents do not transcend the right of a child to an education nor the child's duty to attend school. Parents who fear the negative influence of public education should also examine the damaging effects of teaching a child disobedience to law and defiance to authority."

The next day, a UPI story appeared in major newspapers throughout the country.

> *Marion, Utah (UPI)*—John Singer is holing himself up in his

house with his family and an M-1 carbine, daring the law to
drag his children off to schools that teach "immorality."

Shortly, the Singers were receiving mail and calls from all over
the nation. Some people sent them checks for as much as twenty
dollars. One letter came from a couple named Kitamura in Osaka,
Japan, who had read the UPI story in the *Mainichi Daily News*. The
Kitamuras wrote: "Part of the greatness of America, and many
other nations, springs from people who did not have a formal
education, yet by their integrity and courage of their convictions
were able to be a symbol of good for others. The moral training
and example set by our parents still affect us in life long after sums
and dates and formulas have been forgotten."

Several people from as far away as Denver offered to come up to
Marion with weapons to help John resist arrest, but John turned
them down.

Judge Larson, Ron Robinson, Val Edrington, Governor Scott
Matheson, and Senator Orrin Hatch all received mail from all over
the country, most of it sympathetic to the Singers, and some
vituperative.

On April 8, Utah State Representative Samuel S. Taylor approached Attorney General Robert B. Hansen as they were both on
their way to the parking garage in the state capitol building. Taylor
asked if there was any way the attorney general could intervene in
the Singer case so as to prevent a violent confrontation.

Hansen said, "Well, Sam, I'll do anything I can. What do you
have in mind?"

"The sheriff has orders to arrest Singer, and I think there's going
to be bloodshed if it's attempted at this time. Could you call the
sheriff and get him to hold off until we can perhaps work something
out with the court?"

"I don't have any jurisdiction over the sheriff, Sam, but I would
be happy to call him and talk to him as a concerned citizen."

"I'd appreciate it, Bob."

Another state representative, Edward D. Brown, visited the Singer
farm and met with Attorney General Hansen three days later.
Representative Brown told Hansen, "Those children will take up

arms to defend their father, and I think it would be a scar on this
state if anything happened to the children or their father, or the
sheriff. We should try to get the state out of that case as gracefully
as possible, Bob."

Hansen then called Sheriff Robinson to ask him to hold off on
trying to arrest Singer until he had a chance to talk with Judge
Larson. Robinson agreed to hold off.

When Hansen called Judge Larson a few days later, Larson said
politely but firmly, "I feel perfectly adequate to handle the situation."

Hansen then called Ron Robinson back and told the sheriff he
felt it would be inappropriate for the state to take any action in the
matter. Hansen later made a statement through the press that he
would be willing to meet with John Singer and South Summit
School District officials to try to work out a compromise regarding
the Singers' educational program. John's response, also made
through the media, was: "As an American I don't want to be given
just part of my liberty. I will not compromise my liberties. I would
like Mr. Hansen to study the Constitution and look into the law of
liberty which our founding fathers have guaranteed us."

On Saturday, April 15, Representative Taylor visited the Singer
farm. Sam Taylor, a Democrat from Salt Lake City, would be called
a liberal in most states. But in Utah, perhaps the most conservative
state in the union, he is regarded as radical and controversial. He
was one of a handful of Utah state legislators who were not Mormons.

Taylor checked the state records and found, as John Singer had
claimed, that there was a high percentage of teenage pregnancies
in the South Summit School District. He believed that public school
administrators in the state were arrogantly blind to the problems
of crime, violence, drugs, and promiscuity in the schools, and the
Singers were serving the community by calling attention to those
problems.

Taylor spent most of the day at the Singer farm. He was impressed
by the Singers' home, their life-style, and the tidy little red schoolhouse stocked with books and supplies. Though he kept an eye out
for firearms, he never saw any. He thought the children were healthy
and bright, and on the day of his visit they were playing with
friends and relatives who were their age. At the end of his visit,
after he had listened to John and Vickie explain their religious

beliefs, he was convinced that they were victims of a miscarriage of justice. He promised he would try to help them.

The following Wednesday Taylor asked the House Public Education Committee to form a subcommittee to investigate the Singer case, but the committee voted five to four against involving itself.

Undiscouraged, Taylor wrote to Robert Orton suggesting that Orton ask the court to stay the arrest orders to allow him more time to try to reason with the Singers. "When you're dealing with an unreasonable man, you must reason all that much harder with him, not make a show of force," Taylor advised Orton.

On May 4, 1978, Victor Cline was interviewed on the KSL-TV evening news. Speaking about the Singer children, Dr. Cline said that they were "abused because they are deprived academically and socially." And speaking about John Singer, he stated, "I see him as brain-damaging his children. I see him actually damaging them, because of emotional and social and other kinds of isolation."

John and Vickie had watched the news broadcast and were deeply offended and outraged. "Maybe it's best that we are in an isolated condition," John said, "because the Lord says, 'By their fruits ye shall know them,' and the fruits of this society stink."

Judge John Farr Larson later testified that he did not see the interview on television, nor was he aware of Dr. Cline's remarks.

Former juvenile court judge Charles Bradford, who watched the interview, called Dr. Cline's statements "preposterous."

Shortly after seeing the news broadcast, Harald Singer consulted a reputable neurologist, who told him that it is impossible to diagnose brain damage in children through the testing procedures performed by Dr. Cline, and that it would be difficult to establish such damage even through a neurological examination.

On May 19, 1978, Robert Orton filed a motion for a sixty-day stay of execution, on the grounds that threats of violence might have a devastating effect upon the physical, mental and emotional well-being of the children. The stay would also give Orton an opportunity to communicate with the Singers under less threatening circumstances. Judge Larson set a hearing for the motion on June 13, and a notice of the hearing was mailed to the Singers.

While the motion was pending, Sheriff Robinson once again attempted to execute the arrest and custody warrants. This time he brought two deputies along with him, but left them in the squad car at the gate and walked up the lane unarmed to the Singer house. John and Vickie met the sheriff outside the house. A pistol was conspicuously resting in John's pocket. The sun was peeking in and out of the high dense clouds on that cool and windy day.

"I've come to carry out the court orders," Ron said. "I have to take you two to jail, and . . ."

"We're not going anywhere," John said, hooking his thumbs in his belt; his right hand was inches from the pistol. "I'd rather be buried in my garden than go with you."

Pointing to John's gun, Ron asked, "Would you use that thing to resist arrest?"

"I'll use any means I have to."

Vickie added, "And if you try to take my husband I'll grab you and I'll beat on your head."

Saying no more, Robinson walked back down the lane, got into the squad car, and drove off. From his office he reported to the juvenile court that he felt it would be impossible to execute the warrants without being armed.

Later that afternoon, Mormon Church President Spencer W. Kimball announced that he had had a revelation from God: "He has heard our prayers, and by revelation has confirmed that the long-promised day has come when . . . all worthy male members of the Church may be ordained to the priesthood without regard for race or color." This revision in church doctrine was hailed throughout most of the state as a step forward in the cause of human rights. Among fundamentalists, however, June 9, 1978, is known as "Black Friday."

On June 13 in juvenile court Terry Christiansen opposed Orton's motion for a sixty-day stay of execution. "It would be an extremely dangerous precedent," argued the prosecutor, "if an individual could make it so the law was not enforced against him by the threat of violence. Also, Your Honor, Mr. Singer has made it clear that he will not compromise under any circumstances, and I don't think a stay of execution would influence him to reconsider."

The Singers were not in court, but Bonnie Norder and Edeltraud Lawrence were in attendance.

Judge Larson decided to give Orton a week to see what he could accomplish. "I will grant a stay for a period of seven days, until June twentieth, with the idea, Mr. Orton, that if you feel your efforts during this critical time are fruitful, the court would further consider the matter. It should be kept in mind, however, that this action is not intended to excuse the Singers from complying with the law."

As soon as court adjourned, Orton hurried to his office and dictated a letter to John and Vickie, informing them that the seven-day stay of execution temporarily removed the threat of arrest. He invited them to meet him at the courthouse in Coalville on June 15 to discuss ways to resolve the pending disputes. "For the next week," Orton wrote, "I suggest that we forget the controversy between the State of Utah and John and Vickie Singer, and consider only the question of what is in the best interests of the minor children of John and Vickie Singer."

That evening a report on the Singer case was aired nationally on the CBS television network news.

When Vickie read Orton's letter on June 14, she said to John, "They must think we're stupid, trying to pull such a trick on us! We'd be arrested on the spot if we go to Coalville to meet with him!" The Singers had not set foot outside their farm in six months.

John called Orton's office and told the secretary that he would not be meeting with the attorney the next day or at any other time. That evening, Orton called John and again pleaded with him to consider alternative educational plans for his children—perhaps the court would agree to modify the school district's tutoring plan.

"We already have our own tutoring plan that we are very happy with," John said.

"John, frankly I'm appalled at your lack of interest in the safety and well-being of your children."

"You must be deaf," John said, controlling his anger. "We have already said that we will not compromise our liberties. How much of this mischief do we still have to take?"

As a result of this conversation, Orton was bitterly disappointed. He believed he was doing all he possibly could to prevent the Singer children from being taken from their parents and their home, but now John Singer was treating him like an enemy. John had seemed much more reasonable and less recalcitrant when he visited the family in March; but because of the many statements John had made to the press to the effect that he would never compromise, he had backed himself into a corner and could not retract that position. It seemed to Orton that if there had not been so much publicity, John might have been more willing to compromise at this point.

Daniel and Lynn Kingsley were directors of an independent private school in Salt Lake City. They had been following the Singer story in the media for several months, and finally became disturbed over what they considered infringements on the Singers' rights. In the interest of protecting their own rights also, they decided to get involved.

Daniel Kingsley was a professor at the University of Utah. His wife Lynn was a social worker who had been involved with cases of child neglect, and had worked with juvenile court judges. She also held a teaching certificate. In 1967 the Kingsleys withdrew their youngest child from public school and started teaching him and two neighbors' children in their basement. Over the years their reputation spread throughout the community; they took on more students, and finally moved the classes out of the basement and into an abandoned grammar school building near their home. Lynn Kingsley quit her job with a county agency and became full-time director of Kingsley School, which in 1978 had an enrollment of 350 students in preschool through eighth grade, and thirty certified teachers on the faculty. Kingsley School is not incorporated, or affiliated with any political or religious group, and has never been regulated or monitored by the state or the school district. Its curriculum is designed to prepare Christian students of all races for college.

When she read that Representative Samuel Taylor had become involved in the Singer case, Lynn Kingsley called him to offer help. "I've never heard of any parents in the State of Utah being hassled as badly as the Singers over this compulsory attendance issue," she told the legislator. She also echoed Taylor's concern for the safety of the children because of the threats of violence reported in the media. "Judge Larson knows me and respects our school," she told Taylor. "Maybe it would help if I talked to him."

On June 17, three days before the stay of execution was to expire, Representative Taylor took Daniel and Lynn Kingsley to meet the Singers. The visit lasted four hours. The Kingsleys returned to the

Singer farm by themselves two days later, on a Sunday, and stayed most of the day.

The Kingsleys suggested that if John and Vickie would agree to let them assist in a very small way with their children's education, and if they could report to the juvenile court that the Singers' educational program was now under the supervision of the Kingsley School, then the judge might dismiss the charges against them.

This was the most tempting offer John and Vickie had yet heard, but they braced themselves against the temptation and explained that even such a small compromise would be an acknowledgment that the juvenile court still had the power to approve their educational program and, therefore, it still had the power to withdraw its approval at any time. No, the offer was most generous but they could not accept it.

Lynn Kingsley called Robert Orton on June 19 and told him she would be glad to testify as an expert on the Singers' behalf. She said she still held out hope she could persuade the Singers to let the Kingsley School oversee their home school.

When Orton told Judge Larson on June 20 that Lynn Kingsley was attempting to work out a settlement with the Singers, the judge extended the stay of execution until July 3 and set a hearing for that date to hear Mrs. Kingsley's testimony.

"I could see that the education the Singer children are getting is not the same as they would get in public schools," Lynn Kingsley testified on July 3. "But in some ways their education is superior. . . . Not one of them will ever be welfare cases when they grow up. They are learning responsibility. . . . I would love to have the children in my school visit that farm and learn some of the things Mr. Singer teaches his kids.

"It is a marvelous method to sit around the table with children, on a small-group basis, with a very individualized approach, and this is what the Singers do in their home school. To put the children back in public school at this time would be like leading lambs to slaughter. . . . It would be impossible to control the prejudices of teachers and students in public schools.

"Some of the children who attend our school we classify as poor little rich kids, and they are really neglected. Their parents are never home, cannot be reached; they cannot furnish any homework help, cannot supervise their children at home. The Singers are there all of the time. Where are you going to find a man and a woman who feel that the education of their children is so important that they would subject themselves to what the Singers have subjected themselves to?

"The last thing the Singer children need to worry about is being social. They have more friends and relatives up there to play with than almost any group of kids I've ever known. . . . I wish that all of the children that come to my school looked and acted and behaved as courteously as the Singer children. I felt very much that these children have been taught some social graces."

Robert Orton asked her, "Based on your observations—and I think you said you were a child welfare worker and worked with adoptions and child placement—could these children benefit from being placed in a foster home?"

"Most certainly not."

"Do you think it would be in the best interests of the children at present that they be permitted to remain at home with their parents and attend the private school there?"

"I do."

"Would you be willing to assist in the development of a home-school program for the Singer children?"

"Yes, I would."

Judge Larson then asked her, "Supposing the court vacated the warrants and took off the pressure in this respect, and suppose they did in fact invite your assistance, how is this court going to know if educational standards are being met?"

"Well, I don't really know, Judge Larson, I just think that if I were involved, the education would be superior to the public school's. It would all depend on how much involvement I were allowed, and I hasten to add that Mr. Singer has to have the freedom to choose whether he would like me or anyone else to help him. If it were to be a mandatory requirement that I be the one, I would never get on his property again. Mr. Singer is standing very firm, and may I say that since he has been led to believe that the state might feel more powerful than the parent in the care of the children, he's going to resist any effort to help him until he's free to do it in his own way."

At the conclusion of Lynn Kingsley's testimony, Orton entered a motion to vacate the arrest and custody warrants and to grant probation to John and Vickie Singer. He pointed out that the school board had not decided whether High Uintas Academy was a regularly established private school. "I suggest that the court give the Singers a period of time to establish and carry out the functions of their private school, without testing and without monitoring by the school district or by the state, just as Mrs. Kingsley has been permitted to do with the Kingsley School.

"I admit that this High Uintas Academy could be used as a sham to get around the compulsory education law. But I think that remains to be seen. Whether their standards are going to be adequate remains to be seen. And I'm simply asking, for the benefit of the children, that this be given a chance.

"Now, I don't think justice would be served by either Mr. and Mrs. Singer going to jail. I think they need to be in the home, I think the children need to be there, and I ask the court to give them probation to permit them to prove themselves with respect to their private school.

"I don't think this is so different from many other criminal charges, including felony charges, where a person stands convicted of a felony and upon his first conviction or maybe even a second, and in some cases a third, is given probation."

Orton concluded, "I think it is in the best interest of everyone that this case be concluded here and now, and I think what I am suggesting stands the best chance of being successful."

Terry Christiansen strenuously objected to Orton's motion for probation. "I think that probation many times is warranted," he argued, "but usually when probation is granted, it is the defendant that comes before the court and asks for probation. Now, Mr. Singer has refused to come into the court, and he's refused to comply with the court's orders. These stays were given the last two weeks so that Mr. Orton could meet with the Singers and come up with some sort of compromise program that they would be willing to comply with. Now, this hasn't been done, and based on what has happened in the past, Your Honor, I have serious doubts about whether the Singers will change their attitude and rely on some outside assistance. I simply don't feel what Mr. Orton is advocating has a chance of success."

Sam Taylor and three other state legislators, Daniel and Lynn

Kingsley, a dozen reporters, and a room full of spectators anxiously awaited Judge Larson's decision.

He began, "This court cannot excuse a man from complying with the law based on his representation that God told him not to. If the law should be declared unconstitutional, that's another question. But the constitutionality needs to be raised in this court or in the appellate court, and it hasn't. If Mr. and Mrs. Singer or the children wish to raise the question of constitutionality, even though the time for appeal has expired in this case, this court would cooperate and give them this opportunity. And it would appoint counsel to represent them if they are unable to employ counsel.

"I am going to make the following orders. The previous order placing the children in the custody and guardianship of the Division of Family Services is hereby vacated until further order of the court. With respect to the judgment against Vickie Singer, that arrest warrant is stayed.

"Mr. Singer has been characterized in these proceedings as the patriarchal figure, the one who makes the decisions. . . . The previous judgment and order based upon the court's finding of contempt, that is, the jail sentence, is to remain in full force and effect as to Mr. Singer. The court orders the sheriff to take John Singer into custody until further notice. This court believes that no probation is encouraged to be granted. Probation is a privilege; it is generally granted upon the basis that a party would comply with the law in all future actions. If Mr. Singer comes before this court and agrees to comply with the laws of this state, the court will consider probation.

"Mr. and Mrs. Singer will be given an opportunity free of court order to pursue the private school approach, and I strongly urge that they do this. I strongly urge that Mr. and Mrs. Singer afford themselves the offer that Mrs. Kingsley has provided to establish a private school that is credible, one that meets the educational standards of this state. I also strongly urge that Mr. Singer surrender himself to the sheriff. The sheriff shall, in his sole discretion, employ such means and take such time as are reasonably calculated to avoid the infliction of bodily harm on any person."

The Kingsleys and Sam Taylor drove to the Singer farm after the hearing to tell them of the "wonderful victory," as it seemed to them that the educational issues of the case were all but resolved in the Singers' favor. "The court handed you a ninety-eight-percent ruling in your favor," Taylor excitedly told them. "All you have to do is concede the remaining two percent."

The Singers were not interested in a ninety-eight-percent victory. "If we continue to stand strong, we'll have one-hundred-percent freedom guaranteed to us—and not only to us but the whole United States if not the whole world eventually," Vickie told them.

With tears in her eyes, Lynn Kingsley said, "So all I've done for you in court has been in vain?"

"No," Vickie assured her. "Your labors will not be lost, because you have enlightened the court and the legislators a great deal, and you've made some headway in rescuing more freedom from this unjust system. We are grateful for your help, but we cannot compromise our liberties one iota."

The Kingsleys respected Vickie's position, but Lynn was still in tears when they left the Singer farm with Sam Taylor. The sun already had set behind the Wasatch Mountains and it was dark when they backed down the bumpy dirt lane onto Upper Loop Road.

When they arrived home, Mrs. Kingsley called Judge Larson at his home and reported that the Singers would not accept the assistance of the Kingsley School, and any further action on her part would be futile. She also made a prediction for the judge: "John Singer will become a martyr as a result of this case."

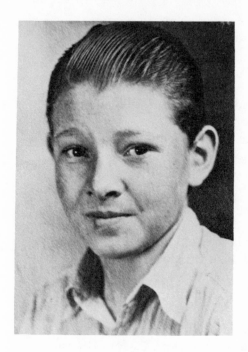

John Singer in 1946, the year
he emigrated from Germany
to the United States,
at age 15. The Nazis had
literally beaten into him
an intense dislike for
regimentation in schools and
authoritarianism in government.

John served in the U.S.
Marines from 1951 to 1953,
part of which time
he was stationed in Japan.

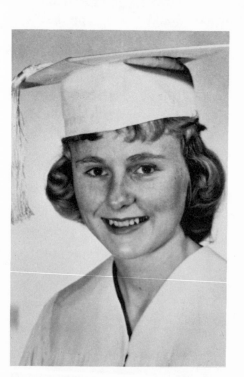

Vickie Lemon graduated from
South Summit High School as
Homecoming Queen in 1961.
When she announced
her plans to marry John Singer
two years later, her parents
were shocked and refused
to give permission.

John and Vickie taught their children in a one-room schoolhouse they built on their 2½-acre farm in Marion, Utah. In 1978, five years after they withdrew their children from public school for religious reasons, they were convicted in juvenile court of child neglect. Psychologist Victor Cline called them an "Old Testament family. . . . a remarkably cohesive and happy family, with much love and affection and mutual support," but also testified that John and Vickie had "deprived their children of intellectual growth by taking them out of school."

(photos courtesy of Vickie Singer; photographer unknown)

John Singer became a polygamist when he married himself to Shirley Black (left) in July of 1978. Shirley brought her three youngest children to live on the farm. Under threat of arrest, John and his two wives who became best friends, continued to teach their ten children at home. Although it is illegal, thousands of Mormon fundamentalists still practice polygamy today. (*photos by David Fleisher*)

Only a few yards away from where lawmen converged on John Singer, Edeltraud Lawrence breaks down the moment she learns that her brother is dead. (*photo by David Fleisher*)

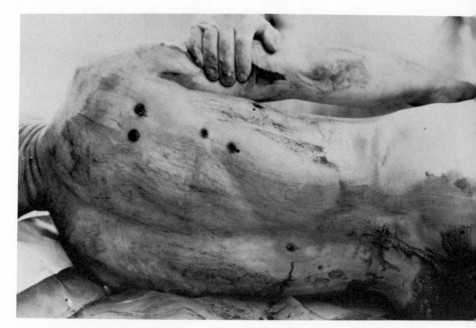

Summit County Attorney Adkins announced that Singer had been shot in the right side, under his arm, while pointing a gun at officers. When the state medical examiner refused to release the autopsy report, a friend of the Singers took photos of John's body at the morgue, which showed entrance wounds in the back. (*photo by Cully Christensen, M.D.*)

An hour after John was killed, Vickie was taken to jail, her children were placed in a shelter home, and Shirley's children were delivered to their natural father. Once a home to six adults and ten children, the farm was now deserted. (*photo by David Fleischer*)

Harald Singer,
at John's burial:
"My brother was
murdered."
(*photo by
David Fleisher*)

Utah Public Safety Commissioner Larry Lunnen, Highway Patrol Superintendent
Robert Reid, and Director of Narcotics and Liquor Law Enforcement Robert
Wadman (left to right) in front of the Summit County courthouse shortly after the
"L.A. Times caper." (*photo by David Fleisher*)

Summit County Sheriff
Ron Robinson admired
John Singer in
some respects,
but was threatened
with contempt of court
if he failed to
arrest Singer.
(*photo by Nan Chalat*)

Famous trial lawyer Gerry Spence filed a $110 million civil rights suit against Utah state, county, and local officials on behalf of John Singer's widow and children. Spence claimed that officials conspired to deprive the Singers of their religious freedom, were grossly negligent in the arrest attempt, and tried to cover up their wrongdoing. (*photo by David M. Freedman*)

The Singer family in 1983. Back row, left to right: Charlotte, Addam Swapp (holding Vanya), Heidi Swapp (holding Annazella), Vickie, Suzanne Bates, Joseph. Front row: Timothy, Benjamin, Israel, Roger Bates (holding Edelweis). (*photo by David M. Freedman*)

Chapter 10

ZION SHALL FLOURISH AND REJOICE IN THE TOPS OF THE MOUNTAINS

Shirley Black was in tears when she called the Singers on July 15. She said she had had a fight with her husband the night before, and had told him she wanted a divorce. Now he was out of town, and Shirley was afraid of what he might do when he returned.

Shirley was seventeen when she married Dean Black. Dean was a heavy-equipment operator; his job took him away from home to construction sites all over the intermountain West, often for weeks at a time. They were divorced after their second daughter was born in 1952, but remarried each other shortly thereafter.

Dean Black was a burly man with black hair and a direct way of speaking that gave the impression he feared nobody. Both Dean and Shirley came from Mormon families, but neither was active in the church. When Shirley converted to fundamentalism in 1961, after her back was miraculously healed by Gus Weller, she quit drinking and smoking and started attending worship services in the Kamas Stake every Sunday. She read the scriptures and prayed at home daily.

In 1964, when her three daughters were fifteen, twelve, and eight,

Gus Weller told her that she should have more children even though she no longer loved her husband. "There are spirits waiting to be born into this world, to be taught the everlasting gospel so that they can live in righteousness and be crowned in celestial glory," Gus had said. She and Dean had four more children. Brent was born in 1964, Nancy in 1966, Grant in 1968, and Julie in 1969. Shirley taught her four youngest children the fundamentalist Mormon beliefs, despite Dean's protestations; but since he was away often on construction jobs, Shirley virtually raised the children by herself.

Shirley was thirteen years older than Vickie, and although they both grew up in Kamas they did not know each other well until they became neighbors. Shirley and Dean were living on Upper Loop Road when Vickie married John, and Shirley quickly developed a close friendship with the Singers. When the Blacks moved away to Kamas in 1963, Shirley and Vickie visited each other or talked on the telephone several times a week. After the Singers were excommunicated and withdrew their children from public school, and after John's split with the Weller family, Shirley remained their only close friend in the Kamas Valley. Her loyalty touched them dearly. Whenever there was an illness in the Singer family, she would bring over a pot of soup and help care for the infirm. Shirley's younger children enjoyed visiting the Singer children, especially because there was always so much to do around the farm.

In 1968 Shirley told John and Vickie about her revelation that she would one day be John's second wife. In the next few years, John and Vickie received revelations supporting Shirley's, but the three of them agreed to wait until God revealed the proper time for them to enter into plural marriage. Vickie was overjoyed to think of Shirley becoming a member of her family, even though she realized there would be major adjustments to make and jealousies to overcome.

In the early 1970s, Shirley's friendship with John was still based mainly on her admiration of him—she saw him as a joyful man with a powerful faith in God, a man endowed with wisdom and understanding, with a great capacity for love, and one who would stand behind his beliefs at any cost. She admired his forthrightness, his sense of humor, and his physical strength acquired from long hours of hard labor.

Shirley was an attractive woman with a soft, gentle, somewhat sensuous way about her. Since Vickie had always satisfied John's need for love and affection, his desire to marry Shirley was probably based less on sexual attraction than on his will to follow the law of celestial marriage as set forth in Doctrine and Covenants, section 132:

> Abraham received promises concerning his seed, and of the fruits of his loins. . . . God commanded Abraham, and Sarah gave Hagar to Abraham to wife. And why did she do it? Because this was the law; and from Hagar sprang many people. This, therefore, was fulfilling, among other things, the promises. This promise is yours also, because ye are of Abraham. . . . Go ye, therefore, and do the works of Abraham; enter ye into my law and ye shall be saved.

Late in 1977 Shirley visited the Singers wearing sunglasses, which she left on even indoors. She told Vickie that Dean had come home one night drunk, and, in the presence of two of their young children, punched her in the temple and in the jaw. For a week Shirley's eyelids were almost swollen shut. A doctor in Salt Lake City told her that she had suffered from whiplash; the nerve running from her spinal cord through her jaw to her eyelids had been pinched, and it would take a few months for it to heal. After a week her eyelids started to open up, but she had to press on her jawbone to be able to see clearly. The doctor confirmed that Shirley's injury had resulted from a blow to her head. The injury continued to cause partial contractions of her eyelids for eight months.

Dean would later deny in divorce proceedings that he ever physically abused his wife, and that 90 percent of the arguments which existed between him and Shirley pertained, in one way or another, to John Singer.

In May 1978, Dean went to Nebraska for six months on a construction job. Their three oldest daughters were now married, and Shirley was left to care for Brent, Nancy, Grant, and Julie. Shirley was convinced that if she stayed with Dean her life would be in danger, so when he came home for a weekend in July, she told him she was going to file for a divorce.

After Dean left again for Nebraska, Shirley called the Singers.

John answered the phone. Shirley told John that she needed to find refuge from her husband before he returned in October. John suggested that Shirley marry him right away and come to live on the farm. He would fix up one of the extra houses for her and her children.

"Shouldn't we wait until I get a divorce from Dean?" she asked.

John read to her a passage from Brigham Young's *Journal of Discourses*, which stated that if a man is unworthy, his wife and children can be given to a more righteous man if the Lord commands it by revelation. This is God's law, John urged, and if they obeyed His commandments He would protect them.

They both agreed to fast for two days and pray for divine guidance. Shirley was planning to bring the Singers a load of groceries on Monday, July 17; then they would talk about it again.

John told Vickie that he believed it was his duty to offer Shirley deliverance from her suffering. Vickie fasted and prayed with him.

It was a great struggle of the spirit for Vickie. "Satan attacked me hard and my stomach was a churning furnace," she wrote in her journal. She wanted to do the Lord's will, but it still hurt to think of sharing her husband with another woman, even one she loved dearly.

Shirley struggled too. She wondered how her friendship with Vickie would be affected if she married John. She wondered how her children would accept plural marriage and a new father. She knew that she would become an outcast in the community, would be excommunicated, and her parents would probably disown her. But these considerations were secondary: she would do whatever the Heavenly Father commanded, whatever the consequences.

On Sunday, Shirley and Vickie talked to each other on the telephone. The best of feelings existed between them, and after hanging up the phone Vickie felt joyous; she told John she felt the Lord wanted them to enter into plural marriage.

As was planned, on Monday morning Shirley brought groceries to John and Vickie's. The three of them took a walk up Hoyt's Canyon. They decided that day to seal themselves together for time and all eternity. John led them to the baptismal font. On their way they teetered between feelings of exaltation and anxiety, knowing the step they were about to take was a big one. It had rained early that morning, and the sun now reflected off small puddles of clear water along the trail, making their path appear strewn with twinkling stars.

Dressed in their everyday clothing, they stood facing the baptismal font and performed the rites of celestial marriage. Vickie stood in the middle with John on her right and Shirley on her left. She took Shirley's right hand and placed it in John's right hand, giving the new wife to her husband according to the story of Sarah.

John began the ceremony. "Are you willing," he said to Vickie, "to give Shirley to me to be my lawful wedded wife for time and for all eternity?"

"Yes," Vickie replied softly.

"And do you, Shirley, give yourself to me to be my lawful wedded wife for time and for all eternity, with a covenant and promise that you will fulfill all the laws, rites, and ordinances pertaining to the holy matrimony in the everlasting covenant, doing this in the presence of God of your own free will and choice?"

"Yes."

"In the name of the Lord Jesus Christ, and by authority of the Holy Priesthood, I pronounce us husband and wife for time and for all eternity; and seal upon us the blessings of the holy resurrection with power to come forth in the morning of the first resurrection clothed with glory, immortality, and eternal lives. I seal upon us the blessings of thrones and dominions and principalities and powers and exaltations, together with the blessings of Abraham, Isaac, and Jacob, and say that we shall be faithful and multiply and replenish the earth, that we may have joy and rejoicing in our posterity in the day of the Lord Jesus."

Shirley had waited more than twelve years for this moment. Far up in the canyon, away from all evidence of civilization, she felt the spirit of God binding the three of them. Tears welled up in her eyes as the ceremony continued.

"All these blessings, together with all other blessings pertaining to the everlasting covenant, I seal upon our heads through our faithfulness unto the end by authority of the Holy Priesthood, in the name of the Father and of the Son and of the Holy Ghost, Amen."

They could not contain their joy as they hugged each other repeatedly.

The Singer children were the first to learn of the marriage, and they were delighted because they liked Shirley and her children very much. None of them knew then that polygamy was against the law.

An hour after the marriage ceremony, Shirley went home to tell her children about it; they all agreed to keep the marriage a secret until a more appropriate time for breaking the news to the world. Shirley would move into the house intended for Harald's family as soon as John could fix it up. Although Grandma's house was complete and ready for occupancy, Harald's house had two more bedrooms and offered more privacy, since it was set back away from the lane, whereas Grandma's house was on the lane, next to the Jepsens' property.

Shirley anxiously awaited her move to the Singer farm, not only because she feared her husband's return, but also because, at the age of forty-nine, she wanted to have children with John Singer.

Traditionally, in Mormon polygamous families, each of the "sister wives" are given separate quarters in which to live and raise her children. The patriarchal husband is responsible for supporting each of his wives and for overseeing the education and welfare of their children.

In communal polygamist groups, a husband normally houses his wives very close to each other, staying at different houses or apartments on different nights. He is expected to give all his wives equal time and equal deference. The wives often develop deep friendships among themselves in this setting and form effective cooperative systems for economic and emotional security.

In a large city, the wives of an independent polygamist may live miles apart, and in some cases the wives may not see each other for months or years.

A polygamist husband is expected to obtain the consent of his first wife before marrying another. In this respect only is the first wife's rank higher than the others'. Sometimes a wife will ask her husband to take her unmarried or widowed sister as a plural wife, for the sake of her salvation or her livelihood, or both.

In the years following the Mormon Church's 1890 Manifesto,

polygamists in the intermountain West—probably at least twenty thousand of them at the turn of the century—were forced to go underground and lead difficult lives as martyrs. Plural wives especially suffered, since they were excommunicated by the church, estranged by friends and relatives, and, when their husbands were prosecuted under the antipolygamy laws, left without support, comforted only by the belief that in the hereafter they would be exalted. Hence the number of practicing polygamists declined in the early 1900s, and most of those who did practice it escaped to the remote rural areas or kept their polygamous relationships secret.

However, since the pro–civil rights climate of the 1960s and the widely publicized murder of polygamist leader Rulon Allred in 1977, the polygamist population has grown and become more visible. The *New York Times* estimated in 1977 that there were twenty to thirty thousand polygamists in the United States; Utah's Attorney General Robert B. Hansen two years later put the number as high as fifty thousand in Utah alone. Exact statistics may never be available, since plural marriages are conducted without licenses.

Rulon Allred, once described by the Associated Press as the leader of polygamist culture in America, presided over a group of about three thousand polygamists living in Utah, Montana, and Mexico. Members of the group paid tithes to Allred, who administered the funds to sustain an extremely wealthy cooperative organization.

A practicing naturopathic surgeon and excommunicated Mormon with six wives and forty children, Allred was known as a good family man, devoted to his fundamentalist beliefs. In 1977, at the age of seventy-one, he was gunned down in Salt Lake County by followers of Ervil LeBaron, the leader of a Colorado militant polygamist sect. Police later held LeBaron responsible for the slaying or disappearance of more than twenty other polygamist leaders in Utah, California, and Mexico. LeBaron's several hundred followers believed their leader to be the "one mighty and strong" annointed by God to set the church in order and rule the world. They were dedicated to carrying out his will, which included the execution of all usurpers who challenged or denied his authority. Ervil LeBaron had been convicted in 1972 of killing his younger brother, Joel, who had led a group of one thousand polygamists based in Mexico, but Ervil was released from a Mexican prison a few years later.

Ervil LeBaron was convicted of ordering the murder of Rulon

Allred. He died of a heart attack in prison in 1981. The investigation that led to his arrest involved 110 local, state, and federal law enforcement agencies and covered nine states and Mexico. As a result, it produced the most comprehensive government study of polygamy ever attempted in the United States. The Salt Lake County attorney concluded that with the exception of the LeBaron group, polygamists were generally peaceful, law-abiding, patriotic citizens. Ironically, the massive publicity of the Allred-LeBaron case helped bring polygamy back above ground.

Although polygamy is a third-degree felony in Utah, there have been only a few minor prosecutions under the law since the 1953 raid on Short Creek, a polygamist commune straddling the Utah-Arizona border, in which 36 men were convicted and 192 women and children were widely dispersed in foster homes. Some prosecutors fear that if the law were challenged today it might be held to be unconstitutional as a violation of the Free Exercise Clause of the First Amendment.

Shortly after Shirley Black secretly became John Singer's second wife, an incident occurred which police called the most bizarre in Utah's history, the backlash from which affected the way state officials treated the Singer case over the next six months.

On July 31, 1978, Immanual David, a thirty-nine-year-old religious cult leader, was found dead from self-inflicted carbon monoxide poisoning. He had driven his truck into a remote canyon north of Salt Lake City and used a garden hose to direct exhaust fumes into the cab of his truck. Three days later his wife and seven children leaped en masse from the eleventh floor of the International Dunes Hotel in downtown Salt Lake. All except one child perished in the fall.

Immanual David was excommunicated by the Mormon Church around 1965 after he had proclaimed that he was God, Jesus Christ, and the Holy Ghost, that he had the original Book of Mormon gold plates in his possession, and that he had received a revelation that he would someday take over leadership of the church. He had also written to the church's General Authorities demanding that tithes be turned over to him. After his excommunication, he organized an anti-Mormon cult with several followers in Manti, Utah, where he lived.

David was a large man who weighed three hundred pounds, with long, braided hair and a beard. According to his former neighbors in Manti, he often carried a three-and-a-half-foot sword which he said would some day be used to lop off thousands of heads. Although he was unemployed, he lived opulently. Possibly, he was collecting tithes from his followers. More likely, he was involved in fraud schemes. One of his followers had been convicted of fraud by wire, and just before his death David himself was being investigated by the FBI for fraud.

The David family had been living in the International Dunes Hotel with a maid and a bodyguard for a year and a half, paying ninety dollars in cash daily for their suite. Hotel employees remembered David as being nonviolent and businesslike. He would come and go every day with his bodyguard, usually bringing back food from the most expensive restaurants in town for his family. His wife, Rachal, and their seven children rarely ventured outside their hotel room, and when they did they followed behind him like ducklings, speaking only on his cue.

After her husband's suicide, Rachal David had been alternately despondent and hysterical for two days. Witnesses to the tragedy on July 3, 1978, said her older children willingly jumped to their deaths, but Mrs. David had to throw the younger ones over the balcony before she herself jumped. The one surviving child suffered massive brain damage.

Immanual David's mother told reporters after his death: "He sheltered his children from society, and felt the rest of humanity outside of his family wasn't worth dealing with." His children had never attended public school.

Bill Low, a protective-services specialist with the Division of Family Services, stated to the press that the David children had been brainwashed by their father, that Immanual David's parenting was a form of "emotional neglect" because he had not sent them to school or allowed them to associate with their peers.

Similarities between the Singer and David families were noted in the press. Representative Samuel Taylor, aroused by the David tragedy, visited the Singers again and urged John once more to present an education plan to the juvenile court, in which case Judge Larson would set aside the contempt citation and cancel the arrest warrant. But John once more refused.

"If I can persuade Judge Larson to come here to visit you, will you talk to him? Maybe show him your schoolhouse and how you teach out there?"

"Certainly we will," John said.

Taylor then wrote to the judge:

> The recent tragedy of the David family . . . with the resulting adverse publicity to Utah prompts this letter to you.
>
> I have never known of any case where parents and children were as demeaned and humiliated both by the courts and by the press as in the Singer case.
>
> For the Singers to have been arbitrarily subjected to the humiliating experiences of tests no other parents were ever asked to take, "brain damage" statements emanating from an incompetent so-called "professional" who demonstrated the lowest form of ethical conduct by his repeated public discussion of the so-called tests given to the Singer children, is for a good trial lawyer to be engaged by the Singers to sue the state for millions of dollars for damages done to the characters and dignity of the Singers and children. It was the state and not the Singers who were guilty of child abuse.
>
> You have asked the sheriff not to use force to arrest Singer. But as long as there remains an arrest order, the possibility of violence still exists. . . .
>
> The Kingsleys and I tried desperately to arrange for John Singer to visit your private chambers. He refuses! What now? The publicity circus and possible tragedy would blight the image of Utah. . . .
>
> In the interest of ending this blight upon the state, I'm suggesting that a visit to the Singers be initiated by you. I will be pleased to make the arrangements. There and then, hopefully, the necessary demonstration of good faith can be effected with a view that, shown such evidence, the court will be in a position to offer probation and to then allow the time to expire with no further fanfare.

In response, Judge Larson wrote Taylor a five-page reply in which he reviewed the history of the Singer case and concluded,

> Any humiliation which the Singers might have suffered has been the result of their actions. It is outrageous to conclude the state has abused these children when the procedures established by law were followed and when the children were duly found to be neglected by parents convicted of a crime for such neglect.

In your last paragraph you suggest I might visit the Singers. As stated before, I have never met these people. They have never accorded the office of Judge the response required of all citizens similarly situated. They have refused, in violation of law, to come to court. . . . I am willing to arrange for a meeting with Mr. and Mrs. Singer either at my office in Salt Lake or the courthouse in Coalville; however, it should be clear that I can do very little for them unless they are willing to, and in fact do, comply with the law which the Legislature and Governor in their wisdom have seen fit to enact.

Undeterred, Taylor fired off another letter to the judge:

I am making another plea to you to go the extra (and not so unprecedented) mile. That sanity may prevail, I ask that you visit the Singers. A firsthand knowledge of the Singer home and environment, devoid of hearsay and guesses, will make for better justice. It is also important to inspect the school and to envision the future potentials of a satisfactory education for the children. . . .

I am further suggesting that it will be possible for another, but face-saving, decision. It will be possible to assuage the "law and order" aspects of this case by requiring John Singer to remain on his property for a period of so many stated months. It will cost the state no monies. (Home confinement sentencing can be used in many other cases, relieving the crowded conditions of jails, keeping families intact, reducing welfare costs, etc.) There would be no violence, the law would be satisfied, and the case would be ended.

Because of their patriarchal beliefs and indoctrinations, the David children were cruelly destroyed. At least, the Singer children can be given a chance at life and the opportunities that life can afford.

This time Judge Larson did not bother to respond. He later stated under oath that he considered Taylor's suggestions "a bunch of bullshit." Taylor later told a journalist that he thought Judge Larson was "arrogant" and "should have been more magnanimous" in his handling of the Singer case.

Around this time, Governor Scott Matheson called Judge Larson and asked for a report on the Singer case. The first three pages of the judge's report were identical to the historical overview contained in the judge's letter to Sam Taylor. Larson's letter to the governor concluded:

The court has been extremely patient with Mr. Singer. He has serious personal problems and has had trouble with the law several times during his adult life. He is extremely paranoid, distrusting almost everyone. While I have a good deal of sympathy for his desire at self-determination, I cannot in good conscience excuse him from complying with the law of this state because of his threats of violence nor his claimed communications from God.

Dick Watson and Don Jepsen, who lived on the lane that connected Upper Loop Road to the Singer farm, and Jared Weller, John's cousin who lived on Upper Loop Road north of the lane, got together and decided they were tired of all the reporters, Singer sympathizers, and other traffic streaming past their homes every day. On August 7 they learned that NBC network in New York was sending out a television crew to interview John and Vickie for its "America Live" program the next morning. On the evening of the seventh, Dick Watson erected a barricade with a "No Trespassing" sign at the entrance to the lane. When John found out about the barricade he went down and dismantled it. But Watson came out a few minutes later and put the barricade up again with a new sign.

Jared Weller's brother Sam called NBC from Salt Lake City to advise them against sending their crew out to Marion the next morning. NBC agreed and, instead, conducted a live telephone interview with John and Vickie on national television.

For two days afterwards, Dick Watson stood by the roadblock and refused to let people by to visit the Singers. Finally, when Shirley Black came with her children, John walked down to the roadblock and escorted them past Watson's barricade, as Watson yelled to his wife Esther to call the sheriff.

Watson, Jepsen, and the Wellers claimed that the lane leading to the Singer farm was the property of Marion Park Estates, a corporation set up to administer the estate of the late Gustav Weller, and therefore they could prevent anyone they wished from trespassing on it. Jared and Sam Weller, the officers of the corporation, even started asking John to pay rent on his two and a half acres, on the basis that Gus had never given John a written deed to the property. In return John maintained that the property had been transferred to him through a sacred covenant with his uncle in 1957. Sam Weller's lawyer then told a representative of the juvenile court that

John Singer was a "land grabber" who refused to pay rent on property that belonged to Marion Park Estates. That summer, Judge Larson privately told an associate that John Singer was "nothing but a squatter."

In order to have Shirley's house ready for her family, John still had to panel and furnish the bedrooms, lay carpeting and linoleum, build and install kitchen cabinets, and put in the bathroom fixtures. He was helped by Timothy and an unemployed friend from Oakley named Alvin Rider.

Al Rider was one of the few people who knew of John's marriage to Shirley. On August 14, after he had been helping John for a couple of weeks, he told John that his wife was suing him for divorce and had kicked him out of the house. He had nowhere to go. John offered to let Rider stay in the house intended for Grandma until Rider could find a place of his own.

Rider was born and raised in Oregon. After converting to Mormonism at the age of thirty, he met Gus Weller's daughter Rachel Summers, with whom John and Vickie had stayed on their honeymoon in Oregon. Rachel told Rider that her father had seen the Savior, and in 1964 Rider and his wife traveled to Marion to meet Gus. They spent three days at the Weller farm and became convinced that Gus was a prophet and a healer, and that the farm would be a gathering place for righteous Latter-day Saints during the millennium.

During their stay, the Riders spent an hour discussing the gospel with John. John told them about his two-part dream in which mobs were on their way to the farm and he and the Wellers were preparing to defend their lives and property against them. John predicted that during the last days before the millennium, mobs would run rampant all over Utah, roaming the hills in search of food and killing people along their way.

Rider was impressed by John's prophecy and by his self-sufficient life-style. Two years later, he and his wife moved to Oakley, three miles north of Marion. He worked as a shingle sawyer and also as a part-time mechanic at Jared Weller's repair shop on Upper Loop Road. The Riders raised five children.

In spring 1978, at the age of forty-eight, Rider suffered from pain for several days when his gums became infected after two root-canal procedures. Instead of going back to the dentist for treatment, he went to John Singer for a blessing. The pain left him almost immediately. Since Rider was unemployed, he expressed his gratitude to John by helping with the construction of Shirley's new house. While working at the Singer farm he met Bonnie Norder and became infatuated with her. But his affection toward her was unrequited.

He was not asked to pay rent, but he agreed to continue helping John with his work. He also felt the Singers' lives were in danger because of their conflict with the state, and he wanted to help support and defend them by moving in. When he moved into Grandma's house on August 14, he brought with him two rifles, a handgun, and five boxes of ammunition, along with his clothing and about a hundred dollars.

Besides helping with Shirley's house, Rider helped John gather firewood, scraped and painted the schoolhouse, dug out the spring to make it wider and deeper, and built an underground cement tank in which to store drinking water. He did most of the shopping for building materials and groceries. Rider took some of his meals with the Singers in the log house, and Suzanne brought him fresh goat's milk daily.

Shirley and her four children moved into their new house on October 4, 1978, a week before Dean Black was due home. Making use of a pickup truck, Shirley moved in with a few pieces of furniture, clothing, kitchenware, a piano, a trampoline, and four goats.

It was an exciting day for all of the children except fourteen-year-old Brent, Shirley's oldest son, who did not care for John Singer, nor did he like Heidi who was the same age as him. But Brent loved his mother, and did not want to be left home alone.

The excitement of the day was snuffed that night for Vickie and her children, when John bid them good night and left the house to stay with his new wife. Before going to bed, Vickie hugged each of her children as she had done every night for more than a decade. But on this night their hugs were more like desperate clings and there were tears in many of their eyes. Vickie stayed up late trying to write in her journal, but her thoughts were confused. She paced the floor. She walked into the children's rooms to talk to them about her anguish. Heidi said, "When Daddy has more wives he'll hardly be able to stay with us anymore." They cried on each other's shoulders.

Vickie was still awake trying to write at three in the morning when John came back into the log house and told her that he and Shirley couldn't sleep either, Satan was bothering them so terribly. By now all of the kids were asleep. John and Vickie walked over to Shirley's house and the three of them prayed together. John walked Vickie back to her house, gave her a hug, and went out again into the night. Vickie continued to pray by herself until sleep overcame her.

As the rising sun warmed the October mountain air, Vickie arose feeling satisfied that she had passed another test of faith. She looked out her bedroom window to see smoke already billowing out of Shirley's chimney, and soon Nancy Black was at her kitchen door asking to borrow some butter. At that moment Vickie's heart was "filled with charity, the pure love of Christ."

"In the next few days," she recorded in her journal, "the Lord did give us burnings in our bosoms and marvelous assurances and short periods of rejoicing. Sometimes He would open just slightly visions in the mind of the greatness of this step that had just been taken by us."

But with the blessings came tribulations.

John spent roughly every other night with Shirley, and their relationship blossomed to the point where Vickie noticed that John was truly in love with Shirley. "You really can't understand these things until you've gone through them," she recorded in her journal.

> It is much harder than I could have ever anticipated, even though I've never doubted for a moment that what we have entered into was of God.
>
> For all these years I've had John to myself, and this is an adjustment that has to come about, and there are feelings of jealousy and hurt.

A few days later she wrote,

> I am being tried quite severely in this new step of progress. Satan molests me almost every night and there are sickening feelings to try and fight down also throughout the day.

There's hardly a moment's peace, it seems. Constant battle to keep down thoughts of pain, depression, hurt, etc. I have a constant prayer on my lips or in my mind, praying for the strength to be faithful in going forward in doing that which the Lord would have me do.

There have been periods of tremendous depression and hurt to where I felt my insides could erupt. I feel like an infant just learning to toddle, and I keep falling down. But John is a very, very fair individual, and very loving and very patient.

It was a source of comfort to Vickie to be able to express these feelings to John and to Shirley. Thus her torment was brought out into the open where it could be vanquished, and her friendship with Shirley was never seriously threatened. Vickie and Shirley got into the habit of taking long walks together up in the canyon, where they poured out their emotions to each other. In fact, as time passed they felt more and more like sisters.

"We are slowly becoming adjusted to our new way of life," Vickie wrote.

I have great confidence that if a person tries ever so hard to overcome self and keep his eye single to the glory of God, and cares and tries only to do what the Lord would have him do, regardless of what others might think and say, and regardless of one's own personal feelings, then a sense of satisfaction and progress is achieved, and the blessings of the Lord pour forth and true happiness is obtained. It sounds simple and easy enough, and might be, if only the hosts of darkness were not continually warring against an individual.

Shirley knew that Vickie was tormented by jealousy and heartache, and tried to empathize with her. "But what can I do?" she thought to herself. "I can't give him up. Every minute I spend with John is an absolute joy."

Except for Brent, Shirley's children loved and respected John. Although the Singer children harbored minor jealousies, they were thrilled to see Shirley's daughters hug and kiss John and receive affection from him that they never had from their own father.

After moving to the farm Shirley kept her children out of public school, without notifying the authorities. She knew that by doing so she was violating the compulsory attendance law; but she too

believed that God's law superseded man's law, and by following
God's law she would be protected by Him, as John had promised.

The Black children attended classes in the red schoolhouse and
Shirley shared the teaching duties with John and Vickie. Shirley
also gave piano lessons once a week to Suzanne, Nancy, Charlotte,
Julie, and Joseph. She found a great deal of pleasure and fulfillment
in teaching, especially because her students were so enthusiastic.

In the afternoon, John taught industrial arts to all the boys and
Vickie taught the girls arts and crafts and cooking. Every day before
supper, unless it was raining, all fifteen of them, including Al Rider,
got together and played baseball or soccer, or played on the
trampoline, or, when there was enough snow on the ground, went
sleigh-riding. For many of the children these were some of the
happiest memories of their childhood.

Each family cooked and ate meals separately, except on Sundays
and special occasions when they all gathered at Vickie's house for
dinner. Once in a while Al Rider attended the Sunday dinners, but
he mostly kept to himself in the evenings, coming and going as he
pleased.

It wasn't long before the Singers' friends and relatives discovered
that Shirley was living on the farm. Bonnie Norder was surprised
that John would take such a step at a time when he was already
being sought by the state on a criminal conviction. But she agreed
that if it was God's will, then it must be done, and she developed
an even closer friendship with Shirley than she had with Vickie.

Harald Singer, on the other hand, could not hide his distress. It
wasn't that he disapproved of plural marriage or disliked Shirley—
quite the contrary. But he felt their timing couldn't have been
worse, since Shirley was legally married to Dean Black; he also
thought the juvenile court conflict was on the verge of being resolved.
Harald was so upset that his relationship with John, his lifelong
best friend, became slightly strained, and he was outright cold
toward Shirley.

John's seventy-eight-year-old mother was also upset. "John, now
what you did!" she exclaimed. She pleaded with him to send his
children back to public school and get the law off his back. But he
said to her, "Mother, if I send the children now to school I send
them to a slaughterhouse." Grandma liked Shirley personally, but
she was so worried about John's perilous legal predicament that

she didn't sleep well for weeks; she lost weight, and came down with a nervous disorder called herpes zoster, or shingles.

One Sunday morning, John and his two wives were gathered in the living room of the log house. John announced that the Lord had revealed that their mission was to establish Zion, a place where "the fullness of the laws of God are to be restored and lived, where the freedoms and liberties and divine powers would be returned." By educating their children at home and fighting society's corrupt laws, by practicing plural marriage, and by instituting all of God's ordinances there on the two-and-a-half-acre farm, not only would they be blessed but, as John told his wives, "This will have an affect on blessings upon the whole world. *Our mission will revolutionize the whole world.*"

John leaned forward in his chair. "We are headed into a new era of time," he declared. "We are in the last days, when a setting in order will take place and there will be destruction and cleansing processes in order to refine and purify a people for Christ's return." The cleansing process, John said, involved physical confrontations between God's people and evil people, in which evil will be destroyed, leaving the clean and pure to serve the Lord and do His bidding.

"We are on the eve of a tremendous crisis when it will be the survival of the fittest. We have to prepare ourselves to be self-sufficient when economic disaster strikes, and educate our children to survive in the new society that will take the place of the old one."

The economic disaster would bring mobs of people from the cities to invade their farm for food and supplies, John said. They would have to defend their property and their lives with firearms, and that meant killing people in self-defense—as a part of the cleansing process.

John also spoke of his future wives, who would come to live on the farm and bear him more children. The Lord had revealed the identities of these women; there were ten of them. Of the ten, eight were presently married. They included Shirley's three oldest daughters and John's own sister, Heidi Hardeman, who lived in Texas. Two were women whom John had asked to marry him years before he met Vickie. One of the unmarried women he named was nineteen years old.

Vickie and Shirley were astonished, but they did not doubt the veracity of John's revelation, for it had come from God. In fact, Vickie later had a revelation of her own which sustained John's, and she assured Shirley, "John's vision will verily be fulfilled."

Vickie and Shirley and a few of the children had dreams of mobs coming up from the valley to attack the farm. But in most of their dreams, the farm was impenetrable and they themselves were invulnerable because the Lord was protecting them.

John revealed his family's mission to Al Rider and said that everyone who lived there, including Al, would play a role in establishing Zion for the Heavenly Father. John and Al concentrated their efforts on getting ready house number four, the one that had been started on the southeastern corner of the farm, for a future wife.

Shirley had filed for a divorce from Dean Black, on grounds of mental cruelty, two days after she moved to the Singer farm. Dean's lawyer was notified and a hearing was set for October 19.

Meanwhile, Sheriff Robinson told county prosecutor Terry Christiansen that he was afraid he would not be able to arrest John Singer as long as the arrest warrant restricted him from using force. The warrant specifically ordered the sheriff to "employ such means and take such time as are reasonably calculated to avoid the infliction of bodily harm on any person."

Christiansen then made a motion in juvenile court to delete the restriction on the sheriff from the arrest warrant. Judge Larson granted his request. In effect, the judge was now allowing the sheriff to "inflict bodily harm on any person," if necessary, in order to arrest John Singer for contempt of court. However, Judge Larson again gave the sheriff as much time as he needed to effect the arrest, in the hope that violence could be avoided.

But the amendment to the arrest warrant did little to ease Ron Robinson's mind. He was still concerned about possible harm to the Singer children—he was unaware that there were now eleven children living on the farm. He also had his own safety to think about. Even if the amended warrant did give him more flexibility in his arrest plan, he was still at a loss to come up with a plan that would guarantee the safety of the children and himself. He decided to go to the Utah Department of Public Safety for assistance.

The Department of Public Safety is an administrative body that governs all five of Utah's law enforcement agencies: the Utah Highway Patrol, Narcotics and Liquor Law Enforcement, Peace Officers Standards and Training, Bureau of Criminal Identification, and the Organized Crime Unit.

Ron Robinson met with Public Safety Commissioner Larry Lunnen in his office at the state capitol. By now almost every public official in the state knew something about the Singer case, so Ron did not have to waste much time on background information. He explained that he had been unable to serve the warrant on Singer without endangering the lives of the children and himself, and asked if the Department of Public Safety could provide him with resources to assist him in effecting an arrest. Lunnen called Robert Wadman, director of Narcotics and Liquor Law Enforcement, and asked him to join their meeting. After a forty-five-minute discussion, Lunnen assigned Wadman to work with the sheriff and provide whatever assistance he deemed appropriate.

Later that afternoon, Commissioner Lunnen dropped into Governor Matheson's office to tell him that his department intended to assist Sheriff Robinson in John Singer's arrest. He asked if the governor had any problems with the idea.

"Certainly not. Do whatever you can," Matheson replied.

During the next two weeks, Sheriff Robinson met three times with Wadman to formulate an arrest plan.

Dean Black came home in the second week of October and learned that his wife and children had moved to the Singer farm. He called Shirley, who told him that she had married John Singer and had removed the children from public school.

Outraged, and concerned for his children, Dean also called Ron Robinson, who reported afterwards to Terry Christiansen and Robert Wadman that John Singer had become a polygamist by taking another man's wife. Christiansen in turn called John Singer to confirm the report, then filed a motion in juvenile court to lift the stay of arrest on Vickie Singer as well as the stay on the order placing the Singer children in the custody of the Division of Family Services. In Christiansen's opinion, a polygamous environment was "extremely detrimental to the children." A hearing on the motion was set for October 16.

The Blacks' oldest son Brent decided to go back to live with his father, in Kamas.

On October 13, the *Salt Lake Tribune* called John to verify a report that he had taken a second wife. John admitted that he was a polygamist, but would not reveal the name of his plural wife, saying only that she was a divorced woman. The story was published the next day.

A few days later, the *Park Record* revealed the name of the second wife and reported that Shirley was still legally married to Dean Black. Explaining why she decided to marry John Singer, Shirley was quoted as saying: "Zion shall flourish and rejoice in the tops of the mountains. And that is what we're trying to establish here." The *Record* also reported that John planned to take more wives in the future.

Other Salt Lake papers picked up the news, and soon Singer was again the center of controversy. In a KUTV interview, Dean Black was asked his opinion of John Singer. "He's out of his mind in this religious bit," Dean replied. "He was a German troop kid over there, and I think he's trying to act like ol' Hitler—he wants to rule the world."

Shirley Black's father, Doug Simpson, who lived on Main Street in Kamas, was also interviewed by the TV station and by *Utah Holiday* magazine. Calling Singer "the Devil's imp," he accused John and Vickie of hypnotizing his daughter and using her for publicity in order to receive more donations and contributions from sympathizers. "Now the coward is hiding behind two women and ten children," Simpson told *Utah Holiday*. "If the law doesn't get him, a hundred people have called and said they'd go up there with me. If there are vigilantes, I'll be the head."

When Representative Samuel Taylor read that John had taken another man's wife, he lost respect for the Singers and dropped out of the case entirely.

Within a week, Shirley was excommunicated.

John, Vickie, and Shirley heard rumors that Dean Black, Doug Simpson, and Vickie's parents were planning vigilante action if the sheriff didn't arrest John soon. The rumors spread to Sheriff Robinson and to Robert Wadman. The lawmen decided they must act soon.

Chapter 11

WE HAVE PUT OUR
LIVES ON THE LINE

On October 16, the juvenile court granted Terry Christiansen's motion to lift the stay on both the arrest warrant for Vickie and the custody order for her children. Recommending that "caution and discretion be used," Judge Larson directed Sheriff Robinson to arrest Vickie and deliver the Singer children to the Division of Family Services.

On the morning of October 18, John received a long-distance phone call from a man who identified himself as Bob Wilson, a freelance writer who had been assigned by the *Los Angeles Times* to write an article on the Singers' "juvenile court problem." Wilson was willing to pay John six hundred dollars for an exclusive interview. John agreed to do the interview but declined to accept payment for it.

Wilson said he would be flying into Salt Lake City on the following day and would like to drive up to see John around six in the evening. He would bring his two photographers with him. John said he would be glad to meet with them at that time.

"Just one thing—I'd like to talk to you in private. There are some things I want to ask you about that I wouldn't feel comfortable discussing in front of your family."

That was all right with John.

"Okay, then I'll see you tomorrow night. Thanks, Mr. Singer."

On the morning of October 19 was Shirley's divorce hearing. She had decided not to attend it, in fear that her father would try to abduct her if she left the farm. Instead, she gave Bonnie Norder a notarized letter to read to the district judge in court.

"My chief reason for desiring a divorce from Dean Black," Shirley wrote,

> is because of his violent, unsettled behavior, which in sundry times past has almost left me virtually crippled and has often jeopardized my life and the safety and welfare of my children. ... His unruly behavior, due to a severe drinking problem at times, left us in mortal dread of his every arrival.
>
> I can say that I have almost raised our seven children single-handedly. He has never cared enough to teach them anything, and his example has been that of a bully and a foul-mouthed tyrant. The care of them has been entirely upon me except for the financial support he has given us.

Shirley suggested in her letter that the court give Dean Black a lie-detector test to prove her allegations.

District Court Judge Peter F. Leary refused to allow Bonnie to read the letter in court but it became part of the court record. Since neither Shirley nor her attorney was in attendance, however, the judge dismissed Shirley's divorce claim on default. Dean's lawyer then submitted a counterclaim seeking temporary custody of the children. He argued that Dean had never physically abused his wife or children and that Shirley Black was not a fit and proper mother because she was emotionally disturbed. She had "joined a religious sect" and had illegally withdrawn her children from public school. She was unlawfully cohabiting with John Singer, thus creating an unhealthy environment for her children. It was therefore in the best interest of the children to have them returned to their father as soon as possible.

Judge Leary awarded Dean a decree of divorce and temporary custody of the four minor children. He also gave Dean exclusive use of his home and three vehicles. Shirley was given half the money in their joint savings account, one hundred dollars a month in alimony, a 1972 Ford station wagon, and four goats. The sheriff was ordered to go to the Singer farm forthwith, pick up the three remaining Black children, and deliver them to their father in Kamas.

Ron Robinson drove to Marion that afternoon with a copy of the judge's orders. John met with him at the gate, armed. "Shirley's kids have made a choice that they want to stay up here," he told the sheriff. "Dean Black can come here and see them whenever he wants to."

Robinson left, and on his way back to Coalville made a phone call to Robert Wadman.

At 5:45 P.M., John got a call from Bob Wilson. Wilson and his two photographers were in Heber City, twenty miles southwest of Marion, and needed directions to the Singer farm. Wilson reminded John that they had agreed to conduct the interview in private.

The sun had not quite sunk behind the Wasatch Range when Wilson drove a black Lincoln Continental inside the gate, followed by a blue van. Both vehicles had California license plates. John came out of the log house alone and greeted them. A tall, distinguished-looking man in his late thirties got out of the car and met John halfway between the gate and the house, extending his right hand. "Mr. Singer, I'm Bob Wilson," he said, and they shook hands. Wilson seemed to be sizing John up, glancing up and down his wiry frame.

"Come on and meet my camera crew," he said, pointing to the van where two stocky, well-dressed men emerged from the side door, one carrying a thirty-five-millimeter camera on a tripod. They left the van door open, and John could see there was more photography equipment inside.

Wilson ushered John over to the van. "I'd like you to meet Grant Larsen," he said, standing behind John as the two men shook hands. Larsen clasped John's hand firmly, and suddenly grabbed John's right wrist with his left hand; in the same instant, Wilson wrapped his right arm around John's neck from behind and grabbed for his left arm. The other photographer dropped his tripod and moved in from the side to grab John's legs. John struggled violently as they dragged him over to the open door of the van. He yelled for Al Rider. Larsen, who had John's right arm, jumped into the van and started pulling John inside.

Most of the family had gathered in Shirley's house to watch the six o'clock news. Suzanne was sitting closest to the living room window which looked out on the driveway. When she heard shouting from outside, she stood up and glanced out the window. The rest of the family was startled by her cry—"They're trying to take Daddy! They're trying to take Daddy!"

It took a couple of seconds to register in their minds. Then Vickie was on her feet and out the front door. Al Rider rushed to the window to see what was happening. He saw John struggling with three men, and he could see that they were trying to get John into the van. Rider ran out the front door just behind Shirley, and was followed by Suzanne, Charlotte, Joseph, Benjamin, and Nancy. Julie, nine, stayed behind with three-year-old Israel.

Timothy and Grant were playing on the trampoline south of the garden when they heard John's shouts. Their view of the driveway was blocked by the barn. They stood still, listening. John was calling for help. Cautiously they trotted to the corner of the barn and peered at the scene in the driveway. They saw Vickie running out of Shirley's house, headed for the melee, followed by Al and Shirley. Timmy and Grant joined the ranks and ran to help John.

Heidi had just come inside from practicing with her bow which John had recently bought her for hunting, and still had a quiver of arrows strapped to her back. She heard shouts, looked out the window, and picked up her bow and ran out to her father's defense.

During this time John had been able to brace his left arm against the door of the van and keep from being pulled the rest of the way in. The man holding John's legs let go of them and tried to grab John's left arm. Seizing this opportunity, John summoned all his strength and, kicking away from the van with his left foot and pushing with his left arm, hauled all three of his assailants away from the van and onto the ground. In a mad flurry of arms and legs and determined faces, the three men regained control of their prey, Larsen holding John's left arm, Wilson again on John's back, and the third man holding his right arm. John's legs were spread wide and his back was bent forward; he was being forced into a crouching position. Larsen pulled a pair of handcuffs from his back pocket. "Get these on him," he yelled to his two cohorts.

In that instant, John freed his left hand, reached under his jacket, and pulled a thirty-eight automatic pistol from his waistband. Still bent over, his hands nearly touching the ground, he cocked the gun and pointed it alternately at the legs of Larsen and the man on the right, yelling, "Get off me or I'll kill you!"

Out of the corner of his eye, Wilson saw the horde of angry family members coming toward him. Still with a grip on John's arm, he shouted at John while trying to stay calm, "We'll leave, Mr. Singer. If we let go, don't shoot. We'll leave, don't shoot."

As soon as he said that, Vickie came crashing into Wilson from the side, grabbing his tie in her left hand and holding her fist in front of his face. "I'll knock your teeth out!" she screamed with a wild look in her eyes. Wilson let go of John and backed away, saying, "No, don't." As he backed away his tie came off in Vickie's hand and she threw it to the ground.

Arriving at the scene, Rider ran at Wilson as he was retreating. Wilson ducked behind the van. Al then made a dart at Larsen, who let go of John and backed away, holding his hands in the air as a sign of surrender. The third assailant was beset by screaming children beating on his back and head. John stood up, ruffled and shaking, and pointed his gun at Larsen, who was standing at the passenger door of the van, then at Wilson, who was on the other side of the van looking over the hood, and at the third man, who was still backing away from the angry children.

"Don't shoot, we're unarmed," Larsen yelled, looking sickly scared, still with his arms in the air.

Al Rider stepped between John and the van. "Who are you and what do you want?" he demanded of the three men.

Larsen said, "We're police officers," and pulled a wallet from his jacket which, when it fell open, revealed a shiny badge.

"We're leaving, don't shoot," Wilson begged.

Still shaking, John said, "Get off my property and don't ever show your ugly faces around here again or I'll blow your heads off."

Wilson ran to the Lincoln as the other two officers got into the van. Both vehicles backed all the way down the lane to Upper Loop Road "faster than anybody ever went down that road forwards or backwards."

Vickie walked over to John and put her hand on his chest. His heart was pounding furiously. They walked arm in arm up the driveway and into the log house. John was so emotionally drained that he had to lie down on the couch in the living room. He still had his gun in his hand and was inspecting it when he called Vickie over and said, "Vickie, don't tell anyone, but my gun wasn't loaded."

When reporters from the *Park Record* arrived an hour later, John was standing sentry in the darkness, his rifle held across his chest, in front of the log house. Al Rider was patrolling the border of the farm with an M-1 carbine. Inside, practically every member of the household was armed: Vickie and Shirley wore pistols in leather holsters, Timmy had a BB-gun, Heidi still wore her quiver, and some of the younger children had knives sheathed to their belts.

More reporters and television crews drove up to the farm. Every time he saw a new set of headlights come up the lane, John picked up his rifle and went out to see who the visitors were. He was nervous as he talked with them.

"Bob Wilson" was really Robert Wadman, director of the Division of Narcotics and Liquor Law Enforcement. Grant Larsen was Wadman's assistant director, and the third man, Bill Riggs, was an officer of the division. All three testified later that they had identified themselves as the police and told John that he was under arrest the moment they first grabbed him. But John did not remember hearing the officers identify themselves until Al Rider had asked them to do so.

The plan had been devised by Wadman and approved by Sheriff Robinson. At the time of the arrest attempt, four sheriff's cars were waiting on Upper Loop Road to go in and "clean up the rest" if the attempt was successful; that is, they would arrest Vickie, put the Singer children in the DFS detention center, and deliver the Black children to their natural father. Grant Larsen later testified that John "was the toughest man I ever grabbed hold of."

A headline in the *Salt Lake Tribune* the next morning, October 20, read: "Singer Foils Masquerade Arrest Try." The church-owned *Deseret News* took a slightly different approach: "Polygamist Pulls Gun on Three Officers."

On the same morning, Summit County Attorney Robert Adkins filed a criminal complaint charging John with three counts of aggravated assault for resisting arrest with a gun. A justice of the peace issued a felony warrant for John's arrest. A felony warrant permits the use of deadly force to effect an arrest.

As soon as the arrest attempt was publicized, journalism societies and news media executives across the country criticized the State of Utah for allowing its lawmen to pose as reporters, thereby "compromising the credibility of the media which rely heavily on public trust." The *Los Angeles Times* called the action "deplorable."

In response to the criticism, Public Safety Commissioner Larry Lunnen stated publicly that he did not regret his decision to allow the officers to pose as reporters; in fact, he would allow such a technique to be used again in an appropriate situation. However, Governor Matheson later apologized to the press and said he would direct Commissioner Lunnen never again to allow state officers to pose as newsmen. He added, "I think they will notify me now of any plans they have regarding an arrest." Matheson met with Lunnen two days later to express his disapproval of the masquerade and asked to be kept informed of any future arrest plans in the Singer case.

The *Tribune's* "Public Forum" is one of the liveliest and most entertaining letters-to-the-editor columns in America. Many of the letters provoke rebuttal letters and, of these, some provoke counterrebuttals. These epistolary debates are sometimes carried on for months over a single issue. The Singer case was such an issue, conjuring forth opinions from the enlightened and the benighted for most of 1978.

After the "L.A. Times caper," as it came to be known colloquially, a letter appeared in the Public Forum from a Kenneth D. Roberts of Salt Lake City in which he wrote:

> This pathetic man has, up to now, only been trying to protect his family from the evils he sees threatening his children. *The Los Angeles Times* escapade has left me with a sick feeling. Why don't the police and the courts spend their time locking up criminals and leave the John Singers alone?

A week later, this response to Roberts' letter appeared:

> In reply to Kenneth Roberts' letter, he, too, must be as sick as John Singer. May I wish him a John Singer for one of his

daughters; then, he'll realize it wasn't such a "crazy" attempt by the lawmen to try to arrest the man.

John Singer does not want to be left alone. He and his wives are begging for publicity.

Wake up and do something about all the John Singers before you find yourselves saluting and saying, "Heil Singer!"

Don't you Singer sympathizers realize the man merely wants more publicity in order to obtain more money?

> Marge Lemon
> Vickie Singer's Mother

The following week, this letter appeared:

My husband, John Singer, and I have borne up long and patiently under years of hateful, rude insults and accusations thrown out by my mother. She has constantly judged us and found fault with us. We . . . haven't held grudges because of these things, nor have we turned our children against their grandparents no matter how bad the situation was between us.

Time for "turning the other cheek" is long since past. We will no longer take these insults sitting down.

My mother accused us of "begging for publicity," which is not true. We have only been polite, honest, and frank with the news media when they have approached us. We have every right to express our beliefs and views, and have found no reason to turn the news media away when, all in all, they have dealt quite honorably with us.

My mother's accusation that John seeks publicity for money is also absurd and a downright lie.

Sign me "Totally Disgusted with My Mother!"

> Mrs. John (Vickie) Singer

Toward the end of October, Judge John Farr Larson held a meeting at his Salt Lake City office with Ron Robinson, Robert Wadman, Grant Larsen, and Terry Christiansen. The judge wanted to know the details of the unsuccessful arrest attempt. After they had dismissed the L.A. Times caper, Judge Larson insisted that John Singer be arrested as soon as possible. Wadman advised the judge that they probably would not be able to arrest John without a violent confrontation, to which the judge replied, "Not only do I want you to carry out my orders, but we will find the sheriff in contempt of court if he does not carry out those orders."

Robinson called Jared Weller. "I'd like to see this whole thing end peacefully," he told Jared. "Do you have any influence over John?"

"No, there's nothing I can do," Jared answered. "Once John makes up his mind about something, nobody can change it."

"You know, it's funny, Jared, in some ways I have a lot of admiration for John," Robinson offered.

As a result of the L.A. Times caper, John and his family grew more vigilant and distrustful of strangers; they were expecting another arrest attempt at any moment. Yet underlying the initial shock of John's narrow escape and the lingering atmosphere of tension was an exhilarating assurance that God had fulfilled His promise to protect the family.

John and Al Rider finished the small, one-bedroom house in the southeast corner of the farm that was intended for one of John's future wives. The yellow paint was barely dry when a recently divorced, homeless man of about thirty-eight showed up and told John he had had a revelation directing him to the Singer farm. While driving his camper in the mountains looking for a place to stop for the night, he had heard a radio news broadcast about the Singers' struggle to establish Zion on their little farm in Marion, in defiance of the state. He felt strongly that he should go there and offer support and protection. Two days later he was living in the new yellow house.

Bob Reynolds was a small man—five foot six and 135 pounds—but fit and strong from working on a construction crew at Park West Ski Resort near Park City. He had been divorced from his second wife, LuAnne, for two months, and was living out of his camper.

He had married LuAnne in 1973, at which time he had custody of his five children from a previous marriage. LuAnne herself had been married three times before, first at the age of fifteen. Four of her six children were married and living in Rulon Allred's polygamist community in Salt Lake County. Her two youngest children, over whom she had legal custody, had been kidnapped by their natural father.

LuAnne helped take care of Reynolds's five children as they flitted across Utah and Idaho from one polygamist commune to another. It was in one of these groups that Bob became engaged to a thirteen-year-old girl. But when the girl's mother found out, she put an end to the engagement.

After Reynolds lost custody of his children, he and LuAnne moved to Park City where his brother owned a construction company that built and maintained ski lifts. Bob and LuAnne were divorced in August 1978, but around mid-October started seeing each other again intermittently to try to reestablish their relationship.

When Reynolds first visited the Singers he had no interest in actually living there on the farm. He just wanted to meet John and offer his support. He told John that he believed "something very great" would result from the Singers' fight for religious freedom.

Reynolds had steel-blue eyes that shifted and squinted just enough to give him a specter of cunning. His well-groomed, thick brown hair was beginning to show gray. He wore tight-fitting clothes that complemented his taut features. The index finger of his left hand was missing as the result of a construction accident.

The day after his first visit to the Singers, Bob brought LuAnne to meet John and tour the farm. LuAnne felt no particular warmth toward John, but she loved the setting of the farm, between Utah's two great mountain ranges; the whole area was peaceful and quiet and appeared to be a place where people could mind their own business and live according to the dictates of their consciences. When they came across the new yellow house, LuAnne said half in jest that it would be an ideal place for her and Bob to try living together again. At the time, LuAnne was living alone in a tiny apartment in Salt Lake.

Bob took her remark seriously, and asked John if they could stay in the house temporarily. John must have liked the couple, for he invited them to live there rent-free. Before they moved to the farm, Bob told LuAnne that he hoped some day to take one of John Singer's daughters as his plural wife.

LuAnne Reynolds was a very attractive woman in her early thirties. She had blue eyes and brown shoulder-length hair, and was the same height as Bob. Up close, her face had a tired, been-through-the-mill look. Her voice was soft and calm. Although she was not especially talkative, neither was she shy.

While living at the Singer farm, Bob worked five or six days a week at Park West, usually from six in the morning to six in the evening. LuAnne went to work with Bob a few days each week.

When she stayed behind she mostly kept to herself, rarely associating with the Singers or with Shirley's family. In fact, she grew to dislike John, calling it a "personality clash." However, she did become friendly with Al Rider, and eventually Al began spending most of his free time with Bob and LuAnne.

The two-and-a-half-acre farm was now home to six adults and ten children. Some of the neighbors on Upper Loop Road started wondering what was going on there. Was Singer starting his own polygamist group?

At about nine on Halloween night the Singers looked out their living-room window to see a ten-foot-tall figure burning in the field across the lane from Watson's and Jepsen's. The blaze lit up the western sky for ten minutes. Early the next morning, John walked over to the spot and found a charred ten-foot pole to which a large feed sack filled with gasoline-soaked rags had been tied and set afire. On Upper Loop Road just west of the pole were the huge letters "KKK" spray-painted in silver.

On November 3 and 4, the Singers noticed a KUTV van parked on Upper Loop Road for most of the day. They also saw patrol cars repeatedly driving past the van.

On November 6, Al Rider walked down to the Singers' mailbox at the intersection of Upper Loop and the dirt lane, two hundred yards from John's property. He found the mailbox almost knocked to the ground, as if someone had tied a rope to it and tried to haul it away with a truck. The aluminum box was battered, probably by some kind of hammer or iron bar.

The next day they noticed a blue car with three antennas parked in the spot where the KUTV van had been. John looked through binoculars and saw four men inside the car looking back at him, also through binoculars. The car remained there most of the day. In the late afternoon John and Al picked up rifles and walked out to the gate; the blue car pulled away.

For the next three days, morning and night, John and Al patrolled the farm with rifles. There was no more sign of trouble.

Early in November, John made some incisive, controversial statements in the press and on TV. He told the *Tribune* that the Mormon Church, no less, was responsible for the "legal hassles" which had forced his family into a virtual state of siege for the past eleven months.

"I was excommunicated because I asked too many questions," John explained to the reporter. "I was too independent and I became too much of an individual. The bishop would accept members who were drunks, but not a questioner."

He was an embarrassment to the church, he claimed, because he was calling national attention to his fundamentalist beliefs and practices. He threatened the church's authority by publicizing its hypocrisy and its apostasy. Mormon leaders could not tolerate a man like John mocking the church on television and in the national press every week. "So the Mormon Church is using these law-enforcement officers as pawns to do their dirty work for them," John charged, although he had no evidence to support his claim.

Speaking of his right to educate his children as he saw fit, John had said: "According to the state's system, my home is just a feeding place. All they want is for me to feed my children and then they want to take them from me and brainwash them to put them into a Sodom and Gomorrah society."

A KUTV newscast showed John telling a reporter, "As I read about Abraham, our forefather, I do not believe that that man would have trusted his children into the hands of outsiders to be educated. It's an impossibility. And I believe if they tried to bring this type of issue against him I think he would have gone through this bunch with his sword, and would have showed them differently."

A letter from John's brother Harald, published in the *Park Record* in November, compared Utah's law officers to the Nazis who were convicted of war crimes at Nuremberg: "They say, 'The law is the law, and the law must be obeyed.' This type of reasoning sends shivers down my back. Because, only a few short years ago I heard that same argument used as justification for the slaughter of six million Jews."

Through an influential Democrat friend, Harald got an appointment to see Governor Matheson at the state capitol. Harald and his attorney met for thirty minutes with the governor and Larry Lunnen, during which Harald warned that any further attempts to arrest John would lead to bloodshed. He also asked the governor to pardon his brother.

Matheson explained that in Utah the power to grant pardons rests entirely with the Board of Pardons, and was therefore beyond his authority. "If you have any suggestions as to a compromise solution that could avert bloodshed, we'd be happy to consider it and take it to the courts," he offered.

Harald replied, "I am not here as a representative of my brother to offer a compromise solution. What I'm asking is for the state to drop the whole thing. The fact is, I feel the next time an arrest attempt is made, somebody will get shot. John has raised his three standards of peace to these people to try to stop them from going against him, and now he feels justified in using force to defend himself. The state would be wise to just forget about this guy, and six months from now nobody will remember him."

"I can't do that," Matheson said. "I am the chief executive of the State of Utah and I am entrusted with enforcing the laws of the state. It is alleged that your brother has broken the law, and he has to be arrested. I am deeply concerned about the safety and welfare of everyone involved in the situation. But the Department of Public Safety is committed to assisting the sheriff of Summit County in this matter."

The governor asked Harald whether there was a possibility of John and Vickie endangering their children's lives as had happened in the case of Immanual and Rachal David a few months earlier.

With emotion, Harald said, "No, my brother is a great respecter of life. He believes that life is a gift from God, and under no circumstances would he ever desire to take anyone's life. He will never become the aggressor, but he will defend himself and his family."

Harald recalled that he also told the governor that his brother would "never fire the first shot" in a confrontation with lawmen. However, both the governor and Larry Lunnen later testified that they did not remember Harald ever saying that specifically.

Harald also claimed that at the close of the meeting, the governor stated that no further arrest attempts would be made without his express permission and approval. The governor later testified that he might have told Harald that he would be kept informed of the state's involvement in the case, but had never said that arrest plans would have to be cleared through his office.

Around the first of December, 1978, a petition seeking clemency for John and Vickie Singer was delivered to Juvenile Court Judge

John Farr Larson by Rhea Kunz of Draper, Utah. Mrs. Kunz was the half-sister of Rulon Allred and was formerly a plural wife herself.

An almost legendary figure in Utah's history, at the age of seventy-four Mrs. Kunz had written the first three volumes of a four-volume autobiography that deals extensively with the practice of plural marriage in the 1900s. Mrs. Kunz presided over an urban commune that included six young men and their plural wives, and ran a state-chartered, nonprofit nursery school for the commune's children. When she personally delivered her petition bearing three hundred signatures to Judge Larson, she warned him that if he did not exercise clemency he would have a "bloodbath" on his hands.

On December 6, Dean Black filed a sixty-thousand-dollar civil lawsuit in Third District Court against John Singer for alienation of his wife's affection. In the complaint, Dean claimed that John had willfully, wickedly, and maliciously prejudiced Shirley's mind against her husband "by employing subtle contrivances, coaxings, protestations of great love toward her and enticements for her to leave and desert" her husband. John's "wrongful conduct" was intended to injure Dean, he claimed.

"Hogwash," John said of Dean's lawsuit. "All he wants is to get more charges against me so I will look more and more like a criminal before the public." John was already being sought for contempt of court and three counts of aggravated assault.

The increasing opposition only strengthened the Singers' conviction that their mission to establish Zion would lead to a worldwide revolution, from which the Kingdom of God would emerge to forerun the second coming of Christ. For why else would Satan be oppressing them so intensely?

John and his coterie were preparing for an invasion by the mobs. They put chicken wire over the windows of the houses where the children lived. They stockpiled ammunition and target-practiced with their weapons. Once in a while they practiced in the dark in case the mobs decided to strike at night.

John taught the oldest children how to use a gun, but told them never to shoot except in self-defense, and then only if a person shot at them first.

Everyone on the farm was affected by the tension and the anticipation. John showed signs of fatigue. He was sick on and off all through December, coughing up bloody phlegm constantly. Still he tried to be loving and humorous toward his family. Even during the roughest moments he would tell Vickie and Shirley how blessed he felt to have them for his wives.

Vickie tired easily as well. Teaching school drained most of her energy, leaving her with barely enough to cook meals and do laundry. She wished she had more time to relax and enjoy her children; instead it seemed that all her hours were spent on mere subsistence.

Shirley was deeply in love with John. It hurt her to see him under such stress, and she gladly would have borne some of his suffering if she could. John told her; "One of these days we will have peace."

But she said to him, "Life with you will never be normal. It will always be one excitement on top of another. And there will be more wives in the future. I'm going to enjoy every minute that I have with you now."

Shirley wanted very badly to have John's baby. But each month she faced disappointment. Sometimes when she looked at him she had a feeling that he would be taken away, and would wonder how many more nights they would have together.

In the last few weeks of 1978 John spent most of his nights with Vickie because from the log house he could look out the windows and see in all directions—the fields, the mountains, the lane. When he was nervous he paced from room to room looking out windows, as if he expected an invasion any minute.

Al Rider was disillusioned. He felt that the atmosphere of love and peace that had pervaded the farm when he first moved there had turned to one of fear. John was no longer friendly, he felt, but cold. In early December, John asked Rider and Reynolds to start paying rent, as the Singers were having trouble making ends meet. They agreed to pay, but didn't.

Then Rider started telling Shirley that John was mistreating her by spending most of his nights with Vickie, that John and Vickie were making all the important decisions and leaving Shirley out. Rider also told Shirley that he and Reynolds desired to organize John's farm into a cooperative based on the United Order of Enoch in the Mormon scriptures. They had not discussed this idea with John, but were trying to rally Shirley's support for such a venture.

In fact, Bob Reynolds had convinced Al that he, Bob, understood the Mormon scriptures better than John did, and that God was now giving revelations to him instead of to John.

Shirley reported all of this to John who, understandably, became very wary of his guests. The final divisive blow came when John learned that Rider and Reynolds had, without his knowledge, proposed to his daughters Heidi and Suzanne, who were fifteen and fourteen years old.

The girls were at an age when attention from older men is flattering. Heidi told her parents that she liked Bob, but had an "icky feeling" about marrying him because Bob told her he wanted someday to have ten wives all living in one big house. Also, she thought Bob was wrong to propose to her without John's consent.

Suzanne had a teenage crush on Al, who told her that he loved her. She had dreams of marrying him. Al told her that he would like to marry her right away if her father approved; otherwise he would wait a few years for her.

In the middle of December John called Al, Bob, and LuAnne into the living room of the log house for a meeting. It was a cold, snowy day; the thermometer read twenty-one degrees below zero.

John censured Al and Bob for proposing to his daughters without his knowledge, and said he would not permit his daughters to marry until they were eighteen, at which time they could decide for themselves whom they would marry. "We have put our lives on the line to deliver our children out of a corrupt, fast-moving world in order to preserve their innocence," John said. "And now that we've kept them away from the world, the courting, the dating, the social mixing that go on, we find that the conditions that we have removed ourselves from have moved themselves right into our midst."

John also dashed any hopes of establishing a United Order of Enoch on his land. If Al and Bob expected him to share his property with them, and allow them to manage it for their own benefit, they were no better than freeloaders, he told them. Besides, in order to live the United Order there must be a revelation from God, and John had received no such revelation.

Bob said he had received many revelations on it, and claimed that John had misinterpreted the scriptures. It was also revealed by the Lord that he was to marry Heidi and Al was to marry Suzanne. "If you refuse to permit these things, you are sinning against my revelations, and if you don't repent you will be destroyed," Bob told John angrily.

John accused Al and Bob of following the god of darkness, and gave them until January 6 to leave the farm.

Al, Bob, and LuAnne fasted and prayed for four days. On the night of the fourth day the three of them agreed that John, by disregarding God's revelations to Bob, had forfeited the divine protection that had once been granted the farm. It was no longer safe there, so they decided to move out as soon as possible.

They rented a U-Haul and moved out on the day before Christmas. The Singers did not hear from them again. Heidi and Suzanne were both relieved when they left.

A few days after Christmas, Al Rider went to Bonnie Norder's house in Salt Lake City and asked her to marry him. Bonnie declined.

On December 30, Dean Black filed an affidavit in juvenile court charging that Sheriff Robinson, who had been Dean's best man twice, had failed in his duty to take his children from the Singer farm and deliver them to him, and that if the sheriff could not give reasons for his failure to carry out the order of the court, he should be punished.

In the Salt Lake City Office of Narcotics and Liquor Law Enforcement, one of the division's agents handed Robert Wadman a report that said: "Mr. Black spends considerable time in the area of the Singer compound and stated to [Jared] Weller a couple of days ago that he is patrolling the road and if he gets the opportunity he will kill Mr. Singer."

Chapter 12

DAMNED IF WE DO,
DAMNED IF WE DON'T

Robert Wadman was born in San Diego in 1941. Both his father and grandfather were policemen. After earning an associate degree in law enforcement at the age of twenty-one, he joined the San Diego Police Department. After seven years on the SDPD, during which he achieved the rank of sergeant, he returned to college for his bachelor's degree in law enforcement. From 1971 to 1974 he worked for the Federal Bureau of Narcotics and Dangerous Drugs, supervising its office on the Arizona-Mexico border. During a heroin bust he was shot through the left arm and in the ribs by a .357 Magnum, and as a result lost partial use of his arm. In 1974 Wadman returned to school and earned a master's degree in public administration. His goal was to be the police chief of a big city.

In 1976 he was hired as chief of police of Orem, Utah, where he was known as a morale builder. By this time he was married with four children. 1976 was the year when a parolee from Oregon named Gary Gilmore murdered Sinclair gas-station attendant Max Jensen and City Center Motel clerk Ben Bushnell in Orem. Wadman was present when Gilmore was arrested, and his department conducted the investigation of the case. After Gilmore's execution by a firing squad in January 1977, Wadman was interviewed extensively by

Norman Mailer, who wrote about Gilmore's story in *The Execution-er's Song.*

In September 1978, Larry Lunnen asked Wadman to help him reorganize the Department of Public Safety. He appointed Wadman as director of the Division of Narcotics and Liquor Law Enforcement, with a promise that within the next few years Wadman would be considered for promotion to assistant commissioner of public safety. He had been head of Narcotics and Liquor for only a month when he was called upon to help Sheriff Robinson apprehend John Singer. After studying the *State* v. *Singer* file, he sympathized with Ron Robinson, who, as sheriff of a rural county, was not equipped to handle the delicate situation.

Wadman was a Mormon, but one who was not active in the church. He knew that John Singer had tried to justify his actions on the basis of Mormon scriptures, and he understood that Singer's actions had been construed by some as civil disobedience. But as a police officer sworn to uphold the law, he felt it would be dangerous if he were given the power to enforce the law selectively; therefore, even if he privately thought John's cause worthy, he nevertheless considered it his duty to assist in serving the arrest warrants.

After the unsuccessful *L.A. Times* caper, Wadman met with Ron Robinson, Larry Lunnen, and Highway Patrol Superintendent Rob-ert Reid to chart a new course. Because John Singer was known to have drawn a gun on police officers once, they concluded that the only effective way to arrest him would be a show of force so overwhelming that John would have no choice but to surrender. However, Wadman pointed out that an excessive show of force was likely to be viewed negatively by the press. "They have portrayed John Singer as a courageous but eccentric individualist who has taken on a massive bureaucracy," he noted. And because the *L.A. Times* caper had so enraged the press, he expected that press coverage would be especially critical of the state's further operations in the case. He also worried about the possibility of a mass suicide, à la Immanual David, if the Singer farm was stormed by troops of police. Wadman summed up his frustration in a way that Ron Robinson could appreciate: "We'll be damned if we do and damned if we don't."

The lawmen decided to consult other law enforcement experts and seek suggestions and comments on alternative arrest strategies.

Superintendent Reid sent a highway patrol helicopter to Marion to take aerial photographs of the Singer compound and surrounding area. Wadman and Robinson made several trips to Marion and Kamas to interview residents who knew about the Singers' habits and life-style. Larry Lunnen interviewed reporters who had been in the Singer home.

They gathered the information in a file labeled "Singer Investigation" and had meetings with the Salt Lake City police chief and commissioner, the Salt Lake County sheriff, and the special agent in charge of the Salt Lake FBI office. Wadman also phoned the Los Angeles Police Department and talked with its Special Weapons Attack Team (S.W.A.T.) leader.

The four then met again to evaluate the list of alternative plans they had drawn up as a result of their discussions with the outside experts. They rejected further undercover operations similar to the *L.A. Times* masquerade—lawmen posing as hunters, as attorneys from the American Civil Liberties Union, or as religious zealots. Singer was likely to be extra wary of strangers.

They considered cutting off the Singers' supply of food and water and shutting off their electricity in the hope that John would be forced to surrender. Such a plan would entail arresting Rider and Reynolds, who were then still living on the compound, for obstruction of justice if they should venture out to get supplies. Summit County Attorney Robert Adkins had agreed to issue warrants for their arrest if this plan was adopted. But it wasn't, because of everyone's concern for the welfare of the Singer and Black children.

Another alternative they thought of was to put a tranquilizing drug called Tazer into the Singers' water supply. Again, this plan was rejected because of concern for the children's safety.

Then they considered driving an armored personnel carrier into the compound so that they could get close enough to the log house to remove the chicken wire from the windows and drop tear gas into the house. They approached Governor Matheson for his permission to use the National Guard's armored vehicle. But the governor vetoed the plan out of his main concern about the potential danger to the children.

They also considered using a S.W.A.T. team to enter the compound and arrest Singer, and appealed to the Ogden and Provo police departments—which had the only S.W.A.T. teams in Utah—for their help. But the Provo and Ogden city attorneys advised their police chiefs against doing so because the cities would incur too much liability in the event of an accident or death.

The lawmen also attempted to enlist the help of a KSL television reporter named John Hollenhorst, who had been trying to persuade Sheriff Robinson to tip him off before another arrest attempt was made. Hollenhurst had urged that it would be in the public's best interest to have an independent witness on the scene. Larry Lunnen hinted to Hollenhurst that he would give his station an exclusive on the arrest if Hollenhorst would somehow use his access to the Singer home to help law officers get in as well. Hollenhorst refused to consider the deal.

Around the middle of December, Wadman, Robinson, Lunnen, and Reid decided on a plan which they determined would be the safest and surest way to arrest Singer, but which would involve a great deal of time and resources in preparation.

Jared Weller owned a farm-machinery repair business on Upper Loop Road about three hundred yards north of Dick Watson's home. In the winter, Weller Repair also rented snowmobiles to tourists. The shop and yard were separated from the property of Singer's neighbors, Watson and Jepsen, by a row of aspen trees. Between the trees and the shop was Gus Weller's old house, now unoccupied but owned by Gus's daughter Eve Hirst, who lived in Salt Lake City. Jared Weller's house and spacious garden were set back about seventy-five yards east of the repair shop.

Around December 15, 1978, Summit County Deputy Sheriff Bob Bates drove up to Weller Repair and asked Jared if he would rent two snowmobiles to the county for a few weeks "for surveillance purposes." Jared agreed and set the rental for two Everest 440 snowmobiles at thirty-five dollars a day each, starting December 27.

On December 22, Ron Robinson went to Eve Hirst's insurance office in Salt Lake City and signed a lease to rent Gus Weller's old house for one month at $325. The lease specified that the premises would be occupied by no more than three adults and no children.

On the morning of December 27, three days after Rider and Reynolds had left the Singer farm, Deputy Bates and two officers from Narcotics and Liquor drove up to the rented house in a

Volkswagen station wagon with Arizona license plates. Three pairs of skis were attached to a rack on top of the car. The officers, dressed in ski clothes, moved into the old house and set up a surveillance station in front of a window facing south, from which they could see, through the naked trees, most of the buildings and surrounding areas of the Singer farm and the lane leading down past the Jepsen and Watson properties to the mailboxes on Upper Loop Road.

Over the next eighteen days, six officers in two shifts held a twenty-four-hour surveillance on the Singer farm. During each twelve-hour shift, one deputy sheriff and two state agents took turns looking out the window through binoculars and touring the area on snowmobiles. They recorded every move that John Singer made, day and night, noting in each entry whether or not he appeared to be armed. They wrote down license-plate numbers of everyone who visited the farm. Each day the surveillance log was turned over to Robert Wadman, and three times a week the deputy sheriffs reported to Ron Robinson. Each of the six officers stationed at the house worked twelve hours a day for eighteen days, including New Year's, with no days off. It was boring, tedious work.

Jared Weller talked to the officers only in connection with the service and maintenance on the snowmobiles. Esther Watson walked over to the surveillance house one Sunday and asked the three officers if they cared to go with her to church. They declined her invitation, saying they didn't have the proper clothing.

On January 3, 1979, Sheriff Robinson was served with an order to appear in Third District Court on the fifteenth to show cause why he should not be held in contempt for failing to take custody of Dean Black's children.

In his seventeen years as sheriff, Ron Robinson had never been faced with the possibility of being held in contempt of court. The Singer case was the most perplexing challenge of his career. "You can't believe the nights I've lain awake trying to figure out how I could talk John Singer into honoring the court orders, or how I could get him away from his house without endangering his children," Ron told reporters. "I've had people from all over the nation tell me that I have no guts—that I just ought to go in there and get that so-and-so."

There were days when he thought to himself, "I wish this thing had never happened . . . I wish it would just go away . . . I don't know how to handle it."

If the stereotypical rural county sheriff is a bigot with mirrored sunglasses and a big pot belly, dedicated to preserving the status quo, then Ron Robinson was the antithesis. He was trim and fit at fifty-two years old, and kept in shape by working on his Chalk Creek ranch in his spare time. He felt that tolerance and understanding were among the most important qualities of a good sheriff. He believed that crime would be reduced if the county offered counseling services for first-time offenders.

The son of a Mormon sheepman, Ron was born and raised in Coalville. He graduated from North Summit High School, then served in the navy in the South Pacific during World War II. After the war he returned to Coalville, joined the police department, married and raised five children, and became Coalville's chief of police. In 1962 he was elected sheriff of Summit County, and was reelected four times consecutively after that.

One Monday morning, January 15, 1979, Ron met with Robert Wadman and Grant Larsen to evaluate the information gathered from the eighteen-day surveillance and formulate an arrest plan.

That afternoon, Robinson appeared in Third District Court and told Judge Bryant Croft that within a week an attempt would be made to take the Black children into custody and deliver them safely to their father in Kamas. Judge Croft continued the order to show cause until further notice.

Larry Lunnen dropped into Governor Matheson's office and told him that an operational plan to arrest Singer had been decided on, and would be executed within days. Their conversation lasted less than a minute.

On Tuesday morning, January 16, the governor attended a breakfast meeting in Salt Lake City's Alta Club. He was seated next to Judge John Farr Larson. Matheson told the judge that there was a plan to arrest Singer "without any trouble," and it would be carried out very soon.

At 10:00 A.M. on Wednesday, January 17, twelve law enforcement officers assembled in the briefing room of the Narcotics and Liquor Law Enforcement office, two blocks south of the Salt Palace in downtown Salt Lake City. No minutes or notes were taken during the meeting; no recording was made. All that is known about the briefing is contained in statements made to the FBI a month later, and in depositions given two years later by the twelve officers who were present.

Robert Wadman and Ron Robinson were in charge of the briefing. Grant Larsen had picked the nine other officers who would accompany him to Marion to carry out the arrest plan. Among the nine were two Summit County deputy sheriffs, six officers from the Division of Narcotics and Liquor, and two officers from the Utah Highway Patrol. Both deputy sheriffs, three of the Narcotics and Liquor officers, and one highway patrolman had served on the surveillance team. The three additional officers had been chosen by Larsen for their physical fitness and their ability to stay cool under pressure.

Sheriff Robinson and the ten members of the arrest team were seated in the windowless room facing a large chalkboard. Robert Wadman handed out aerial photographs of the Singer compound and surrounding areas. He outlined the salient information gathered from the eighteen-day surveillance. According to the log, John Singer left his compound and walked alone to his mailbox on Upper Loop Road, a distance of approximately two hundred yards, two or three times a week. This presented the best opportunity to isolate Singer from his family so that he could be arrested without risk of harm to the women and children. The surveillance team had also discovered an old, abandoned A-frame cabin about one-third of a mile southeast of the Singer compound. Officers could be dispatched from the A-frame cabin as well as from the rented house to converge on Singer and arrest him as he reached his mailbox.

The key to the arrest plan was to surprise Singer with such a show of force that he would realize the futility of resisting arrest, and would submit peacefully.

Wadman laid out the details of the plan on the blackboard, making a rough sketch of the area surrounding the Singer compound. The arrest team would consist of five pairs of officers. Each pair would be assigned a snowmobile. Three pairs of officers designated as Unit One would be stationed at the rented house. Unit Two, comprising the remaining two pairs, would be stationed in the A-frame cabin southeast of the Singer compound. The two units would communicate with each other by the use of walkie-talkies.

Each pair of officers would consist of a driver and a passenger. Drivers would carry standard police thirty-eight revolvers, and passengers would be armed with twelve-gauge shotguns with regulation double-ought buckshot. Each officer would wear a flak vest under a standard-issue raid jacket with the word "POLICE" in seven-inch-high letters on the back.

Both units would watch the Singer compound with binoculars and wait for their opportunity. There would be no time limit on the plan. The arrest team would arrive at their positions at six the following morning and wait until dark if necessary, then go home for the night and return the next morning at six again to watch and wait.

When the opportunity presented itself, Grant Larsen, who was the team leader, would give the signal to execute the arrest plan. Two pairs of officers from Unit One would be deployed on snowmobiles from the surveillance house and proceed south along Upper Loop Road; as Singer headed back up the lane from his mailbox toward his compound, they would turn up the lane and pursue him, identifying themselves as police officers and placing him under arrest. The third pair of Unit One officers would drive due south from the surveillance house, emerging from between Watson's and Jepsen's houses.

Unit Two would deploy from the A-frame and head west until they reached the corner of the Singer farm, then turn to the north and cut off Singer's retreat. Thus surrounded by armed officers, it was reasonable to expect that Singer would surrender and submit to arrest.

Wadman referred to his map on the blackboard and pointed to a fence that stretched from Singer's gate to a point on Upper Loop Road south of the mailboxes. This fence lay perpendicular to Unit Two's path, and a hole would have to be cut in it large enough to let a snowmobile through. One of the officers would have to arrive at the scene before daylight the following day in order to cut the hole without being seen by the Singers.

Wadman gave each of the ten officers their assignments, pairing them up and grouping the pairs into units. Grant Larsen would be stationed at the A-frame house with fellow Narcotics and Liquor officer Tom Carlson, Deputy Sheriff Larry Henley, and Highway Patrolman Floyd Farley. Deputy Henley was assigned by Wadman to arrive early the next day to cut a hole in the fence.

Unit One would consist of Narcotics and Liquor officers Lewis Jolley, Ron Gunderson, Joe Schouten, and David Fullmer; Deputy Sheriff Bob Bates; and Highway Patrolman Robert Hayward. In charge of Unit One would be the senior officer, Lewis Jolley.

Jolley was the firearms instructor for the Division of Narcotics and Liquor Law Enforcement. He had been with the division four years, and before that had been an Ogden policeman for six years. In his ten years as a law enforcement officer and firearms expert he had never had an occasion to fire a weapon at a human being.

Wadman assigned Sheriff Robinson the task of securing five snowmobiles and having them ready for action the following morning. Robinson said he would rent three machines from Weller Repair and make available the Sheriff Department's two emergency snowmobiles.

The officers were to drive to Marion in groups, at least three to a vehicle, so that they would not arouse suspicion by having a large number of vehicles at the scene. Car pools would be arranged at the end of the briefing.

One of the officers asked if there would be any medical personnel on the scene. Wadman said there wouldn't be because an ambulance at the scene would alert Singer and the media that an arrest attempt was imminent. Wadman had informed the University of Utah Medical Center's "Lifeline" helicopter unit that they might be needed in Marion within the next few days. Otherwise, Sheriff Robinson was responsible for all ground emergency vehicles in the area.

Wadman stressed that it would be preferable to effect the arrest without the use of force; weapons should be used only in self-defense. He advised the officers to use extreme caution because Singer had drawn a gun on police officers once before during an arrest attempt; however, he felt that a show of force would dissuade Singer from pulling his gun this time.

Robinson deputized all of the state officers on the arrest team, and when the briefing concluded they arranged to share rides to Marion the following morning.

During the briefing there were no comments, suggestions, or discussions as to the merits of the arrest plan by the members of the team.

Later in the day, however, Ron Gunderson, who had been assigned to drive a snowmobile in Unit One, spoke to Wadman in the hallway of the Narcotics and Liquor office. Gunderson told his boss he thought the plan was dangerous. But Wadman was in a hurry and did not have time to discuss the matter. Not until two years later was Gunderson asked to explain why he thought the plan was dangerous. "The key to the plan was that a reasonable man, when surrounded and confronted by a show of force, would submit," he said. "The problem was, John Singer was not a reasonable man."

A heavy snowstorm hit the Kamas Valley early on Thursday, January 18, and by 5:00 A.M. there were several inches of new snow on the roads. The temperature was below thirty degrees Farenheit. Most of the arrest team arrived late because of the hazardous driving conditions. Deputy Henley, who was supposed to arrive before daylight to cut a hole in the fence, did not arrive until after 7:00 A.M. because Tom Carlson was an hour and a half late in picking him up. Grant Larsen instructed Henley to wait until the next morning to cut the fence, or, if they proceeded with the arrest attempt on that day, he would have to stop and cut it en route.

It was still snowing lightly when the arrest team moved into the rented house with a week's worth of groceries. After a short meeting, the four officers in Unit Two drove their snowmobiles past the mailboxes on Upper Loop Road up to the A-frame cabin, where they set up surveillance and established communication with Unit One. The officers at both stations were a bit nervous and expressed some fear for their own safety should the arrest plan be executed. A few of the officers who had never before been in Marion went out and rode on the snowmobiles to have a look around and get used to riding with their respective partners.

At 8:30 A.M. Unit Two spotted John Singer and Shirley Black taking a walk east of the compound, toward Hoyt's Canyon. John was carrying a rifle. Grant Larsen decided against taking any action at that time. John and Shirley returned to the compound about thirty minutes later.

At the Narcotics and Liquor office in Salt Lake City, Robert

Wadman was informed by the University of Utah Medical Center that severe weather conditions prohibited their use of the Lifeline helicopter that day.

Ron Robinson waited by the phone at the Summit County sheriff's office. The arrest team was instructed to notify him as soon as any action was taken. Not having heard from them by noon, the sheriff went to lunch and left word that he could be reached at Dean's Cafe in Coalville.

At 12:15 P.M. both units observed John Singer come out of his house alone carrying a gas-powered snowblower in both hands, with a rifle tucked under his right arm. He set the rifle down at his gate, pulled a cord to start the snowblower, and proceeded to clear an area inside the gate where a car could park. At about 12:20 John opened his gate and left the compound, clearing a path in the lane with the snowblower. His rifle was still leaning against the gatepost.

As John worked his way down the lane toward Upper Loop Road, Unit Two observed the mailman arrive in a blue Jeep and appear to place a large envelope in Singer's mailbox.

At 12:30, John had cleared a path down to Jepsen's driveway. He laid the snowblower down, the motor still running, and walked west toward his mailbox.

Chapter 13

A SHOW OF FORCE

Saturday, January 6, 1979, was John Singer's forty-eighth birthday. Bonnie Norder had brought John's mother up to the farm for the weekend. Grandma, recently retired at the age of seventy-eight, signed over her latest Social Security check to John, saying she still had a little left from the previous month. John accepted it gratefully.

Grandma had worried herself sick over John's legal predicament. She noticed that John had lost weight and appeared tense. She seemed to suffer from the pressure he was under even more than he did. She said to him privately, "John, I can't stand that you are so worried. I am so sick and tired of living."

"Mother, sometimes I am too," he replied, hugging her.

Shirley brought her kids over for a big family dinner. Most of the food, including birthday cake, was compliments of Bonnie.

John explained the presence of the men in ski clothes riding around on snowmobiles. "They are cops, or else they are hired by the cops to watch us, so they can figure out a way to arrest me. They want us to think they are tourists." The Singers had been watching the surveillance team through binoculars all week.

John pointed out the irony of it. "You know something, that old house where these men are stationed is where I began to learn the gospel. Unk got me on my feet and started training me, and Vickie and I spent many, many times at Unk's house studying scriptures together. Just think of it, those guys are after me, living in that house."

John was in good humor that evening, though, as they all sang songs and danced to the music on the radio. Late in the evening John escorted Grandma and Bonnie to Grandma's house where they spent the night. John brought in wood and lit a fire in the fireplace before he returned home. Bonnie got very little sleep; she thought she heard someone outside the bedroom window, and the roar of snowmobile engines continued throughout the night.

They hadn't seen any snowmobiles for a few days, but on the eighteenth of January there seemed to be at least three of them, and now the police were in uniform.

After John and Shirley went for a walk early in the morning, each family had breakfast and then school. They didn't use the school-house during the coldest months, but held classes in the living room to conserve fuel.

School was over about noon. Shirley and her daughter Nancy began preparing lunch at their house. Vickie was putting away her school materials, Suzanne was cleaning up in the kitchen, and Charlotte was looking out the living room window toward the surveillance house with binoculars. Heidi walked over to Shirley's house to return a book she had borrowed. Most of the other children were chopping wood behind a shed south of Shirley's house. They had not seen or heard any snowmobiles since early in the morning.

John went outside with his rifle and a gas-driven snowblower to clear the lane, because Shirley's oldest daughter Brenda George, who lived in Kamas, had promised to deliver some groceries in the afternoon. John left the rifle by the gate and cleared a parking place in the driveway. Then he started clearing the lane outside his gate. He was wearing a sheepskin-lined blue coat, a blue watch cap, and leather gloves. The snow had stopped falling, but the sky was still a metallic gray.

John saw the mailman come to the mailboxes on Upper Loop Road. Since he could see no snowmobiles in the area, and since he was almost halfway down the lane already, he decided to go down to the mailbox to pick up the mail. He put the snowblower down and trudged west through the fresh snow toward Upper Loop Road.

In the log house, ten-year-old Charlotte Singer was watching her father with binoculars out the living room window.

As soon as the mailman made his delivery, Grant Larsen, knowing John was already outside his compound, told his unit at the A-frame to stand by. "This might be our chance," he said. Officers Henley and Carlson went outside and prepared to start their snowmobiles. Larsen radioed to Lew Jolley at the surveillance house: "You guys be ready. If Singer goes down to get his mail, it's a go."

About the time John walked past Watson's property at the foot of the lane, Esther Watson came out of her house, got into her car in the driveway, and started the engine. She was on her way to a church meeting. She let the engine warm up for a few minutes.

John reached Upper Loop Road and walked five yards south to his mailbox. In it he found two letters to Shirley and a large envelope addressed to Vickie and him.

The officers in the surveillance house could not see the mailboxes because the Watsons' house was in their line of sight. They had to wait for Grant Larsen to give the signal from the A-frame.

As soon as Singer got to the mailbox, Larsen gave the signal: "Let's go," he said to his men and into his walkie-talkie simultaneously. He waited for Jolley's acknowledgment, and then he and Floyd Farley ran out of the A-frame, carrying their shotguns, and jumped onto the back seats of the snowmobiles as Carlson and Henley started the engines.

At the surveillance house, Lew Jolley yelled, "It's a go!" and he and his officers ran to their snowmobiles. The vehicle carrying Gunderson and Fullmer led the way, followed by Schouten and Jolley, out the driveway and south on Upper Loop Road toward the private lane. Bates and Hayward headed for the area between Watson's and Jepsen's houses.

John had already turned up the lane and was walking east toward his farm when the two snowmobiles started south on Upper Loop Road from the surveillance house. John glanced over his left shoulder at them, but seemed unconcerned. He took two more steps and stopped, turned around and looked again, his eyes wide. He saw the shotguns in the hands of Fullmer and Jolley. He realized that as they got close to the lane they slowed down, preparing to turn; John turned again and started running homeward.

As soon as the two snowmobiles turned up the lane, Jolley yelled, "We're police officers, you're under arrest!" Now Schouten and Jolley sped ahead of Gunderson and Fullmer, gaining on John as he was about halfway between Upper Loop and Watson's driveway. As they got closer, John looked back over his right shoulder; seeing that they could overtake him in a few seconds, he pulled a pistol from his waistband with his right hand and waved it back and forth in approximately a forty-five-degree arc, in the general direction of his pursuers. He kept running toward home, but now he was almost sidestepping, his left shoulder pointing east and his feet pointing southeast. He looked alternately back at the officers and forward in the direction he was running.

Gunderson and Schouten slowed their vehicles, just keeping pace with Singer. Immediately Jolley yelled twice, "Halt—police—drop your gun!" Gunderson also yelled, "Police officers—drop your gun!"

When Charlotte saw her father start to run from the snowmobiles, she turned around and called to Vickie, "They're getting Dad! Get the gun!" Vickie rushed to the window. Charlotte handed her the binoculars. Vickie saw John running toward her, nearing Watson's driveway, waving his gun behind him at the officers as if to say, "Get away, leave me alone." Vickie put the binoculars down and ran for Timothy's twenty-two rifle.

Officers Bates and Hayward deployed from the surveillance house, drove south through the aspen trees, and reached the fence separating Watson's and Jepsen's backyards. When they came out of the woods, their snowmobile had to traverse a short hill. Bates accelerated as he reached the hill and Hayward, who was holding his shotgun in both hands, fell backwards off the snowmobile. Bates heard Hayward say "Whoa" and looked around to see if his partner was all right. Seeing Hayward get up and start running after him, and hearing Jolley and Gunderson yell "Drop your gun," Bates decided to continue driving between Watson's and Jepsen's houses toward the lane. As soon as he could see Singer, he stopped the machine, drew his pistol, and pointed it at John's back.

At this point, the Unit Two officers, deployed from the A-frame, reached the fence south of the lane and stopped so that Henley could cut a passage through it with wire cutters. Carlson, Larsen, and Farley watched intently across the field as Singer came to Watson's driveway. It appeared to them that John was pointing his gun directly at Schouten and Jolley, whose snowmobile was now closest to him, about twenty-five feet away. They saw the driver Schouten lean over to his right, ducking his head as if expecting Singer to shoot; Jolley raised his shotgun and took aim.

As Vickie ran to get Timothy's rifle, Charlotte picked up the binoculars again and looked out the window. She saw her father take two steps toward her, lurch forward, and fall; as he fell, his mouth opened and blood flowed out of it. Her mind recoiled in horror.

Vickie heard the distant shotgun blast as she picked up the rifle. She froze for a second, but didn't allow herself to think about what the shot could have meant. She ran into her bedroom to put on her boots.

Timothy and Grant were behind the shed south of Shirley's house chopping wood when they heard the shot. They ran out to see what was happening. They peered down the lane for three seconds, then ran into Shirley's house. Timothy said, "Hurry, I think they've got Daddy!" Grant got his mother's gun out of a cabinet and handed it to Shirley.

Heidi was walking from Shirley's house back to hers when she saw her father running from the snowmobiles. She ran to the log house; she heard the shot as she opened the kitchen door, where her view of the shooting scene was obstructed by the house. She went inside and saw Vickie running into the bedroom with a rifle; Suzanne ran to help Vickie get her boots on. Charlotte was at the window dumbstruck. Heidi went to her bedroom and picked up her bow and quiver of arrows.

Officer Henley was cutting the fence when he heard the shot ring out. He looked up and saw John Singer thrust forward and fall on his face. John braced his arms against the snow and started to get up again, but couldn't make it; he fell once more and did not move again. Instead of cutting the fence, Henley got back on his snowmobile and drove west, parallel to the fence toward Upper Loop Road, followed by Carlson and Larsen. Henley parked his machine at the mailboxes, and he and Farley trotted up the lane to the shooting scene. Grant Larsen directed Carlson to drop him off at the lane and then proceed back to the surveillance house, get his truck, and drive it over to where Singer lay motionless.

Gunderson was driving a few feet behind and to the left of Schouten and Jolley when he heard Jolley's shotgun discharge and saw Singer fall. Gunderson stopped his vehicle, pulled his pistol from its holster, and ran over to where Singer was lying face down in the snow. John's right hand still clutched a gun. Gunderson yelled, "Police, drop your gun," once as he ran, and again as he knelt beside the body and held his pistol at the back of Singer's head. A second later Bates arrived, having run from between the houses, holstered his weapon, and grabbed the gun from Singer's hand.

As soon as Singer had been disarmed, Gunderson holstered his gun and turned John over. His eyes were open and he was still breathing. Blood was running from his nose and mouth. Gunderson tried to console John, saying, "You're going to be okay, we got help on its way. You'll be okay." John didn't respond but looked straight ahead, his eyes not focusing.

Grant Larsen ran up and knelt beside the body. He pulled a second pistol from Singer's waistband—a loaded, twenty-two caliber automatic—and a ten-inch bowie knife from a leather sheath on his belt. Larsen bent John's head back and cleared his air passage.

Bob Bates walked back to where Hayward, who had fallen off the back of his snowmobile, was standing near Jepsen's property. Bates looked at the gun John had waved at the officers. It was a thirty-eight Colt automatic with a live round in the chamber and seven rounds visible in the clip; the safety was off. He clicked the safety into the safe position and pocketed the gun.

Schouten and Jolley slowly drove their snowmobile up to where Singer was lying. Jolley was badly shaken, with a look of alarm on his face.

Esther Watson got out of her car. Grant Larsen yelled for her to go back into her house. Larsen ran into the house after her and asked if he could use her phone. "It's in the kitchen," Esther replied, pointing the way. Esther looked out her living room window and saw the five officers clustered around her cousin's body. She later testified that she had been sitting in her car waiting for it to warm up, reading a passage in Doctrine and Covenants which was to be the subject of a church meeting she was going to attend, when she heard the snowmobiles approach and the officers yell, "We're police officers, you're under arrest." She turned to her left to look behind her and saw the four officers chasing John up the lane in front of her house. She saw John pull his gun and wave it at the officers. According to her statement given to the FBI a week later, Esther turned away from the scene and looked down at the scriptures for three seconds, and in that short time Lew Jolley fired his shotgun at her cousin. When she heard the shot she looked around again and saw Gunderson and Bates converge on John's body at the foot of her driveway.

Inside the house, Grant Larsen called the Summit County Sheriff's office. He was told that the sheriff was out to lunch. He asked the dispatcher to contact the university's Lifeline helicopter. "This is an emergency," he said. "We'll be en route to the county hospital in a blue Dodge pickup with a white camper shell."

On his way out of the house, Esther asked him, "Is Singer dead?" Larsen replied, "I don't know."

Tom Carlson drove his truck up to where Singer was lying. He stayed in the driver's seat as Larsen and Schouten lifted John and placed him on the seat of the cab, his head resting on Carlson's right thigh. Schouten jumped into the back of the truck as Larsen gave orders to his men: "We'll take Singer to the hospital. Take the snowmobiles to the surveillance house, secure the equipment, and wait for orders from the sheriff." Carlson put the truck in gear as Larsen got in, turned around in the Watsons' driveway, and headed back down the lane to Upper Loop Road.

The seven remaining officers looked up the lane and saw Vickie, Shirley, Timothy, and Heidi, all armed, running toward them. Timothy had picked up John's carbine rifle at the gatepost as they left their property.

The officers ran for cover. Deputy Bates yelled from the side of Jepsen's house, "Vickie, stop, or someone will get hurt!" Another officer, crouched behind a snowmobile, yelled, "We're police officers. Go back to your home!"

Vickie and the others stopped running but continued to walk down the lane. They were confused. John was in trouble, and they were not going to turn around and go home until they found out where he was. Shirley had seen the officers load something into the cab of the truck, but wasn't sure if it was a body or not. None of the others had seen John since he started running up the lane. They all saw the blue pickup truck turn left onto Upper Loop Road and proceed slowly south, then around the bend to the west.

Floyd Farley was standing behind a telephone pole in Watson's front yard. When he saw Vickie and the others continue to walk down the lane toward him, he thought to himself, "There's no way I'm going to shoot it out against women and children." Farley yelled at the other officers, "Let's get out of here!" All seven of them scrambled for their snowmobiles and rode back to the surveillance house. As they ran, Heidi yelled after them, "You dirty cowards!"

Vickie, Shirley, Heidi, and Timothy reached the foot of Watson's driveway and found John's hat and the mail, lying beside a round, dark pool of blood that was slowly soaking into the snow. They stood for several minutes looking down, trying to figure out what had happened. They were confused and angry.

Some of the younger children came running down the lane after them, but Vickie told them to go back home, and they did. Vickie and Shirley started to cry, holding each other. Their worst fears were that John had been seriously injured. If John was in the pickup truck they had seen driving away, why was it going so slowly; and why did it turn south, when the hospital was to the north?

Vickie looked toward their neighbors' houses—John's cousins— and felt that they must have played a part in the shedding of innocent blood. She picked up the hat and mail and they walked home, retrieving the snowblower on their way.

Back inside the house, Vickie called Harald in Logan and tearfully told him what had happened. Within thirty minutes, Vickie got calls from KUTV, the *Tribune,* and the *Park Record*—to each she told the story again, still sobbing, in confusing bits and pieces. Shirley and the children gathered around the living room table to pray.

Ron Robinson was trying to decide what to have for dessert when he was called to the phone behind the cashier's counter at Dean's Cafe.

"Sheriff, we got a call from Grant Larsen in Marion. John Singer was shot. He's being brought to the county hospital," the dispatcher told him.

"Oh, Christ," Ron moaned. "Was he hurt bad?"

"I don't know."

"Was any of the officers hurt?"

"I don't think so. Larsen didn't say."

"Does the press know yet?" Ron asked.

"We haven't heard from them."

"Well, don't say anything to 'em until we know what happened. I'll be there in two minutes." He hurried back to his table, picked up his hat and coat, and tossed the cashier a five-dollar bill on his way out.

Driving back to the office, the sheriff was filled with apprehension. He prayed that Singer would not be too seriously hurt. He hated to think of the repercussions if John were killed. He thought of Vickie and her children—he had orders to go up and arrest her and take the kids to the Division of Family Services. The thought of separating those kids from their mother was more distressing now that their father had been shot.

When he got back to his office, he called Vickie. The line was busy for several minutes, but when he finally got through to her he told her that John had been wounded and was on his way to the hospital. And, as it was his duty to arrest her, he would send a couple of officers up there to pick her up. They would also have to take her children to the Division of Family Services and deliver Shirley's children to Dean Black. "We don't want any more bloodshed, Vickie," he implored.

Vickie said she would submit to arrest, much to the sheriff's relief. She asked if he knew how badly John was wounded. Ron said he didn't know yet, but would let her know as soon as he heard anything.

Just before 1:00 P.M., the Highway Patrol set up roadblocks at both ends of Upper Loop Road to keep out the press and the Singers' friends and relatives.

The truck carrying John Singer turned right from Upper Loop Road onto Highway 189 and headed north to Coalville. They had lost about a minute by taking the south leg of Upper Loop Road instead of the north leg. Tom Carlson drove as fast as conditions permitted. Grant Larsen, kneeling on the floorboard, called the sheriff's office on Carlson's CB radio and learned that the Lifeline helicopter was grounded. He told Carlson to drive faster. He reached up to unbutton John's coat and open his collar. John was bleeding from his chest; he didn't make a sound or move a muscle; his eyes were glazed.

It was a thirty-minute ride to the Summit County Hospital. Carlson parked at the emergency entrance, left the engine running, and ran in to get a nurse. Twenty seconds later a nurse emerged with a gurney. Larsen and Schouten, who were already carrying John toward the entrance, laid him face up on the gurney and wheeled him through the door and down the hall to an operating room while the nurse, running beside the gurney, cut open John's blood-soaked shirt and undershirt. Dr. John Kumagai was waiting in the operating room. In less than a minute, at 1:15 P.M., he pronounced John Singer dead.

Officers Larsen, Carlson, and Schouten went directly to the sheriff's office from the hospital. The office seemed to be in a state of chaos, having been deluged by calls from the press.

"Where's Singer?" Robinson asked Grant Larsen.

"He's dead."

A heavyhearted feeling came over the sheriff, and his stomach seemed to sink. He thought, "Why did it have to turn out this way?"

Larsen described the shooting incident, emphasizing that Jolley had feared for his own life when he pulled the trigger.

Robinson called Robert Wadman in Salt Lake City. Wadman said he and Larry Lunnen would be on their way to Coalville shortly. Ron also called Summit County Attorney Robert Adkins, who advised the sheriff to summon all ten of the arresting officers to the sheriff's office and record their statements as to what had happened that day.

Ron Robinson led a convoy of three squad cars to Marion. Grant Larsen accompanied the sheriff because he wanted to make sure his equipment—a camera, walkie-talkies, and binoculars—was recovered. Snow started falling lightly again, though the temperature had risen above thirty-two degrees. They drove up to the surveillance house around two o'clock.

The remaining officers had been waiting in the surveillance house for more than an hour, during which two of them forayed back to the A-frame cabin on a snowmobile to retrieve the state's walkie-talkie and binoculars. The others had loaded their food into cars and were ready to leave. No one had made any effort to secure the shooting scene or preserve whatever evidence might be found there.

While they were waiting for orders from the sheriff, Lew Jolley broke down and cried, not knowing that at that moment John Singer was dead. The other officers tried to console him with such assurances as, "You had no other choice, Lew. Singer might have shot you if you didn't get him first." Jolley told the others that he saw Singer close his left eye, as though he were taking aim, and that's when Jolley pulled the trigger.

Ron Gunderson told Jolley that he too was afraid that Singer was about to shoot. "After I pulled my gun on him, I was squeezing the bastard so hard I must have shot too," he said to Jolley. Most likely he said it merely to console Jolley, but it was a statement he later regretted having made.

Most of the other officers were a bit shaken. Deputies Henley and Bates had never before been involved in a case where a man had been shot. Their feeling was, "But for the grace of God, it could have been me that had to make the decision to shoot."

Gunderson pointed out that there were no medical personnel at the scene, and none of the officers had "so much as a Band-Aid" with them for first aid. "One of us could have got hit. I don't think they planned this too well," he complained.

When Sheriff Robinson arrived, he confirmed their worst fears: "Singer's dead," he said somberly. He waited for it to sink in. "I want you men to follow me back to my office so we can get your statements before you go. Wadman's on his way up there too."

The sheriff called Vickie again from the surveillance house before he left for Coalville. He did not tell her that John was dead. Knowing that they still had guns up there at the farm, he was worried about the possibility of a retaliation or mass suicide. He said John had been wounded in the leg, that he had been taken to the University of Utah Medical Center in Salt Lake, and he would be all right. He told Vickie that Deputy Leon Wilde and Highway Patrol Sergeant Ken Mecham would drive up to get her and the ten children. Since there were no charges against Shirley, she could stay and take care of the farm. Again Vickie promised to cooperate.

The members of the arrest team followed Ron Robinson back to Coalville. They left Marion without having conducted any sort of investigation of the shooting scene: no photographs were taken, no markers were placed at the spot were Singer had fallen or where Jolley had fired, no measurements were made as to how far Jolley had been from Singer when he fired; the shell casing ejected from Jolley's gun was never recovered.

Leon Wilde told Vickie that after they dropped the children at the DFS detention center they would take her to see John at the University Hospital. Deputy Wilde and Sergeant Mecham then loaded Vickie and the children into their patrol cars and headed down to Salt Lake City.

In Deputy Wilde's car, fourteen-year-old Heidi led Suzanne, Nancy, Grant, Julie, and Benjamin in singing a Mormon hymn called "Let Us All Press On." They sang the hymn several times to overcome their fear.

> Let us all press on in the work of the Lord,
> That when life is o'er we may gain a reward;
> In the fight for right let us wield a sword,
> The mighty sword of truth.

> Fear not, though the enemy deride,
> Courage, for the Lord is on our side;
> We will heed not what the wicked may say,
> But the Lord alone we will obey.

It was about three in the afternoon when the two squad cars arrived at the DFS detention center on the southern end of Salt Lake City. Vickie was allowed to accompany the children inside, but was given only a minute to hug each of them and say a tearful goodbye. Once she had gone, administrators separated the Singer children from the Black children, in two different rooms, although the kids fought and struggled to keep from being separated.

Vickie believed she was being taken to the hospital to see John. Sergeant Mecham turned his car into a modern, six-story building in the southeast corner of downtown Salt Lake, where a sign read, "Salt Lake County Sheriff's Office—Salt Lake City Police Department."

"Where are we going?" she asked.

Mecham didn't answer. He drove down a ramp into the underground garage and stopped next to the building by a sign that said, "Salt Lake County Jail." Vickie realized what was about to happen to her. She was handcuffed and led through two heavy steel doors into the booking area of the jail. Mecham removed the handcuffs; before he left, Vickie asked him to find out what John's condition was and let her know.

Vickie was frisked by a tough-looking woman and then booked on the contempt-of-court charge—thirty days, no bail. After her fingerprints and mug shot were taken, she was led through two more barred doors to the female wing of the jail. A matron told Vickie to take out her hairpins and unbraid her hair, which, when let down, hung past her waist. Vickie was placed in a clean ten-by-twelve-foot holding cell that had one small window on the door at eye level. In the cell were a mattress on the floor with a folded army blanket, a wooden bench, a toilet, and a small washbasin. The walls and ceiling were painted beige. The big steel door made a frightful clang when it shut, and Vickie was alone with her anxiety.

She had been in her cell about ten minutes when the matron opened the door and a young male social worker entered to talk to Vickie. He sat next to her on the bench and told her that he was available if she needed someone to talk to or a shoulder to cry on.

A minute later, Sergeant Mecham joined them in the cell. He said, "Vickie, I found out the condition on John, and I'm sorry I have to tell you, he's dead."

"No, you're lying," Vickie said angrily. "John's still alive, but he will be dead because you guys don't want him alive!"

Mecham said, "I'm sorry you feel that way, Vickie, but John is dead."

Vickie burst into tears, covering her face with her hands, and then held the social worker's arm while she cried on his shoulder. Between sobs she moaned, "John, oh my John."

After a minute, though, Vickie abruptly stopped crying and looked into the officer's eyes. "He isn't dead," she insisted. "I know he isn't dead."

Mecham simply told Vickie he was sorry and left the cell. The social worker stayed a few more minutes, asking Vickie how she felt—his job was to determine whether or not she might become suicidal. Satisfied that she was all right, he too left the cell. Again Vickie was alone with thoughts that raced through her mind: "Is John really dead? Oh my God, can it really be? Can this really be happening? My children, where are they? How can they bear this tragedy without their mother? Will I ever see them again?"

Approximately twenty-five minutes after John Singer's body came to the Summit County Hospital, it was transferred by silent ambulance to the state medical examiner's office across the street from the University of Utah Medical Clinic. Summit County Deputy Sheriff Fred Eley rode in the ambulance down to Salt Lake City. A throng of reporters had already gathered inside the building when the body arrived at 2:15 P.M.

John's body was still clothed when it was brought to the autopsy room. The blood that had flowed from his nose and mouth was dried on his face, and his bloody chest was exposed; he was a gory mess.

J. Wallace Graham, Utah's chief medical examiner, performed the autopsy. Also present were his two assistants and Deputy Eley. In John's coat pockets Dr. Graham found two clips to an automatic pistol, seven rounds of thirty-eight-caliber ammunition, and a box of long rifle shells. When he removed the clothing, he found two buckshot pellets embedded in the front of the coat. He cleaned the body and began his examination.

Dr. Graham discovered eight buckshot wounds in John's torso. Six of them were seven-millimeter, round-entrance wounds: one directly under the right arm, midway between the shoulders and the waist; three in the upper right back, from which two pellets were recovered; and two in the lower middle back. There were also two graze wounds on the left shoulder.

Four of the pellets had passed through the body and produced exit wounds in the chest, perforating the heart, lungs, and aorta on their way.

All eight wounds entered the body from right to left and in a slight upward direction, indicating that John had been bending slightly forward when he was shot from behind and to his right.

"It is my opinion," Graham concluded in his postmortem report, "that John Singer, a forty-eight-year-old male, died of multiple buckshot wounds."

Dr. Graham handed over the physical evidence—clothing, ammunition from John's pockets, and four pellets recovered from the coat and body—to Deputy Eley. Eley signed a receipt for those items, and returned to Coalville.

Bonnie Norder and John's mother arrived at the medical examiner's office while the autopsy was still in progress. When Bonnie heard on her car radio that John was dead, her first thought was to go to Grandma's apartment and make sure she was all right.

Grandma learned from a television news bulletin that John had been shot by lawmen. When Bonnie arrived and told her that her son was dead, she wailed, "Oh, I wish I was up there and they had killed me instead of John. Why wasn't I there? I don't want to live any more." She became weak and had to sit down.

Bonnie made several phone calls and learned that John's body had been taken to the state medical examiner's office for an autopsy. Grandma asked Bonnie to take her to see John.

About thirty reporters were gathered outside Dr. Graham's office, clamoring for information, when Bonnie and Grandma arrived. State officials refused to let Grandma see the body until it was transferred to a funeral home. Harald had earlier called to authorize the medical examiner to release the body to Larkin Mortuary in Salt Lake City.

A pressroom was set up on the second floor of the building, well away from Dr. Graham's office and the autopsy room. A secretary told reporters that Dr. Graham would hold a press conference after the autopsy was completed.

Bonnie and Grandma took the elevator up to the second floor and waited with the press. Reporters asked Bonnie if she knew where Vickie and her children had been taken. While Bonnie got on the phone to try to locate them, Grandma wandered around the press area in a daze. Some of the reporters, hungry for any sort of news, interviewed Grandma and recorded her words as she grieved in her thick German accent: "I can't believe he's dead. He was a good boy to me. I'm so sorry I wasn't there that I could be killed too."

Bonnie learned that Vickie was in jail and the children were in the state's custody. After passing this information along to the press, she decided to visit Vickie. She took Grandma home and arranged for one of Edeltraud's daughters to stay with her, and then drove downtown to the jail.

The press waited three hours at the medical examiner's office for the news conference to begin. Finally, the secretary returned to the pressroom and announced that there would be no news conference. Dr. Graham had given her a three-line statement to read to the press, saying only that John Singer's body arrived at 2:15 P.M., an autopsy was performed, and the cause of death was a shotgun wound. Dr. Graham and his staff had left the building and were not available for further comment.

The members of the press were surprised and angry at the apparent clamp on information by the state. One veteran KSL-TV reporter said that he could not remember ever having been so ignored on such an important case.

Bonnie got to the jail around 5:00 P.M. She was allowed to see Vickie in the visitor's room through a thick Plexiglas window, and talked with her by telephone. Vickie looked terrible. She seemed to be in shock and appeared to have been crying copiously.

Vickie was glad to see her friend. Both of them cried as they talked. They longed to hold each other, and Bonnie pleaded with a matron to let her visit Vickie in her cell, but that was out of the question.

Vickie still couldn't believe that John was dead. She was worried that he was alive and the state might be plotting to kill him. Not having seen the body, Bonnie couldn't assure Vickie that John was really dead, or if he was, what was the true cause of his death. Bonnie promised to go to the mortuary and see for herself, then let Vickie know.

After she left the jail, Bonnie called a friend of hers named Cully Christensen, who was an orthopedic surgeon in Bountiful, Utah. She asked him to meet her at Larkin Mortuary and examine John's body to verify the cause of death, and determine whether there was any foul play by the state. Cully said he would meet her there in thirty minutes. In the meantime, Bonnie went to see John's sister Edeltraud and her husband Reinhard Lawrence, who lived in a nearby neighborhood called Sugarhouse.

Coincidentally, Fred Collier was at Cully Christensen's house when Bonnie called around 6:00 P.M. They had heard over the radio that John had been killed by police officers during an arrest attempt, but nothing more was known at that time. Cully grabbed his thirty-five-millimeter camera and they headed for Salt Lake City.

Cully and Fred arrived at Larkin Mortuary before Bonnie. It was dark out and the temperature was starting to drop. The front door was open, but they found no one in the front office or in the dark hallway leading to the chapel. Seeing a light on at the bottom of a wide flight of stairs, they walked down to the basement, where they found a mortician working in the embalming room. The door was open, so they walked in. The mortician was embalming a body that was not John Singer's, and there was another body, covered by a white sheet, on a cart on the other side of the room.

The mortician, whose name was Brent Trimble, looked up and saw the intruders. Startled, he quickly told them that it was against the law for them to be in that room, and ushered them out the doorway. Cully said he was the physician to the Singer family and had been asked to come and look at John Singer's body.

Trimble said they would have to take the body to another room for viewing. Cully and Fred helped Trimble wheel the cart down the hall to a smaller room, where they turned on the lights and lifted off the sheet. John was laid on his back in a pool of blood, zipped inside a clear plastic bag. His chest and stomach had been cut open and loosely sewn back together, and the top of his head had been removed and sewn back into place. His eyes were closed and his mouth was open. Four round buckshot holes were conspicuous on his upper chest, but there were no other visible signs of trauma or injury.

Trimble provided Cully with a flashlight and tongue depressor; Cully unzipped the bag and examined John's mouth and eyes, and then felt over the entire body for evidence of contusions or fractures. He found none. He washed his hands and picked up his camera. With Trimble's assistance, Cully took six color photographs of the body, using a normal lens and strobe flash. He stood on a chair to get a shot of the head and shoulders from above the cart, and then got a picture of the front of the torso from the neck to abdomen. He also took a close-up of the four exit wounds on John's chest.

Trimble, wearing plastic gloves, turned the body as Cully took pictures of the right side, left side, and middle of the back.

When they had finished, they thanked the mortician and walked back up the stairs to the lobby. A security guard and a mortuary supervisor happened to be passing the top of the stairs when Cully and Fred ascended. Thinking they were reporters, the security guard stepped behind Fred and wrapped his arm around Fred's neck. Fred grabbed the supervisor around the waist and told Cully, who had the camera, to run. Fred took a step backward to the top of the staircase—another step back would bring all three crashing down the stairs. The security guard let go of Fred. Cully halted the fracas by telling the mortuary employees that he was a doctor, they were not reporters, and the photographs were for the Singer family, not the media. Cully pulled a business card from his wallet and gave it to the supervisor, who asked Cully and Fred to kindly leave the premises, which they did.

Bonnie, Edeltraud, Reinhard, and Harald had come to the mortuary together and were waiting in the front office for the supervisor to take them down to see John's body when they heard the confrontation at the top of the stairs. Bonnie walked out into the lobby just in time to see Cully and Fred leave the building.

Several minutes later, the four of them were taken downstairs to see the body. Harald and Edeltraud were terribly shaken when they saw their oldest brother lying in his blood with buckshot holes in his chest.

Bonnie called the jail and left a message for Vickie with the matron: She had seen John's body and he was, alas, dead.

Shirley was not alone for more than a few minutes after the officers took Vickie and the children away. Her oldest daughter Brenda drove up with a load of groceries, and she was followed by two *Park Record* reporters and a *Tribune* correspondent. A few hours later, another of Shirley's daughters, Linda Russell, drove down from Logan to be with her mother.

Denise Wheeler, the *Tribune* correspondent, made several phone calls to locate John and Vickie. When she found out that John was dead, she asked Brenda to break the news to Shirley.

"They've killed him, they've killed him," Shirley cried. "Why did the Lord allow this? What has He done?" Brenda and Linda tried to console her.

For the rest of the afternoon the Singers' phone rang incessantly. Reporters from all over the country wanted information; others called just to express sympathy.

When Shirley learned that Vickie was in jail, she decided to go visit her. Denise insisted on driving because Shirley was starting to look ill. The *Park Record* reporters helped Shirley milk and feed the goats and light fires in the fireplaces of the houses so that the water pipes would not freeze overnight. The sun had set and the clouds hung low over the Kamas Valley as Denise and Shirley set out. Dick Watson had erected another barricade at the foot of the lane to keep out the press, which he was successful in doing. He swung the wooden barrier away to let Denise out; Shirley passed by undetected, hiding under a blanket on the back seat of Denise's car.

When they got to the jail, having successfully evaded the press, Shirley was denied permission to see Vickie because jail officials feared that the sister wives would attempt to carry out some kind of suicide pact. Angry, heartbroken, and weary, Shirley and Denise checked into the Ambassador Hotel for the night.

Summit County Deputy Fred Eley returned to the sheriff's office in Coalville around 4:30 P.M. The office was crowded and chaotic. Reporters were waiting for a press conference and phones were ringing everywhere. Members of the arrest team were giving their statements in separate rooms. County Attorney Robert Adkins was there, as were state lawmen Robert Wadman and Larry Lunnen.

Deputy Eley gave Ron Robinson the evidence he had received from the state medical examiner, including John's clothing and the ammunition taken from the pockets. Robinson hung the blood-soaked shirts and coat, still wet, in a steel evidence cabinet, and placed the ammunition in a bin with the pistols and knife that Grant Larsen had retrieved earlier. Whether the sheriff ever received the four buckshot pellets taken from John's body is unclear. He testified later that he didn't remember seeing them at any time. Deputy Eley remembered seeing the pellets in a plastic envelope at the medical examiner's office, but could not positively remember handing them to Sheriff Robinson when he returned to Coal-ville. In any case, those pellets were lost and have never been recovered.

Lewis Jolley's shotgun was turned over uncleaned to Public Safety Commissioner Larry Lunnen. None of the other weapons issued by the state and carried by the members of the arrest team—five thirty-eight-caliber pistols and four twelve-gauge shotguns—were collected or tested to determine whether any of those weapons had recently been discharged.

When the arresting officers finished giving their individual state-ments, they met collectively behind closed doors with county and state officials. It was after dark when they emerged from the room and announced that they would hold a press conference in the county courthouse next door.

At the conference, Robert Adkins issued a statement regarding the arrest attempt: "As officers approached Mr. Singer he pulled an automatic pistol out of his coat, raised it and aimed at the officer nearest him. As Singer's arm was outstretched, that officer fired a shotgun at close range, striking Singer in his right side, beneath his arm. No other shots were fired."

Adkins had not bothered to check with the medical examiner to get his facts straight, and thus left the impression with the press that John had been shot only in the side, when in fact most of the buckshot wounds were in his back.

Adkins told reporters that the county would not release the names of the officers present at the shooting scene because they had already received numerous phone calls threatening their lives. He also stated that the county had called the FBI to request an investigation of the shooting incident, anticipating public demand for such an investigation.

Later that evening at the state capitol, Commissioner Lunnen issued a statement in which he said he was satisfied that the arresting officers had acted in self-defense. "From the officers' standpoint, Singer was obviously prepared to shoot them," he said. "I think under those circumstances, we don't ask law officers to wait until they are shot to return fire." Lunnen also refused to release the names of the arresting officers.

At 5:00 P.M., Juvenile Court Judge John Farr Larson held a press conference at the DFS detention center where the Singer and Black children were being held. He issued a restraining order prohibiting the news media from publicly identifying, photographing, or interviewing the children while they were in the state's custody.

"Today's actions sadden me," the judge announced. And he explained, "My order placing the Singer children in the custody of the Division of Family Services is temporary until such time as Vickie Singer may be able to provide appropriate care and education for the children. There should be no illusions, however. This court will not return the children before changes have been made which guarantee these children a normal life."

Shortly before Judge Larson's press conference, the Singer children were told by Claude Dean, supervisor of the Salt Lake County Shelter Care program, that their father was dead. At that point, the DFS officials were still under the impression that John had been shot in the leg; so Dean told the children that the poison from the bullet had traveled up their father's leg and into his heart. Heidi told her brothers and sisters that the DFS officials were working for the Devil and were telling lies, and their father was still alive—the Lord had promised to protect him. Claude Dean gently attempted to convince the children that he was telling the truth, but they would not believe him. Heidi screamed at him, calling him "Devil," and kicked him in the legs. The other children started crying, except for Charlotte who looked pale and sickly, having been traumatized by the sight of her father falling with blood coming out of his mouth.

Dean Black picked up his three children around 7:00 P.M. and took them home to Kamas. Shortly thereafter, the seven Singer children were given into the custody of Dick and Beth Gehrke, shelter-care parents, who would provide a home for them until they were either given back to Vickie or placed in a foster home.

Dick Gehrke, a social worker, and his wife Beth had participated in shelter programs in California and Utah for sixteen years before Judge Larson called them in the summer of 1978 to ask if they would be willing to provide a temporary home for the Singer children in the event their parents were arrested and put in jail. The Gehrkes were chosen partly because they lived in the same neighborhood as the Kingsley School. When the DFS called the Gehrkes on January 18, it warned them that the children might be violent or suicidal.

Once the Gehrkes picked up the children and brought them home, they found them to be as cooperative and well-mannered as could possibly have been expected under the circumstances. They were all upset, of course, and still didn't believe their father was dead.

Dick Gehrke felt that if Vickie were there to tell her children that John was really dead, they would believe it. So he called Judge Larson to ask him if he would release Vickie from jail so that she could tell her children the truth, and comfort them. But the judge refused.

The kids had not eaten since breakfast. Beth Gehrke prepared a big pot of soup for them, but Heidi instructed the other kids to fast, and so they turned down all offers of food. The children prayed fervently before they went to bed, but got little sleep. Heidi sat in a chair by a window most of the night trying to decide whether or not to lead her brothers and sisters in an escape. She finally fell asleep in the chair.

Edeltraud went to see Vickie in jail late that night. By this time, having received Bonnie's message, Vickie accepted the fact that John was dead. In a soft, angelic voice she said to Edeltraud, "I never imagined that my darling husband could be taken from my side. We have been through so much together, and were so close, we were like one person. Now we're separated. O Lord, give me strength." Vickie broke down crying, and Edeltraud sobbed along with her.

"How on earth am I going to bear this for thirty days in here and not see my children?" asked Vickie. Edeltraud felt an almost overwhelming combination of grief and anger, wishing she could bust through the thick Plexiglas and hold Vickie in her arms.

After Eldeltraud left, Harald's lawyer Steve Gilliland came and talked to Vickie for about ten minutes. Then again Vickie was alone. The cell was warm and stuffy; the lights were left on all night so that she could be kept under observation—authorities feared that she might try to harm herself. Alternately she paced around the room or sat on the bench crying, and did not sleep at all.

She talked to John. "What happened?" she asked him. "Why? I thought the Lord would protect you."

And she asked the Lord, "Why hast thou forsaken us?"

She was overcome by anxiety when she realized that she alone must now shoulder the burden of fighting for the right to educate her children without submitting to government supervision. She suspected the juvenile court would want some sort of commitment from her in that regard before she could see her children again.

Her heart ached and her mind was in chaos. One night in that cell away from her children was almost more than she could bear—the thought of having to spend thirty days there nearly drove her mad.

Chapter 14

A WOMAN CLOTHED
WITH THE SUN

Harald went to see Vickie in jail early Friday morning, January 19. The shock and anger that Harald had felt the previous afternoon gave way to tears this morning. Both he and Vickie sobbed uncontrollably when they spoke of John's steadfast devotion to his religious beliefs.

Vickie told Harald of the anguish she felt, knowing she would be faced with a choice between losing her children and breaking her covenant with God. If she agreed to compromise with the juvenile court and allow the state to supervise her children's education, she would be deserting the principles for which John had given his life. But if she did not compromise, she might never see her children again.

Harald could see the torment on Vickie's face. With tears rolling down his cheeks, he said very solemnly, "The price has been paid. The Lord has exacted the ultimate sacrifice, and He will not ask for more."

Vickie's eyes showed a flicker of light, like the first flash of the sun's rays after a terrible storm. "Are you sure?" she asked.

"Yes."

Back in her cell, she prayed and received assurance that Harald was right. A few precious minutes of peace came to her mind.

Beth Gehrke cooked breakfast for the children, but Heidi instructed her brothers and sisters to continue fasting. Beth could tell the younger boys, Benny and Israel, were hungry, as they eyed the food in the kitchen.

Dick Gehrke took Heidi out on the front porch and talked to her. "Heidi, I know you're upset, and I don't blame you," he said. "But unless you let the kids eat, we might have to separate you." Heidi gave the okay for the others to eat, but she continued to fast for the rest of the day.

Charlotte, still traumatized, would not eat much and hardly spoke a word; she was pale and had stomach pains. The Gehrkes knew that the kids desperately needed their mother. Dick called Judge Larson early Friday morning and also talked to the Division of Family Services staff. Finally, the judge agreed to meet with Vickie at the DFS office at 10:30 A.M., and said that if the Gehrkes would bring the children there they could be reunited with their mother.

Denise Wheeler took Shirley to Larkin Mortuary early Friday morning. They sat for an hour with John's body, which was embalmed and wrapped to the neck in a blanket. Then they drove back to Marion. Shirley's daughter Linda stayed at the farm for ten days to keep her mother company and help with the chores.

Bonnie Norder called a Salt Lake attorney named Kathryn Collard to see if there was anything she could do to get Vickie out of jail and help her regain custody of her children. Collard had until August of 1978 been litigation director of the Utah chapter of the American Civil Liberties Union, and had since gone into private practice, specializing in civil rights and class action litigation.

It was with reservations that Collard agreed to meet with Vickie and possibly represent her in court. The Singer case could be a good opportunity for her, since it involved important issues. But her impression of Vickie, not having met her, was that she was a bigoted religious fanatic, totally subservient to her husband, with no mind of her own. Collard herself had left the Mormon Church in 1961 at the age of thirteen because she considered the church's doctrine racist and sexist: Only white males could enter the priesthood, and Mormon women were discouraged from having careers outside the home.

Her opinion of Vickie would change radically in the following months. In fact, she would consider Vickie a "strong, well-centered person, thoughtful and independent, with a deep desire to understand her own life and religious experience." Collard discovered that Vickie had keen insight into human motivation and, most surprisingly, could deal with her own legal predicament more realistically than most clients. Before the end of the year they would consider each other good friends.

Vickie was escorted, still in custody, to the DFS office where she had quite an emotional reunion with her children. She confirmed for them that their father was dead. "Their hearts were broken," she later recorded in her journal. "You could see the tremendous grief on their faces. The Lord gave me strength and utterance, and I was able to offer great comforting words to them."

Vickie conferred briefly with Kathryn Collard and Steve Gilliland, Harald's lawyer, before going into Judge Larson's office. Terry Christiansen, representing Summit County, and guardian *ad litem* Robert Orton were also present.

By now John's death had been reported in newspapers all over the country, as well as on local and network TV news, and the press had come down hard on John Farr Larson for separating Vickie from her children at such a tragic moment in their lives. Larson had already received several anonymous threats on his life.

After a brief discussion, the judge stayed Vickie's jail sentence and ordered that she be released from custody immediately. Her children would remain in the protective custody of the Division of Family Services, but Vickie would be permitted to stay with them at the shelter home. A hearing was scheduled for January 27, at which time the judge would consider suspending Vickie's sentence and returning the children to her custody, if she and her attorneys could assure the court that she would be able to provide the children "appropriate care and education."

John Singer's death touched off widespread public reaction the likes of which Utah had not experienced in this century. The state's major newspapers were flooded with letters; editorials were written and broadcast; the Concerned Citizens for the Singer Family was founded in Salt Lake to demand a grand jury investigation. The state capitol was evacuated for an hour on Friday after the governor's office received an anonymous bomb threat that turned out to be a hoax. Vandals painted epithets on highway signs—"John Singer is alive"—and across the front of the Division of Family Services building—"John Singer was murdered by the pigs." Graffiti appeared in the bathrooms of several restaurants and bars in Salt Lake and Park City: "Don't sing in the john, they shoot john singers."

Almost everyone who had anything to do with the Singer case received threatening letters, telegrams, and telephone calls at their offices and homes. Ron Robinson had to get a new, unlisted home phone number, so vile were the threats and obscenities. Governor Matheson's children were threatened and had to be kept home from school. Attorney General Hansen started wearing a bullet-proof vest and carrying a gun for protection.

The FBI announced on Friday that it would conduct a "complete, extensive, thorough, and unbiased" investigation of the shooting of John Singer to determine whether his civil rights had been violated.

On Friday evening, after the state received numerous complaints from the media that the details of the autopsy were being suppressed, Chief Medical Examiner J. Wallace Graham issued a press release:

> John Singer was struck with a twelve-gauge buckshot load. Eight pellets, or buckshots, struck the right back and right side of the body perforating the chest from right to left, and back to front, with a slight upward direction. The course and direction of the wounds is consistent with the information that Mr. Singer was pointing a handgun at one or more police officers while evading arrest.

Months later, Vickie's lawyers questioned the propriety of Dr. Graham's comment:

> *Q:* Isn't it also true, Dr. Graham, that the course and direction of the wounds are consistent with the information that Mr. Singer was *not* pointing a handgun at one or more of the officers while evading arrest?
> *A:* Yes, but that information was not submitted.
> *Q:* Aren't your findings also consistent with the proposition that Mr. Singer was not evading arrest?
> *A:* Yes.

Saturday morning's front-page banner headline in the *Salt Lake Tribune* was: "Judge Frees Widow from Jail; Test Shows Singer Shot in Back."

The three days before the funeral were hard for Vickie and her seven children. "The grief that we suffered almost overwhelmed us," Vickie wrote in her journal. "Nighttime was the hardest. The children would groan or make little whimpering noises in their disturbed sleep. It just racked their bodies, their whole souls."

Vickie called Harald and Shirley late at night when she couldn't sleep, and asked them to pray for her. She felt that Satan was trying to kill her: "Such a pressure came upon my heart, and awful feelings attended it, that I felt that I could very possibly be headed for a heart attack. I prayed, rebuked Satan in the name of Jesus Christ, but seemingly to no avail."

During the day, while Vickie dealt with legal matters and funeral plans, the Gehrkes tried to keep the children busy playing in a nearby park, sleigh-riding, and shopping for clothes to wear to the funeral. The children often sang songs, spiritual and otherwise, to keep up their spirits. From talking to the kids about their father, Dick and Beth got the impression that John was a fun-loving man with a keen sense of humor.

At the viewing on Sunday evening, hundreds of people filed past the casket to get a final look at John Singer, the man whose name had inundated the local media in the three days since his death. Vickie and her children, Shirley, Harald, Edeltraud, and Reinhard stood in the receiving line for two and a half hours. Among the visitors who came to pay their last respects were religious leaders of all faiths, a group of fifteen homosexuals who used the occasion to espouse minorities' civil rights, and a Nazi in full uniform who clicked his heels and saluted before shaking hands with Harald and Edeltraud. Two complete strangers proposed marriage to Vickie as she stood next to the casket of her dead husband. One of John's relatives insulted Shirley to her face, and a few people refused to shake Shirley's hand.

John Singer's funeral was held Monday morning, January 22. Three hundred and fifty people attended the service at Larkin Mortuary, and although it was a bitterly cold and windy day, the ubiquitous press and TV cameras hovered outside.

Harald delivered an impassioned, fifty-minute eulogy to an over-flow crowd.

> My dear brothers and sisters, John Singer was born on January sixth, 1931, in Brooklyn, New York. When my grandmother found out that he was born on the sixth of January, which was a religious holiday in Germany called the Feast of the Holy Three Kings, she made a prediction that he would one day become an important religious individual. I think he became an important religious individual because of the love of the gospel of Jesus Christ that he had in his heart and which motivated all of his actions wherever he went. He lived till the eighteenth of January, 1979. Twelve days after his forty-eighth birthday, he was felled by an assassin's bullet. My brother, in my opinion, was murdered!

A murmer of "Amen" could be heard throughout the congregation.

> My brother made a covenant with his Father in Heaven. He kept this covenant unto the day of his death. He died a martyr for the principles of truth and righteousness—for the principles provided in the Constitution of the United States and reiterated in the Doctrine and Covenants. . . .
> His blood cries from the ground into the ears of an offended God seeking that justice be done—not revenge, justice! . . .
> I know that God lives. And I know that John Singer died as His servant, in the name of Jesus Christ, my Savior, Amen.

Heidi sang her father's favorite hymn, "Redeemer of Israel." When the service was over, Vickie and Shirley exited hand in hand and rode together to the Marion cemetery.

Seventy people braved the below-zero temperature and strong winds to attend the burial. As John was laid to rest, Vickie found solace in the belief that he was now whole in spirit, no longer suffering from pain or illness. She wrote:

> When I saw him being lowered into the ground, strength was given to me from on high, and I praised God because at that moment He revealed to me the power of the stand that John had made and the marvelous things that were to come because of it. I felt thankful and joyful to be a part of this great mission.

> I heard John's voice say to me, "Vickie, don't look back—look
> forward to the things to come forth! Don't be sorrowful, but
> rejoice!" For the rest of the day, the words went repeatedly
> through my mind, "The hour of redemption is near."

Vickie and her children stayed at the Gehrkes for nine days,
during which she met with her attorneys to draw up a proposal for
the juvenile court regarding the children's education. Both Harald
and guardian *ad litem* Robert Orton appealed to Lynn Kingsley for
help, and Mrs. Kingsley again generously offered to make the
resources of her private school available to the Singers. On January
27, Judge Larson met in court with Vickie, Mrs. Kingsley, attorneys
Collard and Gilliland, Terry Christiansen, Robert Orton, and an
attorney for the South Summit School District. A plan was agreed
upon whereby Vickie could teach her children at home under the
supervision of the Kingsley School. The Kingsley School would, at
its own expense, train Vickie to be a competent teacher, provide
her with books and materials, periodically test the Singer children,
and report their progress to the juvenile court. Mrs. Kingsley insisted
that the school district have no involvement whatsoever in monitoring the program, and specified that the purpose of the testing
would be not to compare the Singer children to peer groups, but
to measure their individual progress from year to year.

Judge Larson gave Vickie physical custody of her children—
meaning they could all go home to their farm in Marion—but left
them in the legal custody and guardianship of the Division of Family
Services until that agency was satisfied that Vickie could provide
adequate care and education. The court scheduled a hearing for
May 29 to review their progress.

Vickie felt that she had won a partial victory, since she was no
longer under the jurisdiction of the school district. She still hoped
that one day she would be free of all supervision.

After the hearing, Kathryn Collard and Steve Gilliland announced
to the press that they would investigate the shooting of John Singer
and consider filing a wrongful death suit against the state and
Summit County.

The Gehrkes drove Vickie and her children back to Marion later
that afternoon. Their farewell was emotional and tearful. Dick and

Beth had shared some very hard times with the Singers, and the two families would remain close friends for years to come.

All around the farm were reminders of John. It took the family several days to readjust to being home, and to begin working with Mrs. Kingsley on their schooling. They were still overcome with sorrow and mournfulness from time to time, and Vickie still felt that Satan was trying to subdue her spirit and even, at times, drive the life out of her body.

Three weeks after John's death, Vickie had a vision that offered hope in the midst of her suffering. She recorded this in her journal: "I was so overcome by doubt and fear that I went into my bedroom and poured my heart out to the Lord, and then I poured my heart out to John. Then I came out of my bedroom and picked up the scriptures, flipped them open at random, and something was written there on the page that gave me a marvelous, marvelous feeling."

She turned to the Third Book of Nephi in the Book of Mormon. "I shall gather in, from their long dispersion, my people," began chapter 20, "and shall establish again among them my Zion." Further, in verse 10:

> But behold, the life of my servant shall be in my hand; therefore they shall not hurt him, although he shall be marred because of them. Yet I will heal him, for I will show unto them that my wisdom is greater than the cunning of the devil.

"A *strong* feeling came to me," Vickie noted, "that this servant God spoke of is my beloved husband."

> Yea, and then shall the work commence, with the Father, among all nations, in preparing the way whereby his people may be gathered home to the land of their inheritance.

Vickie turned to *The Testament of Levi*, a small book published in 1937 by Francis Darter, a Mormon high priest. In his preface, Darter wrote that Levi, one of the twelve sons of Jacob and the patriarch of the priesthood tribe, prophesied that one day the priesthood would be defiled and the law destroyed. Righteous people would be persecuted and killed. After a period of apostasy, a "new priest"—

the one mighty and strong that Joseph Smith spoke of—would rise up to restore the priesthood to the Saints.

> In the end ye shall kill him out of hand, as you think, not knowing that he shall rise again, and so shall ye receive his innocent Blood wilfully upon your own Heads. . . .
>   Then will God raise up a new Priest, unto whom all the Lord's word shall be opened; and he shall execute true Judgment upon Earth many Days, and his Star shall arise in Heaven. As a King shall he shed forth the Light of Knowledge in the Sunshine of the Day, and shall be magnified over all the World, and be received and shine as the Sun upon the Earth, and there shall be peace thereon.

It all became clear to Vickie: "Something marvelous is coming. Satan wants to kill me because he must know of the marvelous things that will come, and I must have a great part to play in what's coming.

"I believe that John will come back! Something *great* is coming! Praise God for this beautiful hope."

Seeking to understand her own role in the redemption of Zion, Vickie turned to the Book of Revelation in the New Testament. The Revelation of St. John describes the last days before the Second Coming, when God will triumph over the Devil, good over evil, and the Kingdom of God over the kingdoms of corrupt men. Revelation 12:1 speaks of a woman "clothed with the sun, and the moon under her feet, and upon her head a crown of twelve stars." This woman (whom some scriptorians regard as a symbol of the church) was persecuted by Satan because she gave birth to a man-child who would rule all earthly nations from God's throne (symbolic of the Kingdom of God).

Identifying herself with the woman in Revelation, Vickie envisioned that she was to play a vital part in the eventual triumph on earth of God over the Devil, and thus help to establish the Kingdom of God. "My heart was filled with thanksgiving, and tears of joy filled my eyes," she wrote. "I felt that there was nothing to fear, but only something marvelous to look forward to. The reason Satan has been so hard upon me was because he must know that our deliverance is near.

"I lay in bed for hours and enjoyed the warm, happy feeling in my bosom and praised the Lord from whom all blessings flow. I smiled and enjoyed the marvelous plan of the Lord, which is beautiful to behold! It seems that John's spirit hugged me—I felt it! Oh, the Lord is good. Oh that He will bear me through triumphant and all of us enlisted in the fight. I praised and thanked God for this spiritual feast I had that night!"

Chapter 15

TRUTH WILL CUT
ITS OWN WAY

By February 15, 1979, nearly a month after John Singer's death, the FBI, Utah attorney general's office, and Summit County attorney's office had concluded their investigations of the shooting.

Based on the FBI's report, the assistant U.S. attorney in Salt Lake City stated that in her opinion the officials who planned and executed the arrest attempt did not enter into a conspiracy to kill John Singer, and Singer's civil rights had not been violated. The report was sent to the Civil Rights Division of the U.S. Department of Justice in Washington, D.C., for review. Local FBI agents refused to release the report to the public or discuss details of the investigation.

The attorney general's office conducted a limited investigation "to gather whatever information might be needed at a later time" in the event of a wrongful death claim against the state. "Based on the information we have at this point," Attorney General Hansen said, "we feel the state has no liability in this case." He declined to discuss the details of the investigation.

The purpose of Summit County's investigation was to determine whether criminal charges should be brought against any of the lawmen involved in the arrest attempt. County Attorney Adkins concluded that there were no grounds to file any criminal complaints, and told the press that as far as he was concerned the Singer case was closed. The county's investigation was never opened to the public.

Assistant County Attorney Christiansen commented, "There's a popular misconception that Singer was shot because he wouldn't send his kids to school. The fact is, he was shot because he pointed a weapon at a law officer who felt his life was in jeopardy."

Neither the county, the state, nor the FBI would disclose the names of the ten arresting officers, on the grounds that doing so would endanger their lives.

Asked for her reaction to the investigation, Vickie told reporters, "The officials would like the whole thing to be quieted and forgotten now, but there are thousands across the country who want the truth to be brought out, and who want justice to prevail. Innocent blood is laying on the road there."

On February 15, Vickie signed a Notice of Claim, advising State of Utah and Summit County officials of her intention to file a wrongful death action against them. The notice named as potential defendants Governor Matheson, Public Safety Commissioner Lunnen, Sheriff Robinson, three Summit County commissioners, and John Does I through XV, the latter representing the ten arresting officers and other agents and employees of the state or county whose identities had been withheld from the public. The notice alleged, "The actions of said agents, acting in concert, caused the wrongful death of John Singer; and such wrongful death was the result of malice, willful and wanton negligence, negligent supervision, excessive use of force, and violation of the [Singers'] civil rights."

After a two-day custody trial in Third District Court on March 19 and 20, Judge Bryant Croft awarded permanent custody of the four minor children of Dean and Shirley Black to their father. The two girls, Nancy and Julie, had told the judge that they preferred to live with their mother, and Shirley promised to leave them in public school if she was awarded custody. But Dean's lawyer argued successfully that Shirley had exposed the children to immorality and physical danger by taking them to live at the Singer farm, and that she would teach them to break the law of the land whenever she felt it conflicted with God's law.

Judge Croft granted Shirley "reasonable rights of visitation," but added, "In exercising such visitation, Mrs. Black is ordered not to teach the children her present existing beliefs concerning the doctrine of plural marriage."

In April, the U.S. Justice Department advised the Salt Lake City FBI office that there was no evidence to show that civil rights laws had been violated in the death of John Singer.

At Vickie's May 29 review hearing in juvenile court, Lynn Kingsley told Judge Larson that in spite of the tremendous burden of raising seven children and managing a farm and a household, in addition to coping with a recent tragedy that "upset the equilibrium of the whole family," Vickie was teaching her children at home and their progress was satisfactory. "There are no children any place on the face of this earth that are cared for more and who have a parent more diligently interested in their progress," Lynn Kingsley told the court. "Mrs. Singer has the most valiant attitude I've ever seen in any woman. You can rest assured that these children are going to get educated."

Judge Larson ordered that custody and guardianship of the children be returned to Vickie, subject, however, to the "protective supervision" of the Division of Family Services. Another review hearing was set for November 6.

Even though she had won legal custody of her children, Vickie still felt oppressed by the juvenile court's jurisdiction over their education. It seemed to her a constant struggle to muster enough time and energy to administer the Kingsley School program in her home. She had a stack of textbooks and teaching manuals to read through, some of which bored her literally to tears, and as soon as she got halfway through the stack Daniel and Lynn Kingsley would drive up to Marion with another box full of them. Vickie felt that her children's ambition and incentive to learn were smothered beneath all the materials, schedules, requirements, and tests. "I never want the Kingsleys to think that I am ungrateful for what they have done for us," she wrote in her journal. "It's just that my free spirit cannot stand to be in this type of bondage much longer. Oh that we could be free and take the Holy Spirit as our guide in our schooling. We could learn much easier and faster. How I loathe the injustice of this corrupt system."

There were days when the housework and farm chores left no time at all for schooling. Thirteen-year-old Timothy took over most of the responsibility for getting the work done around the farm. He also repaired machinery and appliances, maintained the electrical and plumbing systems in the houses, built furniture, and earned money rebuilding motorcycles and snowmobile engines. Nine-year-old Joseph got a part-time job hauling manure, cutting wood, and taking care of horses at Paiute Creek Outfitters, about a mile up Blake's Canyon east of Marion. Heidi, fifteen, made Indian deerhorn necklaces and sold them for $5 apiece. She also made leather boots for the family. Suzanne, fourteen, made and sold little sock dolls for $2.25 each to help pay for painting lessons at an art school in Kamas. Charlotte, eleven, took piano lessons in Peoa.

Vickie received a $200 Social Security check each month and about $350 in veteran's benefits, which barely kept the family above water.

Shirley lived at the Singer farm for four months after John's death. She helped Vickie with the housework and taught school to the youngest boys, Benny and Israel. She also sold goat's milk to neighbors and a few Kamas residents. Shirley visited her own children for an hour or so each day, or longer if one of them was sick. Julie, the youngest girl, missed her mother dearly.

In May, Shirley took her goats and moved into a small trailer house in Dean Black's yard in order to be closer to her children. Then in August, when Dean went to California for several weeks on a construction job, she moved into the main house. When Dean returned he agreed to let Shirley stay in the house, in the interests of the children, under the condition that she would not associate with the Singer family. They lived at separate ends of the house.

Shirley developed her goat's milk operation into a thriving small business. She and Vickie still considered each other best friends and sister wives, although the two of them met only occasionally, and in secret, when Dean was out of town. Shirley never doubted for a minute that marrying John Singer and taking her children to live at the Singer farm had been right. She believed that she was still sealed in marriage to John, and would be for all eternity.

Vickie was anxious about her November 6 review hearing in

juvenile court. Her family had been so busy that fall harvesting and storing a large potato crop and cutting firewood for the winter that they had not devoted as much time to their schoolwork as they were expected to. Vickie worried that if the court was not satisfied with their progress she would lose her kids again.

To her great relief, the court again determined that the children's progress was satisfactory, and the protective supervision of the Division of Family Services was terminated. Judge Larson scheduled another review hearing for July 21, 1980.

Wyoming attorney Gerry Spence was invited by the Utah Bar Association to be guest speaker at its annual conference in Park City late in the fall of 1979. Spence had recently won a $10.5 million verdict in the Karen Silkwood plutonium contamination trial in Oklahoma, which had vaulted him into national prominence. At the close of the bar association's meeting, a *Tribune* correspondent asked Spence if he had heard of the Singer case and what he thought about it. Spence replied, "If what I've heard on the TV and the radio is true, I'd give my left nut to have a case like that."

The *Tribune* published Spence's remark (substituting "arm" for "nut") the next day. Harald Singer read the story and called Vickie; both agreed that they should contact Spence. Late in November Vickie, Harald, and Fred Collier drove up to Spence's office in Jackson, Wyoming, to discuss the case with him; and on December 11 Spence announced to the press that he had agreed to represent Vickie and her children in their suit against state and county officials. He told reporters that he would file a complaint in "the near future," although he had not yet determined what defendants would be named. At Vickie's request, Spence asked Kathryn Collard to act as local counsel in the lawsuit, and she readily consented.

January 6, 1980, would have been John Singer's forty-ninth birthday. For Vickie, life without him was a struggle. It seemed as though the longing she felt for him at night would never ebb. She still believed that in the last days before the Second Coming John would be resurrected, to dwell again on his farm with his wives and children, and together they would celebrate the start of the millennium. Heidi, Suzanne, Timothy, Charlotte, and Joseph all had dreams of their father's triumphant return, and they came to share Vickie's conviction that John was at that moment being endowed with knowledge and light so that he could one day rise forth to complete his glorious mission on earth.

Gerry Spence dropped a bombshell on the State of Utah in April 1980 when he filed a $110 million civil rights suit in federal court on behalf of the Singers. Named as defendants in the forty-eight-page complaint were Robert Wadman, Ron Robinson, Summit County School District and its superintendent Val Edrington, Governor Scott Matheson, Attorney General Robert Hansen, Public Safety Commissioner Larry Lunnen, Highway Patrol Superintendent Robert Reid, County Attorney Robert Adkins and his assistant Terry Christiansen, Medical Examiner J. Wallace Graham, and John Does A through Z.

Spence's complaint, filed in U.S. District Court in Salt Lake City, asserted three substantive claims for relief. First, it alleged that Summit County officials conspired to deprive the Singers of their constitutional right to educate their children according to their religious beliefs. Spence also charged that county officials maliciously prosecuted the Singers under an unconstitutional compulsory attendance law, discriminated against them because of their religious beliefs, and violated their right to privacy.

The second substantive claim was that state and county officials were grossly negligent in planning and executing John Singer's arrest. Spence charged that it should have been obvious to Wadman and Robinson, and to Governor Matheson who "fully approved the arrest plan," that the execution of the plan would probably result in John Singer's death, "even though the lives of the arresting officers were in no danger."

> Every law enforcement officer knew that John Singer was armed. Every officer knew that John Singer had vowed that he would not be separated from his family. Moreover, the planners knew or should have known that John Singer would certainly pull his weapon to warn off the officers as he had in the past, but would not shoot first [because of his religious belief that he should never act as the aggressor]. There was no doubt that if the officers swooped down on Singer he would pull his gun. There was also no doubt that once John Singer pulled his gun he would be shot! Wadman and his planners knew that their

men were trained to shoot to kill any person who pointed a gun at them. . . .

The third substantive claim for relief was that the defendants conspired to withhold information about the shooting which should have been a matter of public record—including the county attorney's investigative report and the names of the arresting officers—in order to cover up their infringements. In doing so, they deprived Vickie Singer of her constitutional right to due process, that is, the right to freely assert a claim against the defendants.

In addition to actual damages—loss of future income, care, comfort, and consortium—the plaintiffs sought punitive damages because the defendants had acted with "willful, wanton, and reckless disregard for the safety of John Singer," and because the act of imprisoning Vickie Singer and separating her from her children was "depraved and despicable and devoid of humanness . . . and explicitly calculated to inflict severe emotional distress."

Why would the defendants act in such a way toward the Singers? What was their motive? John Singer was embarrassing the state, Spence claimed. "He caused the theocratic power structure to rock and reel with national publicity that focused on the way this simple Mormon excommunicant was being treated by the Mormon moral majority." John Singer had exposed the Utah power structure as being "unreasonable, incompetent, unjust, and immoral. And the power structure would not tolerate it."

So the state, under the pretense of being concerned with the welfare of the children, finally "subdued and conquered this rene-gade Mormon" by shooting him in the back, Spence charged.

To the media, Spence predicted that the case would ultimately result in a landmark decision involving the rights of parents to rear their children as they see fit: "The question is, are we simply the custodians of our children for the benefit of the state, like some poor sharecropper is the custodian of his master's horses; or are we actually parents with the right to determine how our children will be reared, the kinds of influences they will be subjected to, and the kind of education they will receive?"

The *Singer* v. *Wadman et al* case was assigned to U.S. District Judge David K. Winder, a robust, forty-eight-year-old, no-nonsense jurist who had been on the federal bench for four months.

By June 1980, the defendants and their insurers had responded to the lawsuit by hiring the cream of the Utah trial bar to represent them. Chief defense counsel Glenn Hanni was generally regarded as a gentleman and one of the finest trial lawyers in the country, although he never sought the kind of publicity and fame that the flamboyant Gerry Spence enjoyed.

In June 1980, Spence asked Judge Winder to order the Summit County attorney to produce its investigation file and reveal the names of the ten arresting officers who had been listed in the complaint as John Does. The defense lawyers argued, almost a year and a half after John Singer's death, that to reveal the officers' names would endanger their lives. But Judge Winder granted Spence's motion and set a June 1981 trial date.

The plaintiffs had won the first battle of the war, and Spence was confident as he reflected on the issues: "Can you imagine what it would be like if the state police could shoot a citizen, and the citizen's family not be able to find out who it was? Can you imagine that? In a free country? That's what these people did in this case.

"And now the second thing I'd like to ask you to imagine is a press corps in any state which would permit that to happen—the press who is always screaming and hollering about their First Amendment rights, who sat by and let that happen in the State of Utah for a year and a half, and let poor Mrs. Singer finally take that battle on herself! And the press is going to find it out as a result of what Mrs. Singer did today in that courtroom. The people of Utah have her to thank for that."

Spence lionized John Singer: "Here is a man who was raised in Nazi Germany, who saw the effects of Nazism on the minds of men as he grew up, and saw what the Nazis did to people's freedoms. Where you and I might accept some intrusion on our freedoms because we take them for granted, to him it was intolerable to have his freedoms intruded upon, because they were so precious to him. John Singer came to this country and tested with his own life the very principles upon which this country was founded.

"You see," said Spence, "it wasn't a nice little boy or girl whose ancestors came over on the *Mayflower*. It took a poor, little, immigrant German boy who had suffered under Nazism, who really knew the values of those freedoms, to lay down his life for them.

"The American public doesn't know this yet, but John Singer is probably one of this country's great heroes."

In Vickie's July review hearing, Judge John Farr Larson was satisfied with Mrs. Kingsley's report, and upon Kathryn Collard's motion he terminated the juvenile court's jurisdiction over the Singer family. Daniel and Lynn Kingsley withdrew also, promising Vickie their help and support if she should ever need it again.

"This freedom that we've been fighting for has finally come through," Vickie said a few months later. "But it's very ironic, to say the least, because now I'm teaching my kids the same way that John and I did before he died, and I think the state knows it. But all they wanted to do was show us, and show the people, that if anybody tried to come against the system, watch out because this is what can happen to you. And I think they tried to use John and me as an example."

In December 1980, the dispute between the Singers and the Wellers over property rights came to a head, as Marion Park Estates served Vickie with an eviction notice. The corporation, whose president was Jared Weller, gave Vickie three days to pay $200 rent or vacate the premises.

Vickie regarded the action as an outrageous insult. John had worked on his Uncle Gus Weller's 160-acre farm full-time from 1953 to 1964, then part-time until 1968, and never received a penny in wages. Vickie understood that Gus had given him the two-and-a-half-acre parcel of land in 1957 as payment for his labors.

After 1957, property taxes were still assessed on the entire 160 acres in the Wellers' name, but John paid his share of the taxes each year to the Wellers.

Right after John died, Dick Watson, who was Jared Weller's brother-in-law, told a reporter that although the Weller family held legal title to the Singer farm, they would not make it tough on John's widow and children. "We as a family would be very willing to offer neighborly support to make life as comfortable as we possibly can for them," he said. "We will do all we can to be neighborly and considerate and kind."

Not long thereafter, Marion Park Estates, of which Watson was a director, demanded that Vickie pay $100 per month rent on her two and a half acres. When she refused to pay, claiming she owned the land, the company issued the eviction notice. Vickie received the notice ten days before Christmas, 1980.

Kathryn Collard persuaded Marion Park Estates not to evict the Singers until the dispute could be settled in court.

Depositions of the defendants and defense witnesses in the *Singer v. Wadman* case began in September 1980 and continued through the winter. As a rule, Gerry Spence would enter the depositions wearing a ten-gallon hat and blue jeans, to face a battery of defense attorneys in conservative three-piece suits.

Early in the proceedings Spence got J. Wallace Graham, who had performed the autopsy on John Singer's body, to admit that while the wounds were consistent with the report that Singer had been shot once by officer Jolley's shotgun, the wounds could also be consistent with the theory that Singer had been shot more than once and by more than one officer. Dr. Graham's testimony prompted Spence to contact Heinz Karnitschnig, Chief Medical Examiner of Maricopa County, Arizona, whom Spence touted as one of the most outstanding forensic pathologists in the world. After examining Dr. Graham's autopsy report and deposition, the eight-by-ten photos of John Singer's body taken by Cully Christensen, and the clothing John wore when he died, Dr. Karnitschnig signed an affidavit stating that based on the trajectories of the wounds

> it would have been impossible for the wounds suffered by John Singer to have come from a single shotgun blast, but instead the wounds came from one or more shotgun blasts or a combination of a shotgun blast with shots from another weapon or weapons.

In February 1981 Spence filed a sixty-six-page amended complaint, in which the names of the ten arresting officers were substituted for the John Does, and in which Spence added new charges derived from deposition testimony.

Lewis Jolley had testified in his deposition that during the briefing before the fatal arrest attempt, none of the officers were advised of John Singer's religious belief that he could not shoot first. In the amended complaint, Spence claimed that Wadman and Robinson were negligent for failing to so advise the officers. He further claimed, on the strength of Dr. Karnitschnig's affidavit, that the arresting officers negligently used excessive force to apprehend Singer; that the officers shot Singer in the back and then pumped more bullets into him as he lay helpless in the snow.

Spence also filed a motion for change of venue on the grounds that the Singers would be unable to get a fair trial in Utah. Since the population of Utah is predominantly Mormon, he told the court, and since the Singers were considered apostates by the church, "there is simply too great a risk that a juror may see it as his or her religious duty to defend the Mormon Church and to defeat the claim of the Singers." Spence also noted that Judge Winder, a member of the Mormon Church, had been appointed to the state bench and recommended to the federal bench by Governor Matheson, a defendant, and had once been a law partner of Glenn Hanni, chief defense counsel. Could Winder still be fair and impartial in this lawsuit?

The plaintiffs suffered their first setback on April 1, 1981, when Judge Winder denied the change-of-venue motion and dismissed J. Wallace Graham as a defendant. "At worst, Dr. Graham might have given some inappropriate information in regard to an autopsy," the judge said.

In May, Judge Winder postponed the trial to give both sides more time to depose expert witnesses. Because of a crowded calendar, the trial was moved back more than a year to September 13, 1982.

Depositions of forensic experts began at the end of May. Two forensic pathologists testifying for the plaintiffs supported the theory that John Singer might have been shot more than once, based on the evidence. One of them identified a gunshot wound in Singer's right upper back as having a trajectory different from the other wounds.

But three defendants' forensic pathologists refuted the theory, claiming first of all that errors in the medical examiner's autopsy report accounted for the discrepancy in trajectories, and secondly that buckshot pellets do not necessarily track a straight line once they enter a semiliquid or semisolid medium.

A forensic psychiatrist who trained S.W.A.T. teams testified for the plaintiffs that Robert Wadman and Sheriff Robinson should have attempted a "negotiated arrest" before using a show of force. He also pointed out that the defendants failed to properly execute the show-of-force plan because when Singer pulled his gun he was aware of only four of the ten arresting officers. Furthermore, in his opinion, Wadman should have briefed the arrest team on what action they should take in the event that Singer pulled a gun. However, two consultants in police tactical operations testified for the defense that the arrest plan was a reasonable one. Experts for both sides dismissed the strategy of using tranquilizer darts to incapacitate Singer as being ineffective and dangerous.

On April 2, 1982, after a four-day bench trial in Second District Court, Judge Ronald O. Hyde decided that testimony from witnesses "showed clearly, convincingly, and definitely that there was an agreement between John Singer and Gustav Weller whereby Singer was to have the property in question." Subsequently, Marion Park Estates issued Vickie a deed to the two-and-a-half-acre farm.

On June 16, Gerry Spence suffered another setback when Judge Winder dismissed Attorney General Robert Hansen from the *Singer* v. *Wadman* suit, on the grounds that there was no evidence linking him to any alleged conspiracy.

With the trial only three months away, Winder had not yet ruled on motions for summary judgment submitted by the remaining defendants. Settlement negotiations to this point had been fruitless. Reliable sources indicate that Spence was willing to settle for less than $3 million and possibly as little as $1 million. It is doubtful that the defense ever offered as much as half a million.

Vickie was not inclined to accept any settlement unless it was substantial enough to be a clear admission of wrongdoing by the defendants. Both Vickie and Harald believed that the trial of the lawsuit would expose wickedness in high places and help foster a revolution which would result in the emergence of the theocratic Kingdom of God. Pressing this lawsuit was Vickie's mission as "the woman clothed with the sun."

Vickie was asked what she would do with the money if she won a multimillion-dollar verdict. "I'd like to have my driveway paved," she replied, "and put a nice lawn out in the backyard, and maybe get me a new rug for the house." She also said she would establish a trust fund to provide assistance to civil rights plaintiffs.

Sheriff Robinson decided not to run for reelection in 1982 because he was faced with the possibility of spending much of his time in court, and because he had developed ulcers as a result of his involvement in the Singer case. Fred Eley, who had served as Robinson's deputy, succeeded him as Summit County sheriff.

Robert Wadman was promoted in 1981 to deputy commissioner of public safety under Larry Lunnen, and in 1982 was hired as chief of police of Omaha, Nebraska.

Bob Reynolds, who had lived with his former wife LuAnne on the Singer farm in the fall of 1978, committed suicide shortly after he was summoned to testify in the *Singer* v. *Wadman* case.

On September 3, 1982, Judge Winder shocked the plaintiffs, as well as the news media and the public, by granting all the remaining defendants' motions for summary judgment. This meant that the *Singer* v. *Wadman* case was dismissed on the grounds that there was insufficient evidence to present to a jury in support of the plaintiff's allegations.

Winder's 218-page decision picked apart Spence's complaint piece by piece, using adjectives such as "ludicrous," "farfetched," and "spurious" to describe some of its allegations.

The conduct of Summit County officials in prosecuting the Singers under Utah's compulsory attendance law was not unlawful, Winder wrote. Even if the Singers had met the conditions necessary to qualify for an exemption, the school district was not *required* to grant them one. The Singers didn't notify officials that they had incorporated their private school until after they had been convicted of neglect. Moreover, it was up to the school board to determine whether their private school was "regularly established."

Judge Winder ruled that the compulsory attendance law was "not so obviously unconstitutional," and the defendants had good reason to believe that John Singer was in violation of the law. He found no evidence that the prosecution of the Singers was discriminatory, or that the juvenile court judges were influenced by any improper behavior.

With respect to the arrest plan, Judge Winder ruled the plaintiffs had failed to present evidence that Governor Matheson knew the details of the plan. As to Wadman, Robinson, and Lunnen,

> This court does not believe a plan is negligent or grossly negligent merely because it involves a show of force; neither does the court recognize a duty to desist from arresting someone who may draw a weapon, or a duty to insure that a person who draws a gun on arresting officers will be safely taken into custody. In this court's view, no amount of planning can dictate the actions of an arresting officer in a life-threatening situation.

With respect to Spence's claim that the defendants knew or should have known that Singer would never shoot first, Winder wrote:

> Assuming these planners knew that to be a fact—which of course no one will ever know—the court is stymied as to how the planners should have acted on such knowledge, beyond abandoning any attempt to place Mr. Singer in custody.

The judge found no evidence that the arrest plan was devised to cause Singer to pull his gun so that the officers could "justifiably" shoot him.

With respect to charges of excessive force, Winder wrote that John Singer had a duty to submit to officers peaceably; when he didn't, lawmen had a right to use deadly force because they thought their lives were in danger. There was no evidence to contradict Jolley's testimony that he believed deadly force was necessary to protect his life.

Regarding the disputed testimony that there was more than one shot, the plaintiffs presented no evidence as to who would have fired the second shot. If the alleged second shot was fired by Gunderson, it could not have been fired simultaneously with the first shot since Gunderson was driving his snowmobile when Jolley fired. If Gunderson fired later, why didn't Vickie, Shirley, or Esther Watson hear a second shot after being alerted by the initial shot? In any case, the mere existence of a second shot would not be sufficient to prove that the officers used excessive force, the judge ruled.

Winder could find no evidence on the record that any of the defendants entered into a conspiracy, as defined by the applicable federal civil rights statute (Title 42 of the U.S. Code, Section 1983), or that the plaintiffs were deprived of their constitutional rights at any time (the Free Exercise Clause of the First Amendment does not establish a broad right of parents to educate their children according to their religious beliefs without reasonable government regulation, Winder noted). Nor did he find evidence that the defendants' conduct was outrageous or reckless, that they intended to inflict emotional distress on the Singers, or that they conspired to cover up any unlawful conduct.

Calling it a miscarriage of justice, Spence appealed Judge Winder's decision to the U.S. Circuit Court in Denver.

Chapter 16

BY THEIR FRUITS YE SHALL KNOW THEM

Heidi and Suzanne Singer were married in a double ceremony in September of 1980. They were sixteen and fifteen years old, respectively.

Heidi's husband, Addam Swapp, came from a farm in Fairview, Utah, and shared his father's fundamentalist Mormon beliefs. He attended the University of Utah, majoring in mathematics, but dropped out after a year and started his own salvaging business. He was not quite twenty when he married Heidi.

Heidi and Addam moved into the yellow house on the southeast corner of Vickie's farm. By 1983 they had two healthy children, a boy and a girl.

Now a parent herself, Heidi felt grateful that her parents had fought to educate her at home and protect her from immoral secular influences. "I'm so very happy that my parents have gone through what they did for us kids," she said. "I thank the Lord that I am a daughter to John and Vickie Singer."

Heidi and Addam were likewise determined to teach their children at home and resist any attempt by the state to interfere.

They both considered plural marriage a divine law that should be practiced only when the Lord commands an individual to do so.

Heidi said that she looked forward to having sister wives, although she knew there would be initial jealousies to overcome.

Heidi felt that John's death was part of God's plan, and she professed to hold no grudges against law enforcement officers: "Dad wouldn't want us kids looking at a cop and hating his guts, because Christ wouldn't."

Addam believed, as the Singers did, that John would be resurrected. "There's no doubt in my mind that he will come back," he said. "John's death was a great moment in the history of this earth, because his blood being spilled on the ground helped set in motion the Second Coming of Christ." Addam expected the millennium to begin during his lifetime. "Beautiful things are coming. The spirit of the Lord is stronger every day. There is no better time to be born than right now."

Suzanne's husband, Roger Bates, was Addam's first cousin. Roger was twenty when he married Suzanne. They took an apartment in Salt Lake City, where he worked as a self-employed tire wholesaler. Less than a week after the wedding, Roger was excommunicated by the Mormon Church.

Living away from Marion and being exposed to a more diverse culture, Suzanne's outlook became a little less spiritual. She disliked policemen because they killed her father. She had doubts about the doctrine of plural marriage, and didn't like the idea of Roger taking a second wife. But she still considered her father a martyr and believed he would be resurrected.

By 1983, Suzanne and Roger also had two children, both girls. They too were adamant about their children's education. "We are just as capable of teaching our children as public school teachers," said Roger, who was brought up in the public school system. Suzanne concurred: "We won't send our kids to public school *no matter what.*"

"I just want to take each day and learn to relish every minute of it and fully enjoy my children," Vickie said, sitting beside her favorite aspen tree, her "prayer tree," about half a mile up Hoyt's Canyon. "And John felt that way too when he was here. He'd say, 'Let's enjoy our lives, let's really take our children places and let's have fun together.' And we did. We tried to have as full a life as we could. And John used to take us out to restaurants and places with the children, because he was proud to be seen with his children. We would be walking down the street in Salt Lake City and he would be carrying Israel in his arms and all six would be marching behind us. He would just hold his head up high because he was so darn proud of those children.

"They're a lot more rambunctious now than they were when he was here, but deep down they are darn good kids."

Source Notes

The sources of the factual material in this book were:

1. Personal interviews conducted by the authors with every principal character except Jared Weller and Dean Black, both of whom declined to be interviewed. The General Authorities of the Church of Jesus Christ of Latter-day Saints declined to comment on any aspect of the Singer story or the church's involvement in the case, or on questions relating to Mormon doctrine.

2. Another personal interview with John Singer, conducted by James Smedley and Kirk Johnson in the summer of 1978.

3. The court record in the *Singer v. Wadman* lawsuit filed in United States District Court, District of Utah, Central Division (Civil No. C800212W). The authors relied primarily on the original and amended complaints, pleadings, depositions, and Judge Winder's memorandum decision. Exhibits relied upon include John Singer's diary, the FBI investigation report, the Summit County investigation report, the state medical examiner's autopsy report, and minutes of meetings of the South Summit Board of Education. The authors thank Vickie Singer for permission to quote from her journal, which is also part of the record but was sealed under order of the court.

4. Transcripts of the proceedings in the *State of Utah v. Singer* case, District Juvenile Court for Summit County.

5. Court records in the *Shirley Black v. Dean Black* case (Civil No. 5650) and the *Dean Black v. John Singer* case (Civil No. 5684), Third District Court of Summit County, Utah.

The authors do not claim that the dialog in this book, as remembered by the characters involved, represents the exact words used at the time of the events described.

All names in this book are actual except for Daniel and Lynn Kingsley and the Kingsley School. The names of the private school and its directors have been changed at their request.